THEORY AND PRACTICE OF MODERN JOURNALISM

THEORY AND PRACTICE OF MODERN JOURNALISM

Praveen Kumar

CENTRUM PRESS
NEW DELHI-110002 (INDIA)

CENTRUM PRESS
H.O.: 4360/4, Ansari Road, Daryaganj,
New Delhi-110002 (India)
Tel: 23278000, 23261597, 23255577, 23286875
B.O.: No. 1015, Ist Main Road, BSK IIIrd Stage,
IIIrd Phase, IIIrd Block, Bangalore-560085 (INDIA)
Tel: 080-41723429
Email: centrumpress@gmail.com
Visit us at: www.centrumpress.com

Theory and Practice of Modern Journalism

First Edition, 2010

ISBN 978-93-80836-27-0

PRINTED IN INDIA

Printed at Mehra Offset Press, Delhi

Contents

Preface

Journalism is a profession related with the dissemination of news and views and as such journalist should work out of motivation and idealism for the truth, and journalism ethics should be about aspirations and goals rather than minimum standards. The difficulty is that ethical journalists first need to be moral journalists; and to be moral journalists they must first believe in some kind of overriding of conduct and belief. Professional ethics should make all aware of the need for aspirations and principles rather than rules.

Writing about journalism in India is like walking over a minefield. Truthfully speaking, not much of the change, the communication revolution, is of India's making. The Indian expansion, scanned through a crystal ball, will, in the Indian tradition, be thoughtless and planes as was the injection of cable TV into the Indian scene.

Satellite TV has practically killed video for no other reason that it's easy entertainment. Journalism ethics and standards include principles of ethics and of good practice to address the specific challenges faced professional journalists. These principles are most widely known to journalist as their professional code of ethics of the canons of journalism. By emphasising the importance of personal integrity and collective concern for serving the public's right to know the result will be a cohort of journalists who will actively seek the best possible journalism.

Author

Chapter 1

Epistemology to the Practice of Journalism

Objectivity is one of the identifying features of journalism in the United States and perhaps the major contribution American journalism has made to the rest of the world. Anybody who tries to think about our way of doing journalism must grapple with this concept, which is essential to understanding the way the American press sees itself and the way America sees the press.

For the better part of this century, objectivity has been an institutionalized hallmark of reportorial excellence. Yet, despite the longevity of the tradition, in recent years the entire epistemology of "objectivity" in journalism has fallen from grace. Contemporary analyses of the news media have turned the once-transparent notion of objectivity into a hotly contested area of inquiry.

Under scrutiny, its philosophical underpinnings have been challenged, revalued, and ultimately rejected by critics dissatisfied with its rootedness in Enlightenment concepts of reason, its problematic relationship to hegemonies of race, class, and gender, and the fixedness with which reporters' subjective engagements with society have remained unacknowledged in the debates about social responsibility.

In this chapter, I explore an alternative to traditional and contemporary notions of journalistic objectivity and its interpretation in conventional news reporting vis-à-vis impartiality, pluralism, and the like. My argument here is that the underlying principles of objectivity have devolved in practice to an epistemic relativism that fails to meet journalism's emancipatory goals. I propose an alternative of "strong objectivity" grounded in standpoint epistemology, which has the potential to lead to a more engaged journalistic praxis -- a praxis that recognizes and grapples with issues of ideological bias and the problems of alienation of socially marginalized groups from mainstream news coverage. In this chapter, I hope to demonstrate that standpoint epistemology provides a theoretically strong framework to use in redressing some of the problems inherent in current approaches to news reporting.

"OBJECTIVITY": THE EVOLUTION OF A KEY CONCEPT

Journalistic objectivity has always been a slippery notion; its definition has varied over the years and continues to be the locus of considerable debate. Stoker gives a detailed historical account of how constructions of objectivity have reflected the changing economic, social, and moral climates in which journalism has been practiced over the last century and a half. Schudson characterizes objectivity as an ideology rather than a value, dating its ascendance in the American news paradigm to around 1931 and suggesting that its rise was part of a backlash against postWorld War I propaganda. At that time, journalistic objectivity was synonymous with neutrality, or the separation of facts from values and opinions: "Objectivity was understood as an ideal counter to the reality of the reporter's own subjectivity". Yet, right from the start this notion was contested:

Objectivity might be a professional idea, but it is one that seemed to disintegrate as soon as it was formulated. It became an ideal in journalism, after all, precisely when the impossibility of overcoming the subjectivities of presenting the news was widely accepted. Criticism of the "myth" of objectivity has been a contrapuntal accompaniment to the enunciation of objectivity as an ideal from the beginning. The discussion continues to this day; in recent years, critiques of objectivity have been quite rigorous. Tuchman asserts that objectivity comprises a "strategic ritual" used to protect journalists from risk or attack. From the perspective of political economy, Ognianova and Endersby argue that journalistic objectivity is a strategic device that is principally economic in its goals -- i.e., it is a conscious tactic used by news organizations to position journalists as political centrists, in the interests of increasing market shares among mainstream audiences. "Objectivity is a successful tactic used by the news media for maximizing their audience," they contend. Similarly, Chomsky laments the structural factors that mitigate the possibility of objectivity in the news:

What is at issue is not . . . the integrity of those who seek the facts but rather the choice of topics and highlighting of issues, the range of opinion permitted expression, the unquestioned premises that guide reporting and commentary, and the general framework imposed for the presentation of a certain view of the world.

Above all, recent conceptualizations of news as a construction rather than a reflection of reality have cast serious doubts on the possibility of objectivity-as-neutrality in journalism. Because of these criticisms, the gradual evolution of the norm of objectivity in journalism has involved a shifting away from the focus on "neutrality" and toward a foregrounding of "accuracy,""balance," and "fairness." Yet these concepts still involve a separation of the reporter's views from the views being presented -- a separation that is so rigid that it is the equivalent of erasure, the eradication of the reporter's positions from the reporting. Despite the new, intellectually grounded reconceptualization of objectivity, its philosophical basis in value-free facticity remains extant. As Reese points out, "The underlying principles of objectivity nonetheless remain firmly entrenched" in the news paradigm -- these principles being the separation of facts from values and opinions, with the journalist functioning as the impartial relayer of those facts.

Objectivity in the more contemporary sense of impartiality is consonant with another important goal in news production -- pluralism, the journalistic mandate to represent a diversity of positions and voices in the interests of responsibility to the public. Journalists are expected to simultaneously fulfill their obligations to objectivity and pluralism by conscientiously including a multiplicity of viewpoints in a news story, while carefully excluding any manifest evidence of their own. The code of ethics of the Society of Professional Journalists still exhorts journalists to "seek truth and report it" and to "tell the story of the diversity and magnitude of the human experience boldly," all the while noting, "Journalists should be free of obligation to any interest other than the public's right to know."

Similarly, the 1995 report of the American Society of Newspaper Editors, part of an ongoing project to identify journalistic values, lists "balance/fairness/wholeness" and "accuracy/authenticity" as the first two "core values of journalism." According to the report, the former is the imperative "to reflect the 'wholeness' of communities. Coverage needs to capture diverse voices and viewpoints, solutions and problems, the profoundly ordinary as well as the unusual, the good with the bad," whereas the latter requires the journalist "to get the facts right but also to get the 'right facts.' Coverage needs to provide background, context and perspective and it must capture the tone, language, experiences and emotions of people".

In contrast to the SPJ focus on impartiality, the ASNE report includes "judgment" as a journalistic value, urging the journalist "to act as the regulator of the other journalistic values by selecting, shaping and bringing definition to what is important, interesting and meaningful in a community". The report advises journalists to engage in reflexive self-examination, asking themselves what preconceptions they are bringing to the issue and how those biases might affect the framing of the story. Again, however, the eradication of bias is an explicitly stated goal: "Bias influences journalists' news judgments and how they fulfill their values of balance, accuracy, leadership, and accessibility. In the end, bias in a newsroom can affect the credibility of the newspaper". Other examinations of news values prudently stay away from any overt reference to objectivity, yet the philosophical underpinnings of even these formulations remain within its sphere, which is perhaps why Schudson saw fit to refer to objectivity as an ideology rather than a value. Lambeth, for example, offers a list of five principles to be given priority in the reporting of news stories; the first of these is "the principle of telling the truth". Lambeth writes, "The obligation to tell the truth goes to the very heart of journalistic function". Yet he does not stop to problematize "truth" as a concept; his assumption seems to be that there is a monolithic truth that can be discovered and told by the ethical journalist.

The notion that there might be multiple, layered, and conflicting truths about a given issue, and that such truths or versions of the truth might be dependent on one's social location, does not appear to be of concern in Lambeth's conception of journalistic method. This idea of a single recognizable truth that has an independent existence is still grounded in the oldest conceptualization of objectivity -- the notion of the value-free fact.

Practicing journalists struggle with the tensions inherent in maintaining their charge to remain "objective" while dealing with their personal commitments to the stories and issues they are covering and their understandings of the subjectivity of truth. Reese concludes that the production of news involves a continual negotiation of inherently contradictory values; this ongoing negotiation defines the limits of acceptable political discourse and ensures the enforcement of dominant ideologies in the mainstream press by journalists struggling to stay "inside the lines." Notes press critic Jay Rosen, "What is insidious and crippling about objectivity is when journalists say: 'We just present you with facts.

We don't make judgments. We don't have any values ourselves.' That is dangerous and wrongheaded". Rosen is an advocate of "public" journalism (also sometimes referred to as "civic" or "community" journalism), some approaches to which constitute the most recent ventures away from traditional objectivity. Public journalism embodies the notion that journalism is "a theory and a practice that recognizes the overriding importance of improving public life". Public journalists ply their trade as participants in communities rather than as detached observers, and the practice of public journalism is predicated on journalists helping people to translate information into grassroots action and activism. This type of journalism embraces emancipatory goals, which are actually not far off from mainstream journalistic ideals: "Public enlightenment is the forerunner of justice and the foundation of democracy. The duty of the journalist is to further those ends".

Public journalism stands at a crossroads in the objectivity debate. On the one hand, Rosen constructs such a journalistic practice as necessitating the abandonment of "impartiality." On the other hand, Charity locates the public journalist in a middle ground between observer and advocate: As most of them realise, journalists do more than furnish us with facts. They frame and narrate the story of our common life. . . . Without relinquishing their stance as observers and critics, they can try to nourish a particular understanding of American society. Charity concept of public journalism rests on traditional norms of objectivity.

He points out, "Public journalism has a golden rule -- an ethical line -- every bit as sharp as a mainstream journalist's rule, and just as easy to elaborate into a code book of professional norms: Journalism should advocate democracy without advocating particular solutions." Even these sorts of departures have drawn blistering responses from the journalistic mainstream, which tends to view public journalism as "the latest substitute for a healthy editorial budget and solid journalistic instincts, gobbledygook at best, dangerous at worst".

Barney sees potential for moral corruption if journalists become community activists: "The first point of corruption lies in the loss of individuality and autonomy required by membership in the community". A democratic society, he argues, "relies on the individualistic moral sense of journalists to place each of these communities in a perspective that reduces their probabilities of accumulating disproportionate power". This argument is based on the assumption that a journalist has no community affiliations if they are not explicitly declared, a point I will return to later in this chapter. At any rate, the resurgence of public journalism has recentered and intensified the debates over the place of objectivity in reportorial practice, even while journalism's liberatory goals remain resolute.

OBJECTIVITY, POSITIVISM, AND RELATIVISM

The debates that rage over objectivity in journalism closely resemble contemporary problematizations of objectivity in the natural and social sciences -- fittingly, for the evolution of objectivity as a journalistic norm parallels the post-World War II development of scientific theory and method. An understanding of the issues at stake in the terrain of the sciences is called for at this juncture. Interrogating these issues will lay open many of the concepts pertinent to the analysis of objectivity in journalism; it is a necessary step in developing a model of journalistic praxis that could resolve the contradictions and oppositions inherent in the current news paradigm.

Objectivity in the scientific tradition represents "an accurate description of the facts of the natural world as they are" through the application of "nonarbitrary and nonsubjective criteria". "In ascribing (or denying) objectivity to a method we can also be concerned about the extent to which it provides means of assessing hypotheses and theories in an unbiased and unprejudiced manner". These criteria resemble those which journalists are trained to apply in the reporting of news/facts. As in journalism, criticisms of objectivity in the sciences are not new, but with the rise of anti-Enlightenment critiques of positivism, they have taken on new vigor in the latter part of the 20th century.

Cunningham identifies the significant arguments against objectivity as:

- The values argument, which contends that scientists' values, psychology, background, etc., influence the selection of problems and the conclusions drawn.

- The historicist argument, which maintains that scientific enterprise is limited by its historical context.
- The selection argument, which describes scientific method as a series of ad hoc choices made by an investigator from an almost limitless set of possibilities.

All of these arguments impugn the traditional notion of "unbiased and unprejudiced" assessment of data. A common theme in these arguments is the Kuhnian idea that all "facts" are theory-laden, i.e., "how an inquirer could experience, contemplate or describe a subject-matter is predetermined by the theories that he sic holds (however vaguely or unconsciously)". Here Cctheory" means the common sense categories and doctrines embedded in everyday discourse . . . or one's personal Weltenschaung, the very general principles he uses for interpreting his experiences. Or the term might be used to refer to a body of laws and definitions which explain why the regularities expressed in laws of observation hold.

The strongest philosophical refinements of these critiques have come from societal groups whose "theories" were rendered invisible or illegitimate in mainstream scientific practice, and who argue for a reconsideration of the gender, class, and racial biases in so-called objective research. "Knowledge in a male dominant society reflects the experience and interests of men," states Longino; the well-documented works of Keller and Haraway have called attention to the androcentric bias in scientific research that stems from a social history of patriarchal dominance.

When predominantly male researchers use predominantly male subjects to conduct supposedly objective scientific inquiry, the resultant knowledge is "based on the premise that the experience of only half the human population needs to be taken into account and the resulting version can be imposed on the other half" bell hooks argues that even methodologies that have attempted to overcome gender biases remain racist in their epistemological bases: Often the white women who are busy publishing papers and books on "unlearning racism" remain patronizing and condescending when they relate to black women. This is not surprising given that frequently their discourse is aimed solely in the direction of a white audience and the focus solely on changing attitudes rather than addressing racism in a historical and political context. They make us the "objects" of their privileged discourse on race. As "objects," we remain unequals, inferiors. Even though they may be sincerely concerned about racism, their methodology suggests they are not yet free of the type of paternalism endemic to white supremacist ideology.

As powerful as these arguments are, challenges to traditional notions of scientific objectivity have not gone uncontested. The most common rejoinder to the critiques is the equally damning countercharge of epistemic relativism -- the idea that all knowledge positions are equally valid in the face of any supporting evidence. As Laudan asks, if relativism is the only acceptable alternative to bias, then, "Confronted with rival claims about the world (typically in the form of theories or hypotheses) and a certain body of evidence, how do we use the evidence to make rational choices between those rivals?" Thomas Kuhn, one of the first insurgents against traditional objectivity, concluded that such choices could never be made: Different theoretical approaches meant different world views that could never achieve rational closure.

Thus, the alternative of epistemic relativism stymies scholarly inquiry at a certain point and represents an intellectual dead end. Harding observes that epistemic, or judgmental, relativism is a dodge used by socially powerful and dominant groups. "Judgmental relativism is sometimes the most that dominant groups can stand to grant to their critics -- 'OK, your claims are valid for you, but mine are valid for me'". The fallback on relativism obviates the need to further interrogate various truth claims.

This type of relativism is analogous to the concepts of balance and fairness that underpin contemporary conceptualizations of journalistic objectivity, which hold that the goal of good reporting is to present multiple points of view without comment as equally viable truth claims. (A recent standard journalism textbook warns students of "the risk of inserting your opinions into the story"). Journalism has embraced this kind of relativism as an integral part of its practice, as reporters are trained to seek out oppositional views on a given issue as actual evidence of objectivity in reporting. For example, Burnham notes that in coverage of environmental issues, even though the majority of the scientific community is agreed on the greenhouse effect and the gravity of its consequences, opposing views are presented by the mass media as equally valid. Thus the public learns not science, but that there are competing figures speaking on one side or the other, each trying to establish the most convincing authority and media presence. . . . Many journalists, using journalistic standards, have made the judgment call that environmental science is all just a matter of opinion.

Similarly, Rosen points out, "On the one hand the Tobacco Institute says smoking is fine and actually improves your health, but on the other hand the American Cancer Society says smoking will kill you. . . . Journalism shows us that often balance is a flight from truth rather than an avenue into truth". When such contradictory knowledge claims are presented uncritically and unreflexively, the corporate structure of media organizations usually function on a subsurface level to legitimize the more elite positions.

News organizations subscribe to the principle that divergent views should be presented in news content without any evidence of value judgments from the journalists themselves; at the same time, they struggle to increase the diversity of experience and background represented by the journalists in their newsrooms. The people in charge of media institutions recognize clearly that racial, gendered, or class-based exclusion in the hiring of journalists will result in biased news coverage. Yet this diversity of opinion is disallowed from being explicitly manifested in news content or reporting methods.

The most serious consequences of that disallowal is that news content is unexamined in terms of its inherent biases -- biases that stem principally from the social location of the reporter, the news organization, and conventional journalistic practices. The recent ASNE guidelines cited earlier in this chapter have begun to charge reporters and editors with the task of analyzing reportage for such biases, yet the goal remains the elimination of bias, a difficult, if not impossible, enterprise. As long as journalists' efforts remain directed toward eradicating rather than problematizing and dealing with bias, relativism will remain a dominant characteristic of news reporting.

Considered in the context of journalism, the intellectual weaknesses of relativism become serious. The reportorial canon of presenting all perspectives without any engagement with the political valences of such perspectives effectively prevents any progressive or emancipatory politics from developing out of journalism. As in science, the current-day formulation of objectivity in journalism actually functions as a blocking device, stopping the rigorous and informed examination of power in everyday journalistic practice. The relativism of balance and fairness is thus ultimately regressive in its impact, functioning mainly to preserve the status quo by its stolid refusal to acknowledge or address the ideological bases of various truth-claims presented by supposedly impartial journalists. As Harding asks: "What would it mean to assert that no reasonable standards can or could in principle be found for adjudicating between one culture's claim that the earth is flat and another culture's claim that the earth is round?". Still, the rationale of current journalistic practice makes that very assertion.

GETTING AWAY FROM EPISTEMIC RELATIVISM

Although journalistic objectivity has been critically examined by various scholars, alternative models of reportage are few and far between. Stoker developed a practice model of "subjective existentialism" that emphasizes reporters' individual responsibility in reporting the news. This model "accepts the objective world of facts, but reemphasizes the importance of the subjective individual in reducing those facts to an accurate account of the truth". Stoker calls for reporters to engage their individual sense of a moral obligation to society in their reporting of the news. Although Stoker's analysis does successfully confront the ideological and institutional problems of objectivity, his alternative of subjective existentialism ends up representing another kind of epistemic relativism, in that it depends on individual journalists to develop moral codes for constructing authentic accounts of the news. This emphasis on individual responsibility still fails to answer the main question raised in critiques of relativism, viz., how would someone receiving such an account evaluate the knowledge claims being made in the context of the construction of the account?

A more rigorous model for journalism is Sandra Harding's formulation of feminist standpoint epistemology -- a theoretical innovation based on the work of Nancy Hartsock, Hilary Rose, Dorothy Smith, and others. Standpoint epistemology ventures beyond Stoker's formulation in that, whereas it, too, offers an escape from the intellectual quicksand of relativism and the indefensible territory of neutrality and detachment, it involves a reconceptualization of objectivity that offers a concretized way of maximizing the role of reflexivity in reporting without relying on individuals' fragile moral consciences.

FEMINIST STANDPOINT EPISTEMOLOGY

Nancy Hartsock 1983 essay, "The Feminist Standpoint," introduced the concept of feminist standpoint epistemology as a Marxian analysis, of gender and power relations in society; here, the notion of the proletariat was translated into feminist terms -- Hartsock argued that women's oppression in Western capitalist society contained the potential for a critique of domination. Since then, the concept was developed theoretically by various feminist scholars, becoming increasingly more sophisticated. A major rethinking of the theory came from Canadian sociologist Dorothy Smith, who understood social texts and discourses to be "ideological practices and procedures which conceal the underlying relations" of power in society. Central to Smith's critique was the political basis of the supposedly "objective" method of accounting for knowledge -- "that it is a product of the relations of ruling because of the ways it makes alternative readings of the reported behaviours impossible".

Smith's proposed alternative to androcentric science was a sociology that began from the "standpoint of women," that is, an epistemology grounded in women's experiences that takes into consideration the ruptures between women's lives and the dominant discourses of society and science.

This feminist standpoint theory has recently been developed by other theorists into more complex standpoint theories that make an inventory of the variable structures of "constraint" lived by the various marginal, oppressed, or dominated groups . . . such that each form of privation is acknowledged as producing its own specific "epistemology," its own specific view from below, and its own specific truth claim.

Standpoint epistemology uses the socially situated nature of various knowledge claims as the basis for maximizing objectivity. This involves a reformulation of the term "objectivity," taking it away from any notion of eradicating bias toward a method of acknowledging and incorporating bias into the structure of the scientific method. Harding has argued that this approach actually generates stronger standards for objectivity than the supposedly value-free models of science. Harding is the theorist who has advanced standpoint epistemology the furthest; her work has most rigorously scrutinized the tensions and contradictions between feminism and Western science, seeking to incorporate an understanding of diversity and relational forces along with an engaged politics of accountability.

As Pederson writes: Harding's feminist philosophy of science offers a rich and varied account of the world in which we live, a way of holding the dissonance and instability of diverse voices in a creative and productive tension; the question is not only one of knowledge as such but of whose knowledge counts and how that knowledge is put to use. Harding contends that the traditional goal of objectivity --

eliminating social values and interests from research -- was developed out of fear of harmful social consequences in the wake of Nazism and the mindset of the Cold War. This fear allowed objectivity in the American scientific domain to become the intellectual property of dominant groups, who conducted research without critically examining their own political and historical bases and commitments.

An alternative approach requires the constitution of an equivalence between the subjects and objects of inquiry, that is, the subjects and objects of research are placed on the same critical plane. As Hekman explains, "Feminist standpoint theory can and, I argue, should be defined as a counterhegemonic discourse that works to destabilize hegemonic discourse".

In science, this would mean that the scientists, the scientific communities that generate standards of knowledge, the methods of inquiry, and so on, would be put under the microscope, so to speak, as part of the research. This scrutiny would be as rigorous as that to which the "objects" of research are subjected. Notes Harding:

All of the kinds of objectivity-maximizing procedures focused on the nature and/ or social situations that are the direct object of observation and reflection must also be focused on the observers and reflectors-scientists and the larger society whose assumptions they share.

But a maximally critical study of scientists and their communities can be done only from the perspective of those whose lives have been marginalized by such communities. I will return to the second point, which I have marked in italics, after discussing the notion of maximal objectivity as being grounded in an identity location.

In traditional science, supposedly objective knowledge is presented as "the view from nowhere" -- ahistorical, value free, devoid of connections to socially and culturally determined belief systems. This ritual denial of the political bases of conventionally objective knowledge has been described by Haraway as "the God trick." Harding argues that by foregrounding and acknowledging the perspectives, values, and biases of knowledge claims, a less partial and distorted knowledge is possible -- one that makes no claims to universality, but is clearly connected to an ontological, social, historical, and economic position.

This way of approaching knowledge draws on the sociological theory advanced by Karl Mannheim, which holds that all thought is socially determined: Knowledge is related to the social groups to which the knower belongs. According to a recent interpretation by Longhurst, "what Mannheim is saying is that belief is relative to the social location of the social actor, who is constrained by the membership of particular social groups which determine the form and content of the particular ideas adopted".

An inherent problem with this conception of knowledge is that it, too, posits a relativism that does not allow for rigorous arbitration among different perspectives. However, using feminist theory, Longhurst has developed Mannheim's thinking in a manner that escapes the pitfall of relativism. He writes, "There is no need for a contemporary sociology of knowledge . . . to produce a synthetic view of the truth. It is enough to show how those views are produced and utilised by different groups".

The task of epistemology, he concludes, is to show which social groups are important, how they are interrelated, and what this means. This brings us back to Lambeth categorical imperative of telling "the truth" in journalism. Although a single "synthetic truth" or value-free fact cannot be reported, the construction of various truths via social actors in social groups can be.

Central to this exercise would be the acknowledgment that the journalist is such an actor, along with his or her sources. A concomitant step in the process would involve the recognition of privileged discourses in the construction of knowledge via journalism.

That is the critical juncture at which standpoint epistemology could provide a way to destabilize hegemonic discourses in reporting: The development of alternative standpoints within a journalistic text could, in standpoint terms, "deepen the critique available from the standpoint of the proletariat and . . . allow for a critique of patriarchal ideology" .

The Role of Reflexivity

Most scientific accounts, as well as journalistic accounts, are presented from the inside out: Information is collected and interpreted by people who are inside the dominant social order about those who are either inside or outside it, with no overt acknowledgment of these social locations or the implications thereof. When outsiders are part of a news story, they are almost always objects of scrutiny; this position works to delegitimize their knowledge claims.

The question that arises here is this: Can a valid account of a phenomenon be given if the social locations of the reporter and the subjects are not taken into account? Or, as a corollary: How can social phenomena be best observed while taking into consideration the location of the observer? These questions have been given a great deal of scholarly attention in anthropology and literary criticism, where similar issues regarding power and knowledge have arisen.

In an early groundbreaking essay, Geertz noted that the traditionally "objectivist" position in ethnography resulted in "a view of anthropological research as rather more of an observational and rather less of an interpretive activity than it really is". Contrary to this traditional view of anthropology, Geertz argues that all anthropological research is interpretive in that an account of any event is inevitably cast in terms of the interpretation of the observer.

Such accounts, he contends, "are anthropological because it is, in fact, anthropologists who profess them". Similarly, it is my contention here that news stories are journalistic because it is journalists who relay them. Thus journalism, like anthropology, is at best a second- or third-order reconstruction of an event that happened to other people, which brings the validity of the account -- its objectivity, or realism, if you will -- into question. Anthropological research has in recent years dealt with this problem by taking a "reflexive turn". Here, the central argument is that "all claims to knowledge are reflexive of the process, assumptions, location, history and context of knowing and the knower". Hammersley and Atkinson urge that anthropological accounts pay scrupulous attention to the role of the researcher as an active participant in the construction of knowledge. "By including our own role within the research focus, and perhaps even systematically exploiting our participation in the settings under study as researchers, we can produce accounts of the social world and justify them without placing reliance on futile appeals to empiricism".

In a similar vein, the arena of literary criticism uses the notion of reflexivity to describe texts that foreground the nature of their own production. As Stam puts it, reflexive literary narratives "demystify fictions" by unmasking "their own production, their authorship, their intertextual references, their reception, or their enunciation". "Reflexivity," he writes, ". . . points to its own mask and invites the public to examine its design and texture". Reflexivity in literature, and even more so in film, functions as an instrument of social criticism -- its inward look critiques the dominant society that generates the fictions, exposing the illusions created by the narrative as well as the ideological bases of their construction. A parallel move in journalism would correspondingly demystify its practices and ideological bases. The reflexive journalistic text would not present itself as a transparent communication of reality; rather, it would openly acknowledge the factors that went into its construction. This idea is beginning to take hold in established journalistic circles. For example, the new ASNE ethics guidelines incorporate a move toward reflexivity into reporting method.

The ASNE urges reporters to ask themselves the following questions before embarking on a news story:

- *What assumptions and preconceived views do we bring to the table*: how do these preconceived views shape our news coverage before we even begin to frame the story?
- *What is the essence of the story*: how should we frame our coverage to capture where the issue begins, the

nuances of the situation and the meaning people are conveying?

- *How are we listening and to whom*: what voices do we need to cover to illuminate news coverage and how do we need to tap into the many dimensions of our communities to find those voices?
- *How might we think about our coverage over time*: when we think about our coverage over time, what do our conversations within the newsroom need to sound like and what existing perspectives, experience and knowledge do we need to tap within the newsroom?

In anthropological work, attempts to incorporate this type of understanding have led to an abandonment of "a clear statement about validity that goes beyond the researcher's purpose or ideology". In journalism, too, reflexivity in reporting still means that competing knowledge claims go unanalyzed in the news story itself.

Gans has noted, "The news especially values the moral order of the upper-class and upper-middle-class sectors of society. . . . Furthermore, the news reflects a white male social order". Standpoint epistemology hinges on the reverse process, thus providing an avenue for incorporating reflexivity into a clear evaluative method. This methodological departure provides a way of acknowledging and incorporating bias into the news account instead of attempting to eradicate it.

A first step lies in beginning all investigations from the perspectives of those outside the privileged community of investigators. This is a key tenet of standpoint epistemology. Further, both Dorothy Smith and Sandra Harding maintain that the best knowledge comes out of starting from the perspectives of those who are the most marginalized by dominant institutions and practices and looking inward.

Whereas feminist standpoint epistemology originally focused on marginalization that occurred via gender biases in social science, it has been revised in recent years to minimize this essentializing tendency and include ways to understand "the interlocking relationships between sexism, racism, heterosexism and class oppression" in scientific research.

To do this in journalistic practice would push journalists beyond relativism. If all reporting began from the perspective of those whose lives are impacted by events and by the reporting of events, the unrecognized weight of the socially dominant "insider" positions would be counterbalanced. In other words, a critical examination of the journalist and the journalistic institution from the perspective of the most marginalized "object" of investigation would be at the core of every news story. If this starting point is acknowledged and foregrounded, the resulting knowledge becomes less partial and relativistic than the kind of knowledge that is presented by the journalist/insider as value free.

The question then becomes how those who are privileged to study, write, and speak about "social outsiders" can do so without either:

- Replicating conventional biases,
- Inauthentically using others' voices to make false claims of being able to see from their marginalized perspectives
- Legitimating false knowledge claims?

These are dilemmas for journalists, who are privileged to speak about the central issues in today's society. By and large, their background and training, and the authority of their affiliation with a corporate media organization, have located them in this privileged position. Traditional notions of objectivity permit -- even encourage-journalists to speak without acknowledging their own identity locations in relation to the issues on which they report. Public journalism is a contemporary effort to allow journalists to speak as participants in social processes. Even this type of activist journalism, however, may reproduce traditional sex, class, and racial biases, or fail to illumine the differences among various knowledge claims.

Standpoint epistemology can advance journalism by compelling journalists to rethink themselves and their craft from the position of marginalized Others, thus uncovering unconscious ethnocentric, sexist, racist, and heterosexist biases that distort news production as it is governed by the dominant news paradigm. Again, these problems would be acknowledged in news reporting rather than erased. Harding suggests that scientists adopt standpoint epistemology by "reinventing themselves as the Other" -- that is, by seeing themselves and those they study as having complexly related identities. She points out that most scientists act and think out of contradictory social locations -- the "Black intellectual" or the "woman philosopher" are labels that carry inherent contradictions in terms of dominant thought. However, Harding insists that even people whose identities seem not as overtly contradictory (the "White male journalist," for example) can still rethink themselves from the position of the outsider: the point is to develop strategies that encourage men as well as women, whites as well as people of colour, straights as well as gays and lesbians, the economically overadvantaged as well as the working class and the poor to become active agents of historical understanding.

Thus a journalist must strive to conceptualize him- or herself as the outsider, to become engaged in the consequences of the story from the point of view of those most disenfranchised by it, rather than in the simple aggregation of its parts. This repositioning is a critical factor in undoing the locked-in methods by which knowledge is produced in current news practice, and it offers a way for reporters to seriously engage with the "objects" of their investigations in terms of evaluating competing knowledge claims, with a liberatory goal.

Reporters would summon a critical, reflective consciousness as part of reporting, and this consciousness would be made known to media audiences. It is this consciousness that provides a basis for seriously and rigorously understanding various knowledge claims, by revealing the logic, or logics, behind various representations of truth. Harding describes this process as achieving a "traitorous" identity, in the sense of betraying one's privileged position to understand the connections between one's own social situation and that of others, an understanding that goes unexplored in conventional journalistic practice. Moreover, journalists of all races, sexes, sexual orientations, and socioeconomic backgrounds could and should be engaged in this practice, although its more progressive tendencies are best realized when privileged people take on a reflexivity generated from the standpoint of the oppressed.

In attempting to use standpoint epistemology in reporting, the reporter must also be wary of universalizing tendencies. The word "standpoint" should not be misconstrued to indicate a unified, stable subjectivity or an essential, "marginalized" experience. An important aspect of standpoint theory is the understanding that social identities are complex and heterogeneous. Thus, repositioning as "the Other" needs to be accomplished without totalizing or privileging the marginalized experience, which would result in a different kind of bias. Harding calls this tendency "experiential foundationalism"--"the tendency to insist that the spontaneous consciousness of individual experience provides a uniquely legitimating criterion for identifying preferable or less false beliefs".

There is, of course, a difference between experience and knowledge. The trick for the standpoint reporter is to be able to decide on the validity of a knowledge claim regardless of who speaks it, while understanding that who speaks does have a bearing on what is made known. Thus, it is the relationship between knowledge and experience that needs to be problematized in order to get past relativism towards a truly emancipatory journalism.

Incorporating standpoint epistemology into journalistic praxis would require, then, that the starting point for the production of any news story be an examination of the social relationships between the knowers and the known, that is, between the journalist, journalistic institutions, the person who would experience marginalization in the context of the news story, and the knowledge claims at stake.

Using this as a point of departure for reporting on a story would produce an operationalization of what Gans described as "multiperspectival news," a reportorial method that he advocated for its potential to "add a bottom-up view to the current top-down practice" of news reporting. Gans's idea of multiperspectivity has been incorporated into contemporary news practice, but without the grounding of strong objectivity it has relapsed into epistemic relativism.

Standpoint epistemology offers the practice of journalism a means of becoming meaningfully connected to the politics of everyday life. It also offers some hope for realizing the liberatory goals of journalism by providing a method for interrogating and challenging power relations in society via the production of news.

FROM PRINCIPLE TO PRACTICE: A BLUEPRINT FOR CHANGE

Can standpoint epistemology function as a viable journalistic method within the political, economic, and practical constraints of contemporary corporate news organizations? The prospect of this appears at first glance to be dim. As Chornsky observes, "The very structure of the media is designed to induce conformity to established doctrine". A considerable body of analysis indicates that "the media serve the interests of state and corporate power, which are closely interlinked, framing their reporting and analysis in a manner supportive of established privilege and limiting debate and discussion accordingly". Within the fairly rigid corporate apparatus of the mainstream media, the introduction of a radical journalistic practice would appear to be infeasible.

Oddly enough, standpoint epistemology is concordant with the declared ideology of mainstream journalistic practice, which seeks to "afflict the comfortable and comfort the afflicted" according to one of its most overworked clichés. The situation is dilemmatic in that this approach calls for reporters to employ a certain amount of agency, which is mitigated by the dominant ideology of objectivity in the current news paradigm and in its institutional practice. To effectively alter the normalized process of reporting the news within extant institutional routines, standpoint epistemology requires an active and systematic departure from these routines. By adopting a standpoint epistemology, however, a reporter actually gains access to a concrete mechanism for incorporating the class analysis of a story into its reporting, which can be used to counter a common source of bias in current reporting. It is not my intent to promote a naive optimism with regard to the possibilities for standpoint epistemology to flourish as a reportorial method in the repressive ideological environment of contemporary news organizations. I strongly believe, however, that the incorporation of a certain reflexivity has the potential to resuscitate journalism by inverting rather than disrupting the parameters of the current news paradigm, working within the limits of the relative autonomy granted to news reporters in terms of their choice of method. Standpoint epistemology can be seen as a radical intervention to subvert from within the hegemonies in current news practice. Pederson observes that Harding's formulation of standpoint theory offers a way to translate the "instability and dissonance" of multiple perspectives into action. Similarly, Smith connects a "non-objectivist" construction of knowledge with the potential for social activism. For journalism to become powerfully connected to social action, standpoint epistemology needs to be the basis of reportorial practice.

In practical terms, how is this to be done? Studies of journalists' reliance on elite sources indicate that the intense deadline pressures of modern-day print publication preclude them from expending the extra effort required to seek out nontraditional voices or use unorthodox reportorial methods. Already there is some precedent for a reworking of the concept of news sources, though. Even standard reporting textbooks urge reporters to seek out a diversity of sources; Rich, for example, advises students to use multicultural sources in every story, and also notes, "If you want to learn how to sweep floors, talk to a janitor, not to the corporation president. . . . If you want to get the most accurate and vivid information about a story, talk to the people who were directly involved". Incorporating standpoint epistemology into this basic model would require thinking past the first, most obvious source -- the person nearest the action -- to the persons most marginalized in the context of the story. Reporters, especially those reporters with an interest in community journalism, could as easily build a source list of people outside of privileged power groups as they cultivate their "inside" sources. Smith discussion of nonobjectivity links the conceptualization of standpoint theory as critique of dominant ideology to practice. As she puts it, the principled stances taken by the standpoint theorist or nonobjectivist can lead directly to community activism. Yet what action is taken is an open question. In the journalistic context, action is best construed in terms of reportorial methods of destabilizing hegemonic discourses in the news.

The sourcing aspect of applying standpoint epistemology to practice is a fairly straightforward one; the other dimension pertains to the construction of the story itself, with attention paid to the strategic discourses used by various groups, including the reporter as a member of the press corps, to advance their truth claims. This would call for a radical transformation of newswriting so that it would include the elements of reflexivity called for in the new ASNE guidelines. Although the ASNE guidelines urge reporters to be reflexive in their approach to reporting, they do not yet suggest that the process be integrated into the writing of the news story; yet, because this professional organization has recognized the need for such practice, I am hopeful that the journalistic community could adopt such a reconstruction of the news story itself. The news story would need to incorporate the ways in which the various positions on an issue have been structured along gender, class, racial, or other lines.

Examples of such practice are not easily found in contemporary journalism, especially in the mainstream press, but some alternative media strive for this kind of subversion of the norm of neutrality, and there are existing texts that embody at least some of the possibilities of standpoint reporting. The Women's International Newsgathering Service (WINGS), for example, deliberately begins each story from the point of view of women.

Thus, a recent story on the war in Yugoslavia focused on its impact on women as well as the activism of women protesters . However, once more, these stories rarely if ever locate the reporter in the context of the story -- a vital part of "strong objectivity" in reportage. The genre of literary journalism has set some precedent for including the narrator in the narrative; the writings of John McPhee, Joan Didion, and Hunter Thompson are classics of this genre. One much-celebrated piece of literary journalism, J.

Anthony Lukas Common Ground, is a complex and finely detailed piece of reporting that shifts the standpoint of a story about school desegregation efforts in the 1960s among three experiences: working-class Black, working-class White, and upper-class White. Lukas is known as a journalist who sought to capture nuances in his writing, rather than simply recounting facts. Yet even the Pulitzer Prize-winning book, Common Ground, which took 7 years to complete and was critically lauded for its rigor and compassion, is presented from a "God's-eye view": The reporter, his position, his analysis of the situation out of his social location as a Harvard-educated upperclass White male are undeveloped in the narrative. Other works of literary journalism include the author, but fail to rigorously address the reporter's standpoint in relation to others in the context of the reporting process.

The development of a rigorous and ethical method of standpoint reporting in fact calls for a radically new pedagogy of journalism. For reporters to be able to write in these ways, such that they can integrate reflexivity and outsider standpoints into their news accounts while staying on deadline, requires training in an analytical and self-critical style of hard-news journalism that is very different from the newswriting taught in America today. I believe such a writing method can be offered as a practical option for thinking, caring journalists. Whereas the stories might take the same shape as articles in the current inverted-pyramid style, the text would make clear the reporter's social and political location as well as those of other sources; the various standpoints as sites of truth claims would be made apparent. The identification and examination of competing social interests, beginning with the most marginalized, would be at the nucleus of every story. I am convinced that this radical shift in the representation of information would be a positive development in terms of its contributions to journalism's most progressive, emancipatory, and democratic goals.

As Harding has said of science, "Women and men cannot understand or explain the world we live in or the real choices we have as long as the sciences describe and explain the world primarily from the perspectives of the lives of dominant groups". The same challenge applies to journalism. The incorporation of standpoint epistemology into current methods of news reporting would serve to transform journalism from practice to praxis, where praxis is "a general human activity and energy" that is geared to generating new and better ways of understanding.

This praxis would rest on the goal of making people's lives and experiences intelligible in the social, political, and economic context of journalism. The difference would lie in the reexamination of journalistic practices with the explicit goal of redistributing the normalized power relationships inherent to current reporting methods. This redistribution would give relative weight to hitherto underrepresented sources of information so as to reexamine information from those positions. The truth claims of the socially marginalized would be centered and foregrounded.

This process would deploy a system of journalistic self-evaluation that would in fact strengthen the so-called objectivity of reporting, increase journalists' responsibility to marginalized publics, and, most importantly, reveal the ways in which different social locations (of race, sex, class, and sexual orientation, as well as others -- physical and mental disability, age, etc.) can shape the "facts" set forth in news stories. Through such praxis, journalism can effectively serve the interests of a broader cross-section of the public as well as contribute to a progressive politics that would controvert the well-documented problems of normalized and naturalized notions of objectivity in the reporting of news.

Chapter 2

The Emergence of Modern Libertarian Free Speech

When free love editor Ezra Heywood was sentenced in June 1878 to two years imprisonment at hard labour in the Dedham Mass. jail and fined $100 for sending obscene literature through the mail, vice fighter Anthony Comstock rejoiced. Free love advocates promoted a feminist agenda that called for equal rights for women, including allowing women to control their own reproductive systems, regardless of their husbands' desires.

The philosophy, which encouraged women to choose how many children they bore, was a direct assault on Victorian marital, sexual, and social relations. As historian Craig Fisher-LaMay has stated: "To Comstock their social agenda was itself obscene, unsuitable for public presentation, and he naturally sought to confiscate and destroy their literature and prosecute their leaders."

Comstock, who had personally arrested Heywood in his capacity as a special agent of the U.S. Postal Service, viewed the free love movement as a social threat because it exemplified much of what he perceived was wrong with late-Victorian society. As such, he denounced free love adherents, calling them "indecent creatures ... Men and women foul of speech, shameless in their lives, and corrupting in their influences ..." Self respect, moral purity, and "holy living" were crushed by the philosophy. Only "sure ruin and death" awaited its advocates, he said. Heywood, a former Congregationalist minister and critic of Comstock's vice society work which he viewed as censorship, was tried for mailing copies of an anti-marriage, pro-feminist pamphlet he had written called Cupid's Yokes. Although it contained no sexually- explicit language and was an earnest, yet turgid, feminist polemic, U.S. Circuit Court Judge Daniel Clark instructed jurors that Heywood should be found guilty of mailing an obscene publication if they found any part of the pamphlet to have an immoral tendency. They did. Comstock viewed the conviction as proof that decent society agreed that free love adherents were licentious and their discussions were obscene and thus not deserving of any protection.

Repeated arrests and a second conviction under federal obscenity statutes might have consigned Heywood to be little more than a footnote in history, one of many late nineteenth-century radical reformers prosecuted for his non-mainstream beliefs. But Heywood did not exist in isolation; he was part of a much broader group of educated liberal reformers with a variety of views, including free thinkers, former abolitionists, family planning advocates, early feminists, authors, artists, librarians, and attorneys who organized and publicly advocated broad First Amendment protection for ideas, including socially unpopular ones, during an era of vast social and cultural change. Many of these liberals were arrested and prosecuted under the Comstock Act because their progressive views challenged prevailing social norms.

The prosecutions and reactions to them reveal that a substantial segment of the American public, its judiciary, legislators, and some press members embraced narrow interpretations of expression rights with limited debate. By either supporting or not opposing majoritarian will, much of the public was willing to exclude unpopular social expression when such discussion seemed threatening to the public order.

Although some of these nineteenth-century liberals have been the subjects of a number of studies, no definitive work exists on their public campaign to promote free expression rights. This research examines the prosecutions of four noted libertarians: free love advocate Ezra Heywood; Dr. Edward Bond Foote, a well-known New York physician and medical publisher; and two prominent free thought publishers, DeRobigne M. Bennett and Moses Harman and the subsequent libertarian campaign for broad First Amendment protection for all citizens which ensued from their arrests and prosecutions. That individuals were putting forth a libertarian philosophy of free expression in the 1870s (albeit largely under the auspices of individual rights rather than the later interpretation of social benefits), demonstrates the formative period of modern First Amendment development occurred decades earlier than is often acknowledged.

All four men believed individuals should be free to publish information on virtually any topic, no matter how unorthodox, without the fear of legal sanctions. Their support of various feminist causes, including suffrage, birth control, dress reform, divorce, and the right of women to work, presented tremendous challenges to the status quo and inevitably led to their prosecutions by morality crusaders.

The research argues that these liberal thinkers, all too cognizant of the suppression power of obscenity statutes, sought, and eventually helped to create, an expansive interpretation of the First Amendment. As will be demonstrated, these libertarians brought the related issues of the social and legal boundaries of freedom of expression and federal First Amendment protection for ideas, which heretofore were not part of common social discourse, into the public arena. By emphasizing the necessity of free expression rights in a democratic society, the libertarians hoped to spur broad public, legal, and legislative discourse about the First Amendment, its applications, and the limits of state legal controls over individuals and society.

The research first examines two opposing forces: the purity crusaders and libertarian reformers, both of whom clashed verbally about how to remake society. Their views on obscenity and free speech demonstrate the divergent strains of freedom of expression in the nineteenth century-moral censorship for the good of society versus greater openness of discussion for authors of both fiction and non-fiction. The research then turns to the status of obscenity law during the

Gilded Age to provide the context for an examination of the libertarians' subsequent prosecutions. Finally, the research examines the prosecution's and the libertarians' responses-in both words and actions-to the prosecutions and their efforts to promote an expansive interpretation of free expression rights.

The Purity Crusaders and Sesocial Control

At the close of the U.S. Civil War, many members of the middle and upper classes turned their attention and time to reforming the multitude of problems brought about by the nation's rapid industrialization and urbanization, particularly those issues that directly affected their lives or threatened the social status quo. Many of these individuals also were distressed by a series of tremendous cultural earthquakes. Religious beliefs were coming into question as an era of skepticism emerged. At the same time, new philosophical and scientific theories by such men as Herbert Spencer, John Fiske, Charles Darwin, and Henry George challenged traditional views.

Changes in publishing technology and rising literacy rates contributed to the emergence of publishing as a business. Inexpensive magazines aimed at the general public blossomed as a new realism in literature emerged. Works by Frank Norris, Hamlin Garland, Stephen Crane, and Jack London challenged the genteel tradition of romantic literature. Then, too, more lowbrow fare: dime stories, theater, and other working-class amusements, reflected commercialization and a consumer culture rather than the genteel literature and pastimes that mirrored the values the upper classes held as sacrosanct. These social, intellectual, and cultural changes troubled conservatives who realized such profound shifts influenced class, family, and gender.

Middle- and upper-class reformers had cause for concern, particularly when they surveyed the nation's metropolitan areas and saw their political and social influence declining. Writer Henry James voiced the upper class's fears when he remarked that America's emerging social plurality and urban problems filled him with "the dreadful chill of change." Cities were thick with vice, crime, and grinding poverty. Prostitutes plied their trade in broad daylight, gambling dens and saloons were numerous, and obscene and indecent books and magazines were readily available, even to children, from pushcart vendors and news dealers. And, perhaps most alarming, immigrants were changing the nation's urban power structure via voting.

Wealthy reformers, some of whom had been abolitionists, were strongly influenced by the prevailing Victorian linear thinking of the time which held that society was always improving and, relatedly, that virtually all members of society could be perfected. As a result, no reform seemed insignificant and no problem was immune from investigation.

The reformers' interests split them into several camps. One group, which became known as purity crusaders, sought to stabilize society by eradicating prostitution, obscene literature, dime novels and story papers, gambling, pool halls, and drinking. They also engaged in prison reform, campaigned for temperance, and established Sunday Schools to spread a Protestant view of Christianity, particularly to the nation's slum dwellers. Their ranks included Anthony Comstock's New York Society for the Suppression of Vice, the Women's Christian Temperance Union, the Salvation Army, and the Young Men's Christian Association. Purity crusaders also supported Charles Loring Brace's New York-based Children's Aid Society, an organization that removed thousands of poor children from cities and sent them to rural areas.

The purity reformers emerged to fill a void left by the diminished authority of the nation's clergy who once served as near-absolute voices on behavioral and social matters. Not surprisingly, the wealthy citizens who joined the purity crusade promoted their values, including prudence, sobriety, Protestant morality, and clean living, as correct and respectable.

Anthony Comstock's four-decades long effort to eradicate what he perceived as pornographic and immoral publications and art received substantial support by wealthy reformers because his actions mirrored the middleand upper-class view that deviant ideas and individuals had to be suppressed for the good of the community. Comstock seized upon this thinking, pronouncing vice activities as "all-invading," touching the lives of men, women, and children of all classes and leading them to spiritual, social, and economic ruin.

Comstock and other purity reformers used extensive multimedia campaigns as a means to explain their actions, gain support, and, they hoped, produce lasting social and political changes. They gave speeches, wrote articles for magazines and newspapers, and created pamphlets and books about reform issues. Purity reformers used publicity as a tactic after they noted that a number of newspapers had successfully crusaded to eradicate gambling and improve housing conditions in the nation's inner cities in the early 1870s.

Anthony Comstock devoted virtually his entire adult life to stamping out vice. His efforts were born of traditional views about sex, the roles of men and women, and the sanctity of the home and family. More importantly, Comstock, like many Victorian Americans, believed there was a direct link between drinking, gambling, and obscene literature (which he defined as anything even slightly titillating) and criminal behaviour. "When you touch them young people with corruption you have touched the future welfare of society, church, and state," Comstock solemnly intoned in one pamphlet designed to make the public aware of his perceived scope of the problem of obscene literature. The "three great crime-breeders in America" he added, were "intemperance, gambling, and evil reading, and the greatest of these is evil reading."

To drive home his point about the link between vice and crime, Comstock produced books and articles filled with stories of young men who had gone astray physically or criminally because of their love of cheap fiction or obscene literature. The stories, which were designed to frighten readers, fell into two categories. The first told of nameless, "gentle youth" from wealthy, virtuous families who, because of their alleged innocence, fell under the "seductive power" of vice and became regular readers of pornographic literature while they were away at boarding school and thus away from parental guidance, absolving the parents of any blame. Their fascination with pornography led these young men to engage in the "solitary vice" (the Victorian term for the unmentionable masturbation) which purity crusaders believed destroyed the men's health and led them to an early grave. Victims were described as raging with fever, shriveled, their faces ashen, and their brains deteriorated before death occurred.

By contrast, Comstock said poor children were drawn to an equally dangerous, but different, literature: dime novels and story papers. Readers, he said, were often inspired to then commit the very crimes of which they had just read. His book Traps for the Young featured an engraving showing young street urchins reading dime novels then using the knowledge they obtained to rob the wealthy.

Comstock "proved" his claims by lacing the book with alleged confessions by young criminals who claimed that such story papers provided them with both the knowledge and inspiration they needed to carry out crimes. Even without such evidence many of Comstock's supporters believed him, convinced there was a direct causeand-effect link between the media's influence and public actions.

Despite this reality, purity reformers often failed, or refused, to confront the fact that vice activities were not the sole province of the working poor. For example, The Gentleman's Guide, a popular book from the 1860s, listed many of the more than 600 houses of prostitution in New York. Many of the city's finer hotels during the last decades of the nineteenth-century also provided their male guests with business cards from first-class houses.

Furthermore, many wealthy men kept mistresses with whom they could act out their fantasies and desires, believing their wives "were too pure for such actions." The purity crusaders' failure to pursue vice into its upperclass ranks led popular novelist Albert Ross to fume: "We are in the midst of an era of sham. We do not care so much that vice exists as that it be well dressed." Unlike most of the purity crusaders who undertook their work out of fear of social upheaval (or, occasionally, genuine concern for the poor), Comstock's writings reveal the vice fighter truly believed he had been appointed by God to protect women, children, and other individuals with impressionable minds from the evils and dangers of what he perceived to be obscene and immoral material. The vice fighter believed the devil was everywhere, seeking young converts, including the scions of wealthy families, through brazen pornography as well as through dime novels, romance novels, and even classical works of literature and art. Anything even slightly titillating, works which questioned the traditional, Protestant social order, or material which debated the value of Christianity had to be suppressed for the good of society.

Comstock's main tool for fighting vice was federal legislation which the vice fighter and several lawyers introduced on February 18, 1873. The law was, in essence, a time, place, and manner restriction, although such terminology was not used at the time. The statute did not prohibit obscene matter. Instead it criminalized using the U.S. Postal System to send such items. The law left open the possibility materials could be shipped via private freight carriers.

The legislation, popularly known as the Comstock Act, became law on March 3, 1873. The law's language was similar to a federal law enacted a year earlier, but with two important differences that allowed Comstock and other vice fighters broad power. The Act banned mailing obscene materials for the first time. The law also allowed birth control information and paraphernalia (including condoms) to be labeled as obscene matter. The latter change made it difficult for doctors to impart reproductive information to their patients.

The new law failed to define obscenity, an omission that gave purity crusaders great latitude to pursue their quarry under the auspices of protecting public morality. The statute ensured that individuals could not use legal loopholes to gain acquittal. The broadly-worded law banned the importing, advertising, or mailing ob obscene matter and called for the confiscation and destruction of such matter. Two days after the Act's passage, Comstock was appointed as a special agent of the Post Office with the power to arrest individuals who used the mails to distribute obscene matter. He undertook the job with zeal for more than forty years. Comstock, who always portrayed himself as a Victorian David fighting many immoral Goliaths, rejoiced at the Act's passage, both because of its broad applications and because it was enacted, despite the liberals' opposition to it. "There was a most deliberate attempt, on the part of certain of my opponents, to malign me before members of Congress, and to make me odious by their anonymous, and other, letters, so that my word would not be received," he reminisced to free speech attorney Theodore Schroeder in 1905. "But the simple facts which were presented, on behalf of the Law, were sufficient to out-weigh all of the opposition that was hurled against this measure by the great fraternity of smut dealers, who were then organized against it," Comstock added with satisfaction. Comstock's labeling tactic was designed to discredit the law's opponents. This alleged "great fraternity" included prominent publishers, editors, authors, and physicians, a point Comstock would not acknowledge.

The 1873 law gave Comstock and other vice crusaders tremendous license to affix their conservative moral stamp on expression, as well as almost unhindered discretion as postal officials. The 1873 law's lack of a definition of obscenity beyond that of what might corrupt the minds and morals of the young and impressionable meant free thinkers, women's suffragists, birth control adherents, and free love advocates frequently found public dissemination of their beliefs proscribed as did a number of authors of social realism novels.

The purity crusaders' work was a continuation of the American social and legal tradition of censoring unpopular viewpoints, rather than an anomalous new effort by conservatives bent on attacking literature that reflected changing social mores. All printed material, including literature and medical and education books and pamphlets, was open to purity crusaders' scrutiny.

Indeed, Congress's adoption of the Comstock Act during a time of increasing social pluralism led to inevitable and frequently explosive clashes concerning freedom of expression.

Once socially-taboo issues, including divorce and agnosticism, were starting to be discussed in mainstream publications. Other topics, including prostitution, abortion, and family planning, were still largely the province of medical journals or the more daring reform publications, such as The Arena, whose editor was an outspoken supporter of freedom of speech.

Judicial support for the Comstock Act quickly followed the law's enactment. The Act's constitutionality was upheld the same year by a federal appeals court judge in New York who, in affirming the convictions of two men who had used the mails to send abortion powders to customers, held that Congress had the power to determine what matter was permissible to be mailed and what was not.

Five years later, the U.S. Supreme Court affirmed the ruling in a case involving the prosecution of a New York man who had mailed a lottery ticket. In that case, Justice Stephen Field held that the mails could not be used as a vehicle to send obscene matter. Field also affirmed a long-understood nineteenth-century legal convention that judges did not merely announce the law, they were the arbiters of the nation's moral standards. Furthermore, field made clear that Congress's intention was not to violate press freedoms, but it could regulate content by refusing to allow the mails to be used "for the distribution of matter deemed injurious to the public morals." Field's discussion of freedom of the press was limited.

As Frederick Schauer has found, the nineteenth-century interpretation of freedom of the press "was related to political commentary and criticism, and since prohibition of material relating to lotteries and obscenity did not come within the definition of 'press,' there was no constitutional problem."

Congress further aided morality crusaders in 1879 when they passed another postal law aimed at slowing the distribution of unpopular expression. The new law increased the postal system's police powers, allowing officials to revoke the second-class mailing privileges of any periodicals found to be produced for self-advertising. Under the new law, publishers of a number of free thought, family planning, socialist, labour, and other publications espousing non-mainstream views had their permits revoked, including Dr. E. B. Foote's Health Monthly and Moses Herman's Lucifer, the Light Bearer. The editors were forced to use the higher, first-class rates to distribute their publications.

Comstock's arrest powers as a special agent of the post office also were strengthened and broadened by an 1896 U.S. Supreme Court ruling that the 1873 Act included obscene letters. Earlier court rulings had differed on this point with some justices viewing the act as including only obscene books, pictures, pamphlets, prints, and indecent publications. Comstock's tactic of using decoy letters to get allegedly obscene material sent to him through the mails also was upheld by the U.S. Supreme Court.

Comstock was not the first person to use postal laws to stop unpopular expression. The precedent for such postal censorship began during the U.S. Civil War when the U.S. Postmaster General, Montgomery Blair, personally assumed the powerful role of censor by withholding from the mails material he determined was either treasonable or which might aid the Confederate enemy. Despite the unprecedented nature of this action, Congress allowed Blair to continue. By its action (or inaction), Congress determined it had the authority to instruct the postmaster general to declare certain matter nonmailable.

Comstock always claimed the law named after him was necessary, seeing it as a commitment to community security and the status quo of the male-dominated family. "To repeal the present laws would be a crime against society and especially a crime against young women," he told a Harper's Weekly reporter in 1915. His belief in strictly-defined, biblically ordained roles for men and women coupled with his underlying fear that sexually self-determined women would diminish male authority, led to Comstock's insistence that contraceptive devices were obscene because they encouraged immoral practices. Many physicians agreed, claiming contraception was unnatural and stating it would encourage illicit sexual behaviour, and might encourage women to claim "the right to their bodies." Most of the literary works that Comstock initially sought to suppress were not works by noted authors, but instead, novels advertised as "rich,""racy," or "rare," to draw attention to their tawdry character. Comstock explained in his work, Traps for the Young, that such advertising demonstrated that the publisher's intent was to sell an obscene work. "Any person so outraging public decency and good morals ought to be punished," he concluded.

Comstock and his allies (particularly Boston's Watch and Ward Society) at first garnered both the public's and the media's praise for ridding New York and other cities of such works. When Comstock then turned his attention to confiscating cheap reprints of more noted works, including Walt Whitman's Leaves of Grass, Giovanni Boccaccio's TAe Decameron, and Count Leo Tolstoy's Kreutzer Sonata, most of the public, with the exception of a few writers and some journalists, largely failed to object. At a time when books dealing with sexual or unconventional ideas were kept in locked cases in public libraries, such works were not widely-enough known by the public to create outrage at their confiscation.

Indeed, Comstock himself always had a deep suspicion of works of fiction, even works judged classics. He held the common, upper-class, paternal view that such books should remain available only to educated individuals who understood them. The vice fighter stated that classics could be "kept by booksellers only to meet what some consider the legitimate demand of the student, or gentleman's library."

When such works were mass produced, Comstock often tried to stop such sales, worried about the materials' influence on the working class. Then, too, as literary historians have noted, only a few reputable publishers faced arrest by Comstock because most were careful not to produce works that might offend public tastes, even if the work deserved to be published.

Many publishers of the emerging naturalist fiction omitted offending passages, while others withdrew books when threatened by vice societies. This timidity would not subside for decades until cultural attitudes shifted. Indeed, the literary world would not begin a broad, concerted fight against censorship until the suppression of Theodore Dreiser's work, The Genius, in 1916. Publisher Horace Liveright led the anti-censorship crusade, spurred by changing public attitudes.

Comstock's career as a morals policeman, therefore, cannot be viewed as an isolated case of Victorian prudery run amok. Many citizens followed Comstock's lead and formed vice societies, while a number of states passed vice laws. Comstock received broad support for decades, in large measure because "the same society which placed such great emphasis upon race progress, national improvement, and material prosperity could only see sexual promiscuity and the break up of the home circle as the most serious threat to the advance of civilization."

This Victorian aversion to discussion of baser instincts allowed purity crusaders to carry out their work largely unchallenged by politicians, religious leaders, or the public. Although some publications questioned his methods, the scope of his powers, and First Amendment issues, these journals were in the minority for years. And, although religious strictures slowly eased throughout the nineteenth century, societal pressures kept traditional moral views on such subjects in place.

Individuals who challenged the prevailing social norms often were pushed to the fringes of society and frequently prosecuted under obscenity statutes. Shortly before his death in 1915, Comstock proudly boasted of arresting more than 3,600 people during his four-decade career and confiscating hundreds of thousands of pounds of books, articles, pictures, photographs, movies, and other items he considered obscene (particularly condoms) as well as a substantial amount of gambling paraphernalia.

The sheer quantity of material demonstrates Victorian society's public demonstrations of respectability and religious rectitude did not necessarily match private realities of the time. Yet, Comstock "set for himself the herculean task of trying to make Victorian America conform to the image of rectitude and virtue to which it pretended." And his efforts and the public's support of those efforts say much about America's willingness to censor unpopular ideas as a method of social control.

LIBERAL REFORMERS AND FREEDOM OF EXPRESSION

Despite their efforts, purity crusaders found themselves at odds with another group of reformers who wanted to correct the same social ills, but who championed more radical reforms, including suffrage, family planning, free thought, and free love. Virtually all were ardent libertarians who believed the public must be well informed if social change was to occur. The Doctors E. B. Foote Sr. and Jr., for example, regularly stated that broad social reforms could not be accomplished without free and open debate about the country's many problems:

There is certainly great need of social reform; the social as well as the financial world is honey-combed with corruption. No one brain is capable of devising successful means -for improving our condition. It would seem necessary therefore that suggestions should come in from all sources, however radical, and all these suggestions to meet with extensive circulation and wide consideration must necessarily be printed; furthermore the mails must be used for their transmission," the Footes said in explaining their opposition to the Comstock Act.

Purity crusaders had no use for reformers who questioned the traditional social order, including birth control advocates and free thought writers whose beliefs in feminism and individual autonomy led them to debate the value of marriage and religion while seeking to elevate women's status and power in society. Comstock echoed the wealthier classes' fears of these reformers when he stated that they "ruthlessly trample underfoot the most sacred things, break down the altars of religion, burst asunder the ties of home, and seek to overthrow every social restraint." The libertarians' beliefs were derived from an amalgamation of influences, including abolitionism, free thought, free love, suffrage, and individual autonomy. The individualist anarchist philosophy of Josiah Warren was particularly important to the radical libertarians' social and legal thinking. Warren believed autonomous individuals, rather than governments, should make their own decisions about private matters, including sexual relations. Government regulations, he said, would impinge on individuals' freedoms.

Warren's and John Stuart Mill's philosophies also directly influenced the liberals' views on free expression. Warren's teachings stated autonomous individuals had "the absolute privilege of expressing themselves freely, totally unrestrained by any programmatic or ideological restrictions." Similarly, the liberals also believed wholeheartedly in Mill's disdain of censorship expressed in his work, On Liberty. Mill viewed governmental police powers, including those to regulate expression, as limited to preventing harm to others. The most often quoted passage expressed this philosophy: "If all mankind minus one were of one opinion, and only one person were of the contrary opinion, mankind would be no more justified in silencing that one person, than he, if he had the power, would be justified in silencing mankind."

The venerable former abolitionist Elizur Wright eloquently elaborated on this view, stating that the founding fathers were opposed to most attempts to suppress expressions. "No doubt the liberty of the press has its evils and dangers," he said in an 1883 letter to the Boston Evening Herald. "But the framers of our constitution and the people who adopted it seem to have emphatically decided that nothing the liberty of the press could do would be so dangerous as any attempt to restrain it," he added. "Did they not bravely trust that the press would correct its own moral errors more safely and surely than any arbitrary censorship?"

Liberals also viewed free expression as a natural right and as an essential means by which autonomous individuals could achieve self-fulfillment. Liberty was "not simply a means to an end, but an end in itself," National Defence Association President J. H. W. Toohey stated during an 1878 rally in Boston to support Ezra Heywood.

The liberals' philosophy often blended early feminist and abolitionist beliefs to assert that married women were little more than sexual slaves to their partners. Many rejected conventional marriage relations as well as church and state sanctioning of marriage, at least in theory, because most were married. They also demanded that women be given full civil rights, including the right to vote, to work if they so chose, to control their own reproduction, and to dress as they saw fit for health, safety, and personal preference.

Liberals knew many of their causes were far from mainstream. They also recognized that repealing the Comstock Act was an uphill battle since anti-vice crusaders wrapped their actions in the cloak of morality. Dr. E. B. Foote Jr. stated in 1890 that libertarian arguments for free expression were slow to gain ground in Congress because Comstock always countered that morality was at stake: "It is about as hard to get an egg back after the hen has laid it, as to repeal a law that has for its ostensible object any moral purpose," he told a Michigan liberal.

Despite the purity crusaders' rhetorical upper hand, liberals determined the best tactic to use in seeking the repeal or modification of the Comstock Act was to make broad philosophical and Constitutional arguments to persuade the public to support speech and press protections for all viewpoints, even unpopular ones, because they viewed free expression as a core value in democratic society. Thaddeus Wakeman, an attorney who defended several liberals who fell afoul of the Comstock Act, reiterated this position during the 1878 rally supporting Ezra Heywood. "The imprisonment of an editor for anything he may print, except libel, is one of the most dangerous stretches of power possible in a free republic, and worthy of our gravest consideration," he said.

Noted orator Robert G. Ingersoll explained the broader societal ramifications of censorship during a speech to an audience of several thousand at the Cooper Institute in New York in the late 1880s. The public, he said, was entitled to know "a man's honest thoughts." He added: "When you say that a man shall not speak, you also say that others shall not hear." Ingersoll reiterated the importance of free expression as a central value both to individuals and to democratic society during an 1888 debate at New York's Metropolitan Opera House sponsored by the Nineteenth-Century Club. "This liberty of thought, this liberty of expression, is of more value than any other thing beneath the stars," he stated.

These libertarians argued that two principles-the right of all individuals to express their views and the need for social tolerance to allow expression to flow unhindered-would allow both individuals and America's democratic society to flourish. Ingersoll stated these points during his closing argument in 1887 for a man accused of blasphemy:

I deny the right of any man, of any number of men, of any church, of any state to put a padlock on the lips-to make the tongue a convict ... Have you not the right to read, to observe, to investigate and when you have so read and so investigated, have you not the right to reap that field? And what is it to reap that field? It is simply to give your thoughts to your fellow men. If there is one subject in the world worthy of being discussed, worthy of being understood, it is the question of intellectual liberty. Without that, we are simply painted clay; without that, we are poor, miserable serfs and slaves.

Free thought publisher Moses Harman made a similar libertarian argument after facing arrest for publishing four articles that graphically discussed various aspects of sex, sexual relations, and the related issue of women's rights. That his frank discussions violated social norms should not matter, he argued during his trial. He added that the right of citizens to express and disseminate their views was a bedrock democratic principle as well as a natural right.

The object of this appeal ... is not to get a decision on questions of propriety or of taste, but simply upon the question of a citizens right to speak, to utter, to publish and to send by mail, all of one's honest thoughts, whatever they may be, provided always that no personal rights of property or reputation are invaded by such acts of utterance or of publication. This right of or to freedom to speak, to write and to publish is, in the humble opinion of this writer, the fundamental franchise, the rock-bottom right, upon which all rights of persons and of citizens must rest. Freedom of the press is the right preservative of all human rights-the franchise preservative of all other franchises. Let this franchise be once surrendered to the demands of a censorship, no matter how elected or appointed-no matter how honest or benevolent the man may be who exercises that censorship-and it needs no prophet to foretell the speedy destruction of the still unfinished temple of American liberty (civil and religious) in the upbuilding of which so many valuable lives have been sacrificed during the last two or three hundred years.

Liberals also argued that fearful and reactionary citizens should support broad protection of free expression rather than censoring controversial ideas, because support for expression would allow the truth to emerge through debate. "The only safety of the Republic against social as well as political heresies is the perfect freedom of publication, allowing every man to load his literary gun, whether with wisdom or folly, sense or nonsense, and fire it in the face and eyes of the common sense of the public," Elizur Wright stated.

The libertarian radicals, therefore, held expansive views of the First Amendment based on their beliefs in natural law, individual autonomy, and limited governmental police powers. Although they did not accept the late nineteenth-century normative view that political speech was deserving of more protection than expression about private issues, they believed expressive conduct was a civil liberty deserving of broad First Amendment protection, largely free from government censorship, particularly when it came to matters of taste or content. The libertarians' belief that individuals had a near-absolute right to self-expression meant they saw value in ideas which they might not personally support, especially viewpoints considered by much of Victorian society to be immoral or unpopular.

This core group of liberals was never large in number either before or after the Civil War, however, like the purity crusaders, they reached a national audience via publishing, legislative petitions, and speeches. Although some members of society viewed them as a "lunatic fringe," whose ideas flew in the face of Victorian propriety and social norms, the libertarian sex radicals had much in common with purity crusaders: They fervently believed their causes were just, they were hardworking, and most lived proper, virtuous, middle-class lives.

Unlike the purity crusaders, who believed broad public ignorance of sexual and reproduction issues was necessary to protect society, the libertarians believed the opposite- that early education about human physiology was crucial to reduce crime (particularly against women) and necessary for broad moral reform of society. The liberals also argued that censoring controversial material under obscenity laws would not lead to a more moral society. "Good morals and habits can be better fostered by education, persuasion, industry, and healthy amusement, then by force and government interference," Elizur Wright told the third annual conference of the National Liberal League in 1879 in Cincinnati.

After Comstock Act prosecutions began, many liberals felt themselves under siege from purity crusaders, the courts, and Congress who, they believed, were imposing an undemocratic, unconstitutional "state-enforced Christian dogma" on the public. Robert Ingersoll stated in the liberal's position in an 1878 letter to the Boston Journal seeking repeal of the Act stating: "Certain religious fanatics, taking advantage of the word 'immoral' in the law, have claimed that all writing against what they are pleased to call orthodox religion is immoral."

Liberals spent decades arguing that obscenity laws subordinated the rights of individuals to the will of the majority. Since they viewed free speech a "fundamental right of personal autonomy," libertarians disagreed with judges and legislators who believed that broader concerns about the public's welfare could justify speech restrictions.

The libertarians recognized their cause would not be successful unless they popularized their case to the American public via newspaper and magazine articles as well as through speeches and petitions. Two of the most prominent of these libertarians, a well-known father-son physician team based in New York City, the Drs. E. B. Foote Sr. and E. B. Foote Jr., spent years developing and nurturing a moderately successful grassroots campaign to spread the libertarians' philosophy to the public via the Footes' Health Monthly magazine.

The Footes, as well as other nationally-known liberals, including free thought publisher D. M. Bennett, noted orator and agnostic Robert Ingersoll, novelists Albert Ross and Julian Hawthorne, biographer James Parton, veteran abolitionist Elizur Wright, and the Revs. Minot J. Savage and Hugh O. Pentecost, lobbied Congress as well as state legislatures to repeal laws or stop new bills aimed at censoring the press. They also penned articles and letters to the editor in newspapers and magazine, including the Boston Evening Herald, the Boston Journal, the New York Herald, The Arena, the North American Review, and the Twentieth Century, created pamphlets, and gave lectures extolling the necessity of embracing a libertarian view of free speech and press. These liberals recognized they had to gain legislative, judicial, and public support for their interpretation of First Amendment freedoms to effect change.

Achieving such support proved exceedingly difficult in the late nineteenth and early twentieth centuries. State and federal legislators rarely debated the definition or boundaries of freedom of expression. Much of the public seemed indifferent to their cause and judicial hostility to First Amendment claims often was the norm. Prior to the 1920s, judges viewed press freedoms as applying almost exclusively to political commentary. Most jurists accepted Sir William Blackstone's narrow, common-law interpretation of free speech. Blackstone opposed prior restraints, but supported post-publication punishment for material that negatively affected morality and the social order.

In applying Blackstone's theory, American judges regularly invoked the bad tendency test to punish unpopular speech and ignored First Amendment claims in order to protect majoritarian interests. The libertarians, by contrast, recognized that the vast, on-going changes in society, politics, economics, and culture necessitated subsequent shifts and reinterpretations of laws. They argued that federal First

Amendment protection, broadly interpreted and applied to all citizens via the Fourteenth Amendment, was necessary because narrower views no longer served society adequately. The libertarians' expansive interpretation of the First Amendment, which included protection for earnest discussions of unpalatable topics, was a clear departure from the traditional conservative libertarian tradition which linked expression and personal property together as related aspects of individual liberty.

Liberals, therefore, objected to the Comstock Act and sought its repeal or modification on both philosophical and legal grounds. The law, they stated, blurred the lines between church and state because vice societies, which were largely supported by religious authorities, were given police powers to bring alleged law breakers to court. Furthermore, liberals said the law was not narrowly tailored since the Act had no definition and it gave a relatively small number of purity crusaders the license to use the Act to punish authors who put forth serious discussions of such reform issues as family planning, women's rights, and free thought.

Libertarians strenuously argued the public should be awakened and alarmed that their federally-guaranteed freedoms were being eroded by a small group of paternalistic individuals. "Nothing is so unsafe, in an alleged free country as to permit interference, on any light pretext, with a free press. What is agreeable to one may be offensive to another, but that gives no excuse for police regulation," novelist Albert Ross wrote in an 1891 article published in The Arena. Ross's article was motivated by Comstock's autumn 1890 raid of a New York book wholesaler which netted a number of works Comstock proclaimed obscene, including three by Ross.

The liberals were not always in complete accord as to what boundaries, if any, state and federal officials should impose on individuals' free expression rights. A few libertarians, including Heywood, were absolutists on First Amendment issues. Others, including Elizur Wright, the Drs. Foote, and free thought publisher D. M. Bennett, supported some restrictions on freedom of expression, providing those laws were written with clearly defined language and were narrowly tailored so as to not stop more speech than was absolutely necessary. Veteran abolitionist Elizur Wright explained the libertarians' concern that the Act's lack of a legal definition for obscenity invited the potential for prosecutorial abuses. "Nobody here, I think, would object to a law regulating the transmission of literature through the mails, if it could so define obscenity as not to exclude a great part of our most valuable literature, including the Bible, and so as not to violate the true and constitutional liberty of the press."

The Doctors Foote and noted biographer James Parton agreed. In numerous articles and letters to the editor, they opined that giving free reign to a small group of censors to determine what was indecent meant that many classics, including works by Shakespeare, Byron, and even the Bible, could be vanned because "certainly a grovelling mind can find plenty of material to feed on in all these books." Bennett, citing Mill's philosophy on the libertarians' views of a state's police powers, stated the issue more simply: "Law exists solely to prevent people from injuring others."

The liberals also frequently reminded the public that purity crusaders seized more than literature, they also censored works relating to divorce, birth control, feminism, agnosticism, and atheism. The Comstock Act, Elizur Wright told a Boston crowd, was used to suppress honest discussion of "the most vital questions of society, with no word more indecent than can be found in the most revered works in our libraries, and with no opinions even more heterodox or erroneous... than can be found in the writings of John Milton." Attorney Thaddeus Wakeman concurred, stating that works "put forth in sincerity and good faith" containing no "obscene words, phrases, or pictures" should not be held to be obscene under the law.

Liberals noted that vice society seizures of physicians' literature, in particular, appeared class based, a paternalistic effort designed to keep reproductive knowledge out of the hands of the poor who most needed such information. Birth control information had been relatively widely disseminated prior to 1873. The Act's passage relegated most discussion to the confines of medical journals and books. "Nothing can be more fatal to human progress than the suppression of free discussion," Dr. E. B. Foote Sr. stated in an 1878 editorial in his Health Monthly in support of dissemination of medical knowledge."

Although many libertarians, including the Footes, Heywood, Wakeman, and Bennett, sought the full repeal of the Comstock Act, they recognized that if that could not be achieved, they would have to focus their efforts on lobbying Congress for three crucial modifications to the law. First, they sought to have the term "obscenity" and its application narrowly defined to promote untrammeled discussion of issues, including highly controversial ones second, and related, they sought procedural changes during trials so that courts would have to consider the obscenity of the work as a whole rather than in part. Finally, the libertarians, drawing on their belief in minimal federal police powers, said that if obscenity statutes must exist, they belong as the sole province of the states. Attorney Thaddeus B. Wakeman stated in his writings and lectures that the Constitution's framers feared two things: 'the granting of criminal jurisdiction to the general government, and the use of ... 'incidental' or implied powers." James Parton agreed. He called for full repeal of the Comstock Act, adding that state and municipal laws were "sufficient for detection and punishment" of individuals.

Liberals also raised several procedural, legal, and philosophical points relating to vice societies and their agents operating as extralegal organizations. First, they questioned whether or not state and federal governments had the authority to give vice societies such powers. They also questioned the qualifications of society members and postal officials to separate material attempting to discuss serious social issues from that which was meant to arouse passions.

To liberals, the prosecutions smacked of paternalistic censorship and fear of the common man. The Comstock Act, James Parton wrote, is "so liable to abuse by a narrow-minded or provincial officer."" The Arena's editor, Benjamin Flower, agreed. Flower believed literature's greatest strength was its ability to highlight social problems and suggest solutions. Defending Tolstoy's Kreutzer Sonata, which was deemed obscene by postal officials under the Comstock Act because it dealt with an extramarital affair, Flower said suppressing the work was "another striking illustration of conservatism ... assailing all who seek to purify life ..."

Novelist Albert Ross concurred, stating in The Arena that adults had the ability to judge for themselves what was acceptable reading matter: An over-governed people will soon cry out loudly in defence of its right to read what it pleases and form its own judgment as to what is good for it. How does the agent of a society that decides to 'suppress' a book know any more whether it should be suppressed than a hundred thousand others who are waiting for the opportunity to purchase it? We are not all gifted with equal pruriency of mind. There are paintings in the great galleries of the world in which one set of men will see glorious beauties and another only the naked forms of women.

Paralleling this, libertarians charged that the postal system's legal apparatus had no adequate systems of checks and balances regulating its inspectors' actions. Wakeman reiterated the libertarian view that putting police powers in the hands of a few individuals to act as moral censors for the seeming betterment of society was a dangerous legal precedent. He further argued there was no Constitutional basis for granting such unlimited powers. Albert Ross warned that such actions would stifle speech and harm democracy by not allowing ideas to flourish: "All the shafts of the professional 'suppressors' are kept for the writer who gets on thin ice where men and women love 'not wisely but too well'," Ross stated. "And yet there is nothing in fiction that affords such opportunities as the love that goes astray."

The liberals also regularly objected to Comstock's use of decoy letters to obtain information, despite the U.S. Supreme Court's affirmation that the practice was a legally accepted tactic. James Parton, in an 1880 letter, said he abhorred works which had a corrupting effect on youth, yet he argued

Comstock's actions were worse: "And yet it seems to me that the espionage of the mails by an illiterate person is even a worse evil than that. It menaces the very citadel of liberty."

Ross and the libertarians argued the public should not passively accept the vice societies' claims that they were attempting to rid the world only of "obscene" literature. He urged readers to recognize the discussion of once-taboo topics reflected changes in American society and culture. "The reading public is broadening its ideas," Ross said, then argued that the mere discussion of often-controversial topics should not be considered a social danger. Writers, he said, frequently try to awaken the public to new ideas. Stopping the discussion of such topics was the danger. "It is not revelation that is dangerous, but silence," he added. Libertarians also expressed the disdain many educated individuals held against purity crusaders, whom they viewed as largely uneducated and thus unable to make reasoned judgments about what literature was prurient and what was genuinely artistic in its portrayal of the sexes. For example, Walt Whitman viewed Anthony Comstock as an uneducated buffoon and derisively referred to the vice fighter as "Saint Anthony," in a letter to a friend after Comstock stopped an 1882 reprinting of Leaves of Grass, claiming several poems were obscene. Whitman defended the changing nature of literature and social thought in an article published by the venerable North American Review. "It is not the pictures or nude statue or text, with clear aim, that is indecent; it is the beholder's own thought, inference, distorted construction," the poet stated.

Whitman's private criticism was more pointed. In A letter to a friend, he said Comstock had not "discovered the difference between virtue and vice: he is not so much a knave as an ass: he goes stumbling about as a bull in a china shop." Albert Ross concurred. "Ignorance shall not convict intelligence," Ross said, adding "men whose knowledge of literature is confined to the Farmers' Almanac and the Sunday School Advocate (and I speak respectfully of both publications) shall not say that Balzac and Dumas and Tolstoi are indictable." Comstock diluted the libertarians' effectiveness in persuading the general public by pejoratively labeling liberals as "friends of obscenity" in his writings and speeches. The tactic forced liberals to be forever on the defensive about separating themselves from obscenity. For example, when novelist Albert Ross denounced Comstock's censorship tactics in The Arena, he quickly noted: "It is hardly necessary to say that I do not favour ... a single printed line of obscenity.

These are things about which we should all agree..." Elizur Wright made the same argument in 1878 at a Boston meeting to protest Heywood's imprisonment. "Nobody here doubts that there is such a thing as obscenity in literature and art, and that is a bad thing," Wright said. Yet, he reiterated that serious discussion of controversial social issues needed to be protected and separated from prosecutions of works meant only to titillate. Similarly, two of Comstock's targets, marital advise writer Ida Craddock and Ezra Heywood, felt forced to proclaim that their lifestyles were morally upright and not licentious, as Comstock had stated. They made clear that self-control, mutual respect, and love were necessary in any relationship.

The schism between liberal reformers' legal and social views and those of purity crusaders remained immense for decades. As legal historian David Rabban has stated, "the libertarian radical vision of individual autonomy often struck social purists as a threat to their goal of a morally cohesive community." Lawmakers and much of the American public were supportive of this cohesiveness, casting aside "the antebellum model of unfettered exercise of individual rights" in an effort to stabilize society. Yet, this "new found strength of the state's regulatory arm jeopardized free speech guarantees." Despite broad opposition, the libertarians stayed the course intellectually, challenging the "American Inquisition" for almost fifty years.

THE PROSECUTIONS AND THE LIBERTARIAN RESPONSE

Although Comstock personally arrested more than 3,600 individuals during his 42 years as a purity crusader, the vice fighter's prosecutions of four particular individuals, prominent New York physician and popular medical book publisher Dr. E. B. Foote, ST., free love publisher Ezra Heywood, and free thought publishers D. M. Bennett and Moses Harman, set the stage for a protracted, and very public, battle concerning the meaning and boundaries of the rights of free speech and expression. These four individuals found themselves at the centre of a First Amendment maelstrom precisely because their discussions of individual rights, religion, women's rights, and family planning were uncommonly frank as well as a direct challenge to many long-held upper-class views about gender roles and family order in American society.

The four men also found themselves targets of Comstock's wrath because they were very public in their criticism of the vice fighter and his methods. Heywood, for example, called Comstock a "religious mono-maniac" who was mistakenly allowed by Congress "to use the Federal Courts to suppress Free Inquiry." The Footes regularly referred to Comstock's work as the "American Inquisition" in their magazine. Bennett wrote a particularly vitriolic attack, vilifying Comstock in 1878 in his work, The Champions of the Church: Their Crimes and Persecutions. Then, too, Bennett also attracted Comstock's wrath for his efforts in trying to get the Bible declared obscene.

These four men differed from most of Comstock's other quarry in several significant ways: they were better educated, were bitten by the Victorian reform impulse and, therefore, truly felt driven to promote their reform agendas. And, when convicted, they were willing to fight the convictions because their intent was to inform and not to titillate. They also had or were able to obtain the finances to launch vigorous court fights. Finally, in the cases of Heywood and Harman, some of these men were willing to be martyrs to the cause of freedom of expression.

Edward Bliss Foote, a popular and wealthy New York physician and his physician son, Edward Bond Foote, bankrolled much of the libertarians' efforts after the elder Foote ran afoul of the Comstock laws in 1876 for publishing a pamphlet on birth control. The doctor believed that Comstock pursued him because Foote testified his opposition to a New York state legislative that was considering enacting an anti-obscenity bill in 1872 that was initiated by Comstock. Despite Foote's efforts, the bill became law.

Foote had personal, professional, and philosophical reasons for opposing Comstock's work. Imbued with the truest democratic and egalitarian sympathies, the doctor spent many years as a journalist prior to pursuing medical studies with a botanical physician and taking a course of study at the well-respected Pennsylvania Medical University. He worked as a printer's devil as a teen at the Cleveland Herald, then left Cleveland for a type-setting position at the New Haven Journal. At nineteen, he took over the editorship at the New Britain Journal and made it the state's largest selling weekly. He later became the associate editor at the Brooklyn Morning Journal, but left that post after two years to study medicine, the field to which he aspired.

In 1858, two years before he received his diploma, the 29-year-old Foote published a work that would bring him wealth, a measure of fame, and eventually, Comstock's attention. The book was Medical Common Sense, a medical treatise for the general public that explained the workings of the human body and subsequent treatments for illnesses. The work would sell more than 250,000 copies by 1870. Foote enlarged the book in that year and claimed that the retitled volume, Plain Home Talk, Embracing Medical Common Sense, sold more than 2,000 copies a month. By 1870, Foote not only had a flourishing medical practice in New York, but he also had a successful mail order botanical drug company and a publishing operation, from which he issued numerous other medical works and sold condoms and other preventives.

A philosophical journey from Methodism to Unitarianism to agnosticism led him to the free thought and libertarian principles he held so fervently throughout his adult life. Similarly, as a graduate of what was then termed an eclectic medical school, his training led him to embrace a wide range of treatments and cures, including ones not always popular with more traditional medical training. His acceptance of treatments he did not use (or even advise) led him to rally to the aid of a number of the sex radicals and other physicians later in life. A eugenicist and a neo-Malthusian, Foote's first edition of Medical Common Sense contained a brief, three-page section entitled "The Prevention of Conception." In it, the doctor warned readers of the dangers of associated with many popular preventives, but failed to offer any alternatives. Despite the brief nature of the section, its inclusion is important because most medical schools, textbooks, and many popular medical works aimed at the general public did not discussion prevention.

Foote expanded his discussion of birth control in an 1864 revision. As one medical historian has noted, "Foote sloughs off his previous timidity and presents a complete approach to contraception, giving his philosophy, an exposition of the commonly employed contraceptive methods, and details on the reliable devices he recommends." Although a number of other popular medical books existed before Foote's treatise, the book's popularity helped to prepare the public's acceptance of birth control.

Although Foote's beliefs on birth control were progressive, the doctor also at times adhered to mainstream Victorian thought. He preached against abortion and masturbation, believing the latter led to a variety of debilitating physical and mental conditions. He warned in Plain Home Talk that proper sex education and hygiene should be taught to boys and girls so that they would not abuse their bodies. He published a multivolume work in 1874, titled Science in Story, to do just that and advertised the work in every issue of his Health Monthly.

Foote's neo-Malthusian beliefs also shaped his views on birth control. He stated in the 1864 edition of Plain Home Talk that "excessive child-bearing may be truthfully said to be the bane of general society." He told readers that too many pregnancies not only were physiologically bad for women, but led to "innumerable ills" both social and genetic. Prevention, rather than abortion (a practice he vigorously denounced), was the solution, he advised. The doctor's strong belief in prevention led to his arrest and indictment under the Comstock Act in June 1876 after Comstock himself used a decoy letter to request Dr. Foote Sr.'s contraceptive-advice pamphlet, "Words in Pearl," as well as a copy of Medical Common Sense, which explained the male and female reproductive systems. The book brought about Comstock's ire because Foote had the audacity to suggest that married couples should determine how often they have sex based in part upon the pleasurable nature of sex rather than recommending sex only for reproductive purposes. Then, too, both Foote and his son were ardent feminists and birth control advocates whose many publications reflected their belief in women's rights. The doctors felt it important for men and women to know about their bodies and reproductive systems for health reasons as well as personal selfgovernment.

Even before the elder Dr. Foote fell afoul of the Comstock Act, the doctor recognized that the passage of New York State's anti-obscenity law placed his publishing empire in peril. He moved the entire operation to Connecticut. Although Foote derived substantial income from his publishing company, the doctor was genuinely gripped by a democratic impulse to impart medical advice to the general public. By contrast, many physicians of the time wanted to keep their knowledge from the public.

A second crusade in 1876 to stop the New York State Legislature from prohibiting the manufacturing and sale of contraceptives only confirmed Foote's suspicions. Many physicians aligned with Comstock to support the bill. As historian Hal Sears has noted, however, Foote "was at a disadvantage in his efforts." Under federal indictment, Foote's counter legislation was rejected when Comstock labeled the doctor an abortionist and introduced a letter signed by "leading New York doctors, stating that only quacks and frauds prescribed contraceptives."

"Words in Pearl," the publication which led to Foote's arrest, had been in circulation for six years before Comstock, using a decoy letter, requested the pamphlet as well as a copy of Medical Common Sense. Although it was one of Foote's employees at his Murray Hill Publishing Company who sent both the publications to Comstock, and not the doctor himself, the physician was indicted on charges of mailing an obscene pamphlet and providing information about "an article designed for the prevention of conception can be obtained," tried, convicted, and fined $3,500. Foote avoided jail time, however, because District Judge Charles Benedict stated the doctor's patients would suffer. Judge Benedict required Foote to eliminate the information on reproduction from the book after he rejected Foote's argument that "medical advise given by a physician in reply to the inquiry of a patient" via the mail should not fall under the purview of obscenity laws. The judge said other means were available, besides the postal system, to inform patients, a ruling Foote unsuccessfully disputed.

The conviction forced Foote on the defensive. He explained his views and work in an article in the August 1876 edition of his Health Monthly and, in October, issued a special supplement that ran excerpts of sympathetic articles from newspapers large and small, including the New York Ti/nes, the New York Commercial Advertiser, the Bergen Index of New Jersey, the Suffolk Gem of Virginia, and the Chicago Daily Times.

The supplement also included letters from outraged readers, including one from a woman who noted: "I have read your pamphlet Words in Pearl, and wonder why that could in any respect be called obscene. I suppose wiser people would attribute that to my ignorance; but any one, however stupid, can tell which is the greatest offence-the harmless prevention of conception, or the terrible crime of abortion?"

Foote was not allowed to turn his trial into an opportunity to discuss the limits of freedom of expression. Although Foote objected that his indictment did not contain precise information on the allegedly obscene material, his objection was overruled and his attempt to get the material entered into the record failed. Judge Benedict relied on an 1821 case, Commonwealth v. Holmes, which established the precedent that indictments "must contain the exact words unless the indictment alleged that the words were too indecent to be reproduced. The judge also ruled that the Comstock Act proscribed the mailing of obscene material sent by sealed, first-class post. "It is not the form in which the matter is mailed, but the character of the matter itself, which fixes the criminality of the act," he wrote.

Foote faced the postal censors' wrath again in August 1881 when A. A. Freeman, the assistant attorney general for the post office department, notified Dr. E. B. Foote Sr. that his magazine's second-class mailing permit was being revoked. Freeman said the Health Monthly was a "publication designed primarily for advertising purposes" and thus not within the scope of publications worthy of the second-class permit. The assistant attorney general gave as proof the fact that many of the advertisements were for books and products offered by Foote's Murray Hill Publishing Company or his mail-order medical business. He also stated that since three-quarters of the 12,000 circulation were sent out as free copies, this was proof that the publication did not have a "legitimate subscription list."

The doctor again believed that the post office's decision to revoke his permit was based on his advocacy of "advanced ideas" as well as his outspoken criticism of Comstock. The elder Foote hired lawyer T. B. Wakeman to fight for the return of his second-class permit, a battle Wakeman won. In the interim, Foote moved the publication to J. S. Robertson & Brothers Printing House in Whitby, Ontario, in an attempt to avoid further censorship.

Comstock's pursuit and prosecution of the elder Foote led both father and son to become central figures in the battle for free expression. Indeed, after Dr. Foote Sr.'s obscenity conviction, both physicians devoted many non-working hours to opposing the Comstock Act. Their greatest achievement was the formation of the National Defence Association. Prior to 1878, the liberals' biggest weakness in fighting the Comstock Act was their lack of organization. Although they frequently consulted with one another in person and via letters, much of their early work was done in isolation. This changed in 1878 when Doctor E. B. Foote Sr., indignant at being convicted for doing what he believed was his duty as a physician, established the National Defence Association. The organization was devoted to "investigat[ing] all questionable cases of prosecution under what are now known as the Comstock laws ... and to extending] sympathy, moral support, and material aid to those who may be unjustly assailed by the enemies of free speech and free press."

The Association, which patterned itself after a similar English group, held weekly meetings, raised money to hire attorneys and paid court costs for dozens of individuals, including many doctors who ran afoul of the law for disseminating birth control information and lobbied Congress and state legislatures to repeal or modify laws. They spread their libertarian views to the general public by holding rallies advocating free expression rights for all individuals that attracted thousands of citizens, organizing an active speakers bureau, and penning numerous articles and letters to the editor that appeared in some of the nation's most prominent newspapers and magazines. NDA members also met Comstock's challenges in person by attending Comstock's annual NYSSV meetings to put forth their views and disseminate their literature.

The NDA's membership read like a who's who of Northeast liberal intellectuals. Its members included noted abolitionist Elizur Wright; Biblical scholar Prof. A. W. Rawson; nationally-known sculptor Wilson McDonald; Harriet Beecher Stowe's publisher John P. Jewett; abolitionists Elizur Wright and Stephen Pearl Andrews, Dr. E. B. Foote Jr.; and feminist and co-editor of The Dial Margaret Fuller who served as vice president. The Footes were the main promotional force behind the NDA. They issued numerous pamphlets on free speech issues through their Murray Hill Publishing Company and used their popular medical monthly magazine, Dr. Foote's Health Monthly, to promote the NDA's activities as well as to spread their liberal views nationwide. The doctors created a special section in their magazine titled "The Outlook" which dealt exclusively with free speech issues. Readers found appeals to the NDA's legal defence fund and articles that allowed them to follow the cases of doctors, feminists, birth control advocates, free thinkers, and other editors charged with violating the Comstock Act for publishing medical books or pamphlets on physiology.

Every issue of "The Outlook" section also featured reprints of articles supporting free expression that appeared in mainstream newspapers. Letters from Health Monthly readers thanking the doctor for his medical advice or opposing purity crusaders' attempts to suppress birth control information also were strategically placed in each issue in an attempt to demonstrate broad public support for progressive ideas as well as to counter Comstock's claims that only a small group of "smut lovers" and urban liberals sought out such information.

The Association was proactive rather than reactive in its approach. NDA members lobbied state legislatures and Congress to repeal or quash any legislation or potential legislation aimed at stifling press rights. For example, when Congress considered broadening the Comstock Act by making it a crime to distribute "filthy, or disgusting" materials, the National Defence Association sent members, including Dr. E. B. Foote Jr., to Congress to testify against the changes and submitted a brief stating the group's objections. The Association also lobbied against state purity laws with some success. Their speakers, petitions, and counter bills helped to defeat an 1882 obscenity bill in Wisconsin and another measure in New York in 1887.

The NDA achieved several notable victories, including getting the charges dropped or obtaining acquittals of a number of doctors who disseminated family planning literature, securing Ezra Heywood's pardon from President Hayes, getting charges against D. M. Bennett dismissed after he sold a copy of Heywood's tract, Cupid's Yokes, spearheading a petition drive in 1878 to get Congress to repeal the Comstock Act, and helping Walt Whitman get the 1882 edition of Leaves of Grass published and sold openly again after it was suppressed.

The NDA's 1878 petition drive demonstrates the difficulties that liberals faced in trying to convince an often-indifferent public and a hostile Congress to adopt a more progressive, tolerant approach to freedom of expression. Bennett, the Doctors Foote, and a number of other liberals printed thousands of copies of the petition and sent them to leading liberals, doctors, publishers, and freethinkers. The Footes also reproduced the petition in their magazine for several months during the winter of 1877-78 and used editorials to encourage readers who believed in the cause of free expression to sign the petition and/or write to members of Congress.

The petition's wording was strong, yet cautious at times. Stung by four years of accusations that they were smut lovers, liberals made certain that one massage clearly stated their objection to obscene works: "It is not desired by any good citizen that lewd and lascivious books should be tolerated in the country, but in discriminating against them special care should be exercised that the rights of the people are not destroyed."

Despite this tempered approach, Comstock arrived at Congress with several NYSSV board members, including Samuel Colgate, and proclaimed many of the signatures, including those by noted doctors, publishers, journalists, and ministers, were forgeries, a claim liberals vehemently denied. Comstock provided no proof, yet his statements created doubts among the members of Congress and the liberals' herculean efforts fizzled out. Comstock rejoiced at his success against his enemies. He denounced liberal thinkers as "lawless" and stated the National Defence Association was "composed of ex-convicts, free-lovers, and other creatures that seemingly believe neither in God, religion, or morals."

As the National Defence Association entered the 1880s, several of the older reformers who formed the first vanguard died. Dr. E. B. Foote Jr., who had previously served as treasurer, shepherded the Association into the new era. The younger Foote was an ardent feminist; a strong supporter of numerous social, political, and economic reforms; an outspoken liberal; a founder of the Manhattan Liberal Club; and a life-long advocate of birth control. Ned, as he was called by family and friends, along with his physician wife, Mary, worked as partners, devoting much of their time and personal finances to the organization and other progressive social causes.

Foote also was in accord with his father's belief that medical knowledge was not the purview of physicians, but should be made as available as possible to the public. Current Opinion editor Leonard D. Abbott said Dr. Ned Foote's views never wavered: Foote Jr. "did not ask whether he saw eye to eye with a man before he would help him. He had the large conviction that there could not be real progress in the world unless we each one of us have the undeniable right to express the truth as we see it."

Not surprisingly, the younger Dr. Foote also was responsible for broadening the Association's outlook and work as the twentieth-century dawned. Although he continued to help sex radicals who ran afoul of the Comstock Act, including Moses Harman during his repeated arrests, Ned Foote merged the National Defence Association into a new group, the Free Speech League, in 1902. The new group worked to defend radicals of all sorts who faced First Amendment suppression and repeated arrests after President William McKinley was assassinated. The League became better known than the NDA, in part, because of the work the Association's members had done to popularize free expression rights as well as broader public acceptance of progressive views. But numerous government attempts to censor the speech of labour unions, socialists, communists, and anarchists also contributed to the group's popularity.

Like the NDA before it, the League's membership boasted a number of nationally-known individuals, including journalists Lincoln Steffens and Huchins Hapgood, editor Leonard Abbott, and attorneys Gilbert Roe and Clarence Darrow. The group, which was led by nationally-prominent attorney Theodore Schroeder, used the same public relations tactics as did the NDA. Members produced vast quantities of printed works, gave speeches, petitioned the President for pardons, and addressed Congress and state legislatures on freedom of speech issues. The League existed for two decades, dissolving only when its members decided that the newly-formed and better-organized American Civil Liberties Union could better continue the fight.

Like Dr. Foote, free love publisher Ezra Heywood also was a man of principle. Unlike the doctor, however, Heywood failed to understand or accept that social propriety had limits. This very inability to know when to stop led him down a path he embraced, First Amendment martyrdom, but it proved physically and financially ruinous for the editor.

Heywood's early life sheds light on his willingness to follow causes. A Massachusetts native, Heywood preached briefly as a Congregationalist minister after receiving a divinity degree from Brown University. He soon joined the anti-slavery cause after college and was a close friend of William Lloyd Garrison. A pacificist, Heywood broke with Garrison in 1861 after Garrison supported the war as a means to end slavery.

Following the Civil War's end, Heywood was intellectually adrift, very much a man without a cause. He gravitated toward the individualist anarchism philosophy of Josiah Warren and established a journal in May 1872 titled The Word, which was devoted to labour reform, land reform, currency issues, and, strongly encouraged and influenced by his wife Angela, women's rights. Although Warren's and Heywood's friendship dissolved because Warren found Heywood's views extreme and his writing frequently "hasty and injudicious," Heywood remained forever influenced by Warren's philosophies.

Heywood did not arouse Comstock's attention or ire until The Word began discussing sexuality frankly. Although the issues of sex and marriage had received considerable attention throughout the nineteenth century, the magazine's articles provided a "candid and occasionally hedonistic treatment of sexuality ... A liberation from the Victorian ethos" unseen in any other reform periodical of its time.

Heywood was arrested five times, in 1877, 1882, 1883, 1887, and again in 1890, for violating the Comstock Act. He went to trial three times, although the National Defence

Association secured Heywood's pardon from President Rutherford B. Hayes after Heywood had served six months in the Dedham prison for his first conviction in 1878. The outspoken free love advocate was not so lucky during his 1890 trial. He was sentenced to two years and served the time. The NDA's petition to President Benjamin Harrison seeking a second pardon was unsuccessful. This conviction also proved ruinous to Heywood's health.

Ironically, Heywood had much in common with Comstock. Both men believed the lower class exhibited unrestrained sexuality and both feared this. Although Heywood believed that relationships should be "free compact[s], dissolvable at will," he said he was not arguing for "unrestrained licentiousness." Heywood differed from Comstock in that he believed that self-control was an individual's responsibility and not the state's. Furthermore, he also believed that men and women needed sex education and birth control to properly regulate their lives.

Heywood produced his anti-marriage, pro-feminist Cupid's Yokes because he wanted to put forth his belief that neither the state nor religious institutions should be able to interfere with an individual's sovereignty. Then, too, he also wrote the work as a protest against the Comstock Act. Heywood was angered at Comstock's arrests of several other free love advocates and sex reformers, including Victoria Woodhull, Dr. Foote, John Lant, and George Francis Train and referred to Comstock as "the mercenary assassin of liberty."

Cupid's Yokes was far from titillating. Instead, Heywood produced a lengthy, and at times turgid, tract about why women should be emancipated, both sexually and socially, as well as why marriage should be abolished. He argued that love should always be the guiding force for sexual union. Drawing upon his abolitionist training, Heywood pronounced that marriage was institutional, state-sanctioned slavery He added that society forced women to be the sexual slaves of men. The metaphor was an easy one for Heywood to draw upon. Heywood, like other free lovers, saw white males as the oppressors of both women and African Americans. He denounced Victorian America's limited socially-acceptable choices of marriage or abstinence, the latter he termed a "suicidal evil." Heywood said that "marriage obliterated individual freedom and denied women the right of self-government."

Heywood and other free love advocates believed that relationships between men and women "should be the result of 'mutual discretion-a free compact, dissolvable at will.'" As Heywood biographer Martin Blatt has written: "The key for Heywood was that any human association be based on freedom, mutual respect, and reciprocal treatment."

At his first trial in 1877 for mailing two allegedly obscene publications, Cupid's Yokes and R. T. Trail's popular work, Sexual Physiology, Heywood discovered the judge would not allow his courtroom to be used as a libertarian soapbox. The prosecutor determined which passages were obscene and then presented his findings to the grand jury, which returned the indictment with only the titles of the books mentioned. Nowhere did they cite the specific, offending passages. Nor were those passages presented by prosecuting attorney Charles Almy Jr. during the trial in an attempt to keep from spreading the allegedly obscene materials. The jury only received copies of the publications upon their adjournment to begin their deliberations.

Heywood also was given no opportunity to argue the issue of obscenity. The editor was deeply angered that either work would be labeled obscene. He had penned Cupid's Yokes to generate serious discussion about anti-statism, the role of marriage, and women's rights. Judge Clark ruled that jurors would decide if the material was indeed obscene. Heywood also found himself prohibited from discussing the reason why he wrote the publication and was prohibited from explaining the philosophies and beliefs he expressed in Cupid's Yokes. His attorneys also were not allowed to introduce medical books into evidence to demonstrate that these were similar to Trail's book. The judge held that the texts were irrelevant to the case; whether or not medical works could be considered obscene or not was not an issue for the jury, Clark stated.

The NDA and many libertarians rallied around Heywood. An editorial in The Health Monthly argued that no one could find Heywood's tract obscene since it was a dry, philosophic study not aimed at polluting the minds of the innocent. Young readers, the editorial said, "would not be likely to proceed for more than a page or two without throwing it down as devoid of interest." The publication challenged the district attorney to enter the nation's best libraries and proceed according to the standard he has erected for the arraignment of Cupid's Yokes. Other liberals took the stand to defend Heywood, notably veteran abolitionist Elizur Wright, Dr. J. M. Bruce, Boston Attorney A. E. Giles, and free thought editor Sidney H. Morse, but none were allowed to give their opinion on the nature of the publications nor on Heywood's character.

In his closing argument, Heywood's attorney told the jury that freedom of the press was central to the case. The District Attorney rebutted this in his closing argument. Press freedom, criticisms of Comstock and his work, Heywood's character and his reform work were not relevant, the district attorney stated. The only facts the jury needed consider as relevant, he said, were that the publications were obscene and that Heywood had mailed them.

Judge Clark's instructions to the jury also took the focus away from the issue of freedom of expression and greatly influenced the decision. Heywood's free-love writings "would turn Massachusetts into one great house of prostitution," the judge stated. Relying on Regina v. Hicklin, Clark invoked the bad tendency test by instructing the jurors "that an obscene book was one that was offensive to decency by exciting impure or lewd thoughts or by inciting the practice of impure desires. An obscene book need only to contain an immoral tendency, and only part of the book needed to be obscene for it to come within the meaning of the Comstock law."

Upon Heywood's conviction, Elizur Wright, on behalf of the NDA, wrote President Rutherford B. Hayes asking him to pardon Heywood. Wright told the President that despite the conviction, he believed Heywood had not produced an obscene work. Wright also expressed the libertarians' concerns about heavy-handed paternal censorship and excessive federal police power: "I do not think the government of the United States has any jurisdiction over the morals of the peoples of the states ..." he told Hayes.

Libertarians celebrated Heywood's pardon by honoring him at Paine Memorial Hall in Boston. According to the Boston Globe (which devoted an entire column to the reception), between 6,000 to 7,000 people attended, including Bennett, NDA President A. L. Rawson, and spiritualist Laura Cuppy Kendrick. The sheer numbers must have shocked purity crusaders who always argued that liberals were a very small group. The libertarians passed several motions during the reception, including an affirmation that free expression is a precious, natural right, a demand for the repeal of the Comstock Act, and the removal of Comstock as a special agent of the postal service.

Heywood ran afoul of Comstock for a second time on October 26,1882, when he was arrested for championing poet Walt Whitman's right to free expression. Comstock stopped the distribution of a new printing of Whitman's Leaves of Grass after determining that three poems, "A Woman Waits for Me,""To a Common Prostitute," and "The Dalliance of Eagles" were obscene. Comstock's letter to Suffolk County District Attorney Oliver Stevens was enough for Stevens to contact Whitman's Boston publishing house, Osgood and Company. Steven's letter, coupled with Boston Postmaster L. S. Tobey's declaration that the book was unmailable in its present form, forced the publishers to request that Whitman remove the poems. Whitman's refusal caused his publishers to break their contract and return the printing plates to the poet. Comstock's actions had a broad chilling effect on Whitman's work. Another publishing house, Rand & Avery, also refused to print Leaves of Grass, afraid, Whitman said, of being indicted.

Indignant that the vice hunter would go after Whitman, Heywood decided to engage in civil disobedience to test the limits of First Amendment protection for expression. He produced a single sheet called the Word Extra which contained two of the Whitman poems and ran an advertisement in an issue of The Word for a contraceptive device Heywood dubbed "The Comstock Syringe." Not surprisingly, he was arrested however, Heywood fared far better in his second trial, which began in the spring of 1883. Trial judge T. L. Nelson threw out two of the four counts in the indictment against Heywood, claiming that neither the Word Extra sheet nor his magazine were "too grossly obscene and lewd to be placed on the records of the court." Heywood then faced only one count of obscenity for advertising the vaginal syringe for sale.

The editor defended himself in spirited fashion. The judge allowed Heywood to call more than thirty-six witnesses who testified as to his character, the honorableness of his work and ideas, and that freedom of expression was indeed under assault. Heywood concluded his defence with an almost five-hour summation to jurors that restated his beliefs in limited government, press freedoms, women's rights, and his willingness to be a martyr to these causes. He also tore apart the Comstock Act and the vice fighter's methods. After only two hours of deliberation, the radical editor was acquitted, an action that deeply angered Comstock.

Less than a month later, Comstock had Heywood arrested for the third time, this time on state charges for an article on birth control edited by Heywood's wife Angela. Liberals, led by Stephen Pearl Andrew, organized a defence committee and a petition drive to get the charges dropped. After trial postponements and changes in both the judge and the district attorney, the charges were indeed dropped in May 1884. Three years later, Comstock again arrested Heywood on obscenity charges, but U. S. District Attorney George M. Stevens declined to prosecute.

Liberals hailed these two victories both in print and via receptions, but a fifth and final trial in 1890 would occur. More importantly, the case also reaffirmed the application of the bad tendency test, the principle that obscenity was not worthy of First Amendment protection, and the fact that Congress did indeed have the power to regulate the mails. Heywood's final arrest in May 1890 on both state and federal charges for sending obscenity through the mail. While Comstock was behind the federal charge, the state charges were initiated by the New England Watch and Ward Society, a group closely affiliated with the NYSSV. Although Comstock had repeatedly asked the Princeton, MA. postmasters to stop Heywood from depositing his publications in the mail, they steadfastly refused until U.S. Postmaster General John Wanamaker, at the urging of Comstock, replaced Princeton's postmaster (who had publicly proclaimed himself an infidel) and replaced him with a new official willing to seek Heywood's arrest.

The editor faced three counts for three separate works that appeared in The Word: a reprinting of the "O'Neill Letter," a New York anarchist physician's account of devious sexual practices which previously had appeared in Lucifer, a letter from a mother who called for proper sex education for children that also detailed how she explained the sex act to her young daughter; and, finally, a reprint of an 1883 article by Angela Heywood defending birth control.

The final trial went as badly for Heywood as did his first in 1878. Judge Nelson, who had presided at Heywood's 1883 acquittal, was ill so the editor drew Judge George M. Carpenter, a conservative who supported the Comstock Act. Judge Carpenter followed the 1879 Bennett ruling, which had declared that a publisher's purpose in publishing material was not an issue and did not allow Heywood to testify that he was trying to promote sexual education and not lewd conduct.

The judge also did not allow the defence to call character witnesses, nor was Heywood allowed to explain that he either was acquitted or charges were dropped during prior arrests. Instead, the judge limited the defence to the issue of whether or not Heywood had mailed the material. Judge Carpenter's instructions to the jury that only "proper fit and decent" material had First Amendment protection undoubtedly sealed Heywood's fate. Jurors found him guilty and the editor was sentenced to two years imprisonment in Charlestown State Prison at hard labour and denied an appeal.

Liberals were unsuccessful in obtaining a presidential pardon; however, they again penned numerous articles for the nation's periodicals. Novelist Julian Hawthorne wrote a pamphlet titled "In Behalf of Personal Liberty" published by the Twentieth Century in support of Heywood's right to free expression. Hawthorne made clear he disagreed with Heywood's ideas, but said controversial works on sex reform should not be obscene.

Liberals gave Heywood a rousing reception in Boston upon his release from prison. Although the editor returned to publishing The Word, the final imprisonment had sapped his health. He died within a year after contracting a cold. His wife and children were left paupers. Within ten days of pursuing Heywood in 1877, Comstock also descended upon free-thought publisher DeRobigne Mortimer Bennett, editor of the Truth seeker. A former Shaker, seed salesman, and pharmacist, Bennett was the leading exponent of anti-clerical free thought following the Civil War.

The publisher came to the philosophy relatively late in life, in his midfifties, after reading Thomas Paine's Age of Reason. He launched his journal, the Truth seeker, in Paris, Illinois, the same year the Comstock Act was passed, then quickly moved his periodical to New York. As historian Hal Sears has stated, Bennett's "techniques were openly and puckishly iconoclastic, confounding the clergy in their own contradictions and human failings, while at the same time devoting a fair amount of exposition to earthy portions of the Bible."

Although soft-spoken and genial, Bennett's views were perceived by many individuals as so radical, his opponents branded him "the devil's own advocate." Unlike Heywood, Bennett had little use for sex radicalism. Yet he became an equally outspoken opponent of the Comstock Act, seeing it as both a state-sanctioned move by religious groups to impose their Christian beliefs on the public as a whole, as well as a violation of liberty of conscience. As a result, Bennett helped lead a petition drive that netted 70,000 signatures, including those of journalists, editors, attorneys, and ministers.

The free-thought editor brought Comstock's wrath upon himself by vigorously opposing Christianity, and the grudge between the two men was deeply personal. Comstock's position on Bennett was clear. In his arrest log, Comstock listed Bennett's religion as "infidel" and his occupation as "publisher of obscene and infidel works." The vice fighter also wrote a lengthy and very personal diatribe about Bennett in the vice society's arrest records:

This man has published, almost weekly, most outrageous and infamous attacks against Comstock, charging all manners of offenses, blackmail, perjury, and everything bad. He continues to publish the most infamous and obscene matter in his pamphlets, and because he mingles blasphemy with it, the community seems unwilling to have him interfered with ... His history of Comstock are lies, without hardly a shadow of truth. His book Champions of the Church is a huge libel; and his tracts" Open letter to Jesus Christ" and etc. are not only obscene, but so blasphemous that they almost make ones blood run cold ... He has not failed any week, almost without exception, to libel Comstock and attack him in some malicious and cowardly manner. He has sought to repeal the U.S. Law and got up a monster petition of about 70,000 names to have law repealed.

Comstock was so fearful of the social changes that freethinkers advocated that he told one liberal that freethinkers "are entitled to no mercy" and that he would "show them no quarter." The vice fighter arrested Bennett in New York in November 1877 on charges of blasphemy and obscenity for mailing two pamphlets, a scientific tract written for TAe Popular Science Monthly by H. B. Bradford called "How Do Marsupials Propagate" and a satirical and heretical work by Bennett, "An Open Letter to Jesus Christ," that posed Biblical and uncomfortable personal questions to Jesus.

Although Bennett, like Heywood, would become a near-martyr to the cause of free speech and his health ruined by his imprisonment, he was not a First Amendment absolutist. Bennett supported broad protection for freedom of expression, but believed that both libel and obscenity laws were necessary. In one of history's many ironies, however, the Bennett case established the precedent for prosecuting individuals under the Comstock Act for five decades. Upon the free-thought editor's arrest in 1877, Dr. E. B. Foote Sr. provided the $1,500 bail money, then he and noted orator Robert Ingersoll, both friends of Bennett, acting on behalf of the NDA, used their influence to convince the postmaster general and other Washington, DC officials to dismiss the charges against the Bennett, much to the furor of Comstock.

Comstock received some satisfaction a short while later when Bennett was again arrested, this time in Watkins Glenn, NY. Bennett's crime was helping Heywood's sister-in-law sell Cupid's Yokes at a meeting of the New York State Freethinkers Association. Although local officials had arrested him, Bennett was convinced that Comstock was behind this second prosecution. The free-thought editor vowed to openly sell Cupid's Yokes to anyone who requested it. Not surprisingly, Comstock used a decoy letter to purchase the pamphlet and some other works. Libertarians worked feverishly to try and get the charges dropped again, but to no avail. Thaddeus Wakeman, a committee chairman with the National Liberal League, an organization devoted to the separation of church and state, wrote to Elizur Wright asking Wright to contact prominent friends in Washington to put pressure on the U.S. Attorney General to drop the case. Wright correctly surmised that Bennett might well lose his case if it got to court. Despite his best efforts, the most Wright was able to do was to obtain a continuance.

Bennett's conviction resulted in a "landmark decision," a $300 fine and a thirteen-month prison sentence at the Albany Penitentiary. Although the judge in the 1878 Heywood case had cited the English Hicklin ruling, it was not until U.S. v. Bennett, that a justice fully considered and used the English case to determine a test for obscenity. In Bennett, Judge Samuel Blatchford, relying on Ex parte Jackson, re-affirmed the constitutionality of the Comstock Act. Blatchford then Lord Chief Justice Cockburn in Hicklin to rule that the test for obscenity was "whether the tendency of the matter charged as obscenity is to deprave and corrupt those whose minds are open to immoral influences, and into whose hands a publication of this sort may fall." The judge also relied on

Hicklin to rule that an indicted work can be judged by isolated passages rather than the work as a whole. Relatedly, Judge Blatchford held that the intent of the author in producing the work did not matter. That a publication contained obscenity was enough. Finally, the Bennett case re-affirmed that the indictment for obscenity did not have to contain the precise, alleged obscene words and passages in the court records so long as the work was sufficiently identified so that the defendant knew the work's identity.

The elderly and sick editor appreciated the liberals' efforts to free him. Robert Ingersoll sought a pardon from President Rutherford B. Hayes, pointing out that although he did not agree with the contents of Cupid's Yokes, he was convinced that it was not obscene and that Bennett was really being prosecuted for being a non-believer. Ingersoll was confident that since Hayes had previously pardoned Heywood for the same publication, Bennett also would be freed. Purity crusaders launched a vigorous crusade to block the pardon, especially appealing to Hayes's deeply devout wife. The pardon attempt failed.

Although Bennett appreciated his supporter's efforts to free him from prison, he regretted liberals were using his ill health as the main reason in their appeal. Bennett told friends in a letter that "If I cannot be liberated on the merits of the case, why not let me stay here until my time is served out." He was released in 1880. Liberals threw him a rousing reception at which they presented him with funds for a trip around the world. Two years later, Bennett died.

MOSES HARMAN

Libertarians rallied again in 1887 when Kansas free-thought editor Moses Harman, his son George, and co-editor Edwin C. Walker were arrested in February of that year for publishing a reader's letter concerning forced sex during marriage. An ardent feminist, Harman strongly supported equal rights for women in all realms and ignored the Victorian code of socially respectable discussion in order to expose social evils as "the first step in healing them." This tradition of exposure came easily for the editor since he had used such tactics previously as an abolitionist in Kansas. Following the war, Harman became involved in free thought and established the Valley Falls Liberal in 1880.

Money was always in short supply, so Harrnan changed the publication's name to the Kansas Liberal hoping for a broader audience. He also made a brief move to Lawrence and shared the editing responsibilities with Annie L. Diggs (who later became a noted Populist Party editor). When Herman's editorial vision clashed with Diggs's, he returned to Valley Falls and took Walker, an individualist anarchist, as coeditor in 1882. Walker had previously contributed articles on anti-statism to Liberty, The Truth seeker, and the Kansas Liberal before obtaining a fulltime position with Harman.

The Kansas Liberal had been strongly anti-clerical, feminist and somewhat socialist before Walker's arrival. The new coeditor quickly broadened the journal's editorial vision to include individualist anarchist thought, a philosophy with which Harman approved. In August 1883, Harman courted more controversy by changing the publication's name to Lucifer, the Light Bearer, The editor explained he had done so because the word "liberal" was overused and that Lucifer was both the name of the morning star and "the first teacher of science."

The name change, however, may well have been calculated to arouse publicity. The tactic worked. However, mainstream publications heaped scorn upon the editors for both the journal's name and its subject matter. Harman responded by regularly printing articles supporting freedom of speech, claiming that it was a natural right and a necessity if social evils were to be exposed. "No reform work can succeed without the assistance of the press," he stated in a January 1897 issue of Lucifer.

Herman's beliefs about male-female relations and limited state police powers were derived from personal experience (his first wife died in childbirth), his abolitionist background, and his adherence to Herbert Spencer's doctrine that freedom meant that a human being had "'the right to do as he pleased, so long as he does not invade the equal rights of others,'" Harman said. "Liberty, wedded to responsibility for one's acts, is the true and only basis of good character, or of morality," he added. Freedom, said Harman, meant equal freedom of conscience and private judgment for all, especially when it concerned moral or personal matters.

Harman incurred Comstock's wrath following his announcement in the spring of 1886 that he would not censor the words or ideas of any submissions, including those that graphically discussed sexual issues. In essence, he put into practice the "free language" ideas of Stephen Pearl Andrews who argued against the idea that words could actually be obscene. Words should be used "unblushingly." Harman explained to his readers that "the right of a free press should be unqualified by considerations of taste or propriety." To these ends, Harman published a number of articles and letters from readers on women's rights, birth control, and sexual relations.

The first, known as the "Markland letter," as mentioned above, led a U.S. Deputy Marshall to arrest Moses and George Harman as well as Walker in early 1887 and a grand jury in Topeka to indict them on 270 counts of obscenity. While awaiting trial, Harman published three more letters, one of which was a protest against contraceptive use, the second was an article about a couple who, believing the world was about to end, confessed their affairs to each other, and the third letter commented upon two methods of abstinence.

Harman's beliefs in gender equity only partly explain why he would publish such sexually frank material. As historian Hal Sears has noted, Harman sought notoriety for both himself and his journal and "plunged with fervor into the role of First Amendment martyr." The editor was well aware that social tolerance for radical thought, while never strong, had decreased markedly since the Chicago Haymarket incident.

Even liberals found Harman's philosophy and his editorial practice of those beliefs reckless. For example, George E. MacDonald, the editor of the Ttuth seeker, supported Harman's right to print as a matter of principle, but called the indicted letters "mostly tommyrot and hogwash ...

physiologically puerile and socially impossible." MacDonald added, however, the articles were merely "foolish stuff" that could not injure anyone's morals. Even his co-editor, E. C. Walker, quit over the policy, stating that radical philosophy worked best "if pitched in conventional language." Walker called Harman's plain word policy "perverse persistence." Surprisingly, Walker never discussed the libertarian issues at stake. Local and national journals, by contrast, referred to Harman as a fool, a crank, and a cheap notoriety seeker.

A number of liberals, including the Footes and Heywood supported Harman's First Amendment rights by again raising a defence fund to pay his court costs. They also penned articles, pamphlets, and letters to various publications supporting Harman's free expression rights. The Reverend Hugh O. Pentecost, a noted New York Congregationalist minister, social reformer, and attorney, explained his support of Harman in the Twentieth Century by stating: "It is the principle involved that interests me ... I do not believe it is possible to keep art or literature pure by law. If human beings are impure they cannot be improved by law."

Pentecost also expressed the wary concern many libertarians held that many radical reformers would not receive a fair trial. "I believe it is quite impossible for any one holding very unpopular opinions to be fairly tried by an jury or judge," he added. After citing examples of several individuals who were jailed or fined for their unpopular reform views, including single tax proponent Henry George and several spiritualists, he charged: "Juries and judges are almost sure to decide in favour of established ignorance and enthroned wealth."

Harman's radicalism made it difficult for the NDA to raise the money to pay his court fees. An article in the Health Monthly reiterating a call for money to defend the editor said there was a "strange lukewarmness" by First Amendment supporters. The article reminded readers that free expression was the issue and not Harman's political or social views. The Footes told readers that Harman did not publish the articles and letters with the intent of inflaming passions, but instead, devoted himself whole-heartedly and purely to the emancipation of women. Harman had achieved notoriety even before the letters were printed. His daughter Lillian and Walker had been arrested, jailed, and found guilty of violating Kansas's marriage license law after the two, with Moses Herman's blessing, engaged in a non-church, non-state marriage. Harman's attorneys, David Overmeyer and Caspar C. Clemens, were the editor's saving grace. They got the initial indictment quashed after it was discovered the grand jury could not explain the exact instances of obscenity for which the two Hermans and Walker were charged. The jury claimed the paper was so obscene as to make it impossible. The grand jury then refiled. Charges were only brought against Moses Harman for publishing the four offending letters.

Four years of delays ensued before the trial occurred. Although the NDA and several other organizations had petitioned Judge Caius G. Foster to acquit Harman on the grounds that he was a sincere sex educator, Harman's continued insistence on flouting the law led the trial to go forward. While under indictment, the editor reprinted the four offending letters, a section of Genesis 38, a particularly earthy chapter of the Bible, and another letter known as the O'Neill letter. Written by anarchist New York physician Richard O'Neill, the letter graphically detailed a variety of sexual abuses and deviant practices he had seen and treated.

When the case finally came to trial, Harman made the mistake of dismissing his attorneys and choosing to defend himself. Judge Foster appointed an attorney to help Harman, which proved to be Harman's undoing. The attorney, Colonel Bradley, ignored Harman's First Amendment arguments and sought an acquittal based on insanity. The tactic failed and Harman was only allowed to address the court briefly on the constitutional issues. A jury found him guilty on four counts. He was sentenced to five years in the penitentiary and fined $300. David Overmeyer, one of Harman's original attorneys, returned and gained the editor's release on a technicality after Harman had served just four months of his sentence. The editor was then tried on new obscenity charges for publishing the O'Neill letter, found guilty, and sentenced to one year in prison. Again Overmeyer obtained Harman's release on a technicality. The editor had served eight months of the sentence. Harman was then tried again for reprinting the Markland letter and sentenced to a year at hard labour.

The O'Neill trial in 1891 established an important precedent for determining obscenity by establishing a community standards test. Judge Foster modified the Bennett ruling by holding that matter was obscene if it "is offensive to the common sense of decency and modesty of the community" as well as whether the material "is of such a character as to deprave and corrupt those whose minds are open to such immoral influences." As with Foote, Heywood, and Bennett before him, Harman found that the judge applied the bad tendency test. For Harman, two decades of intransigence and imprisonments, including a year at hard labour breaking rocks at age seventy-five in Joliet, destroyed his health. Yet, the editor managed to savor a few minor victories throughout his two decades of persecution. His journal repeatedly discussed the women's rights and sexual issues he believed important. He also was one of the few sex radicals able to raise the issue of citizens' constitutional First Amendment rights during his 1891 federal district court trial.

British playwright George Bernard Shaw penned a 1907 letter to the New York Times supporting Herman and noting he would never visit the U.S. for fear of being imprisoned after purity crusaders declared some of his works obscene. "If the brigands can, without any remonstrance from public opinion, seize a man of Mr. Harman's advanced age, and imprison him for a year under conditions which amount to an indirect attempt to kill him, simply because he shares the opinion expressed in my Man and Superman that 'marriage is the most licentious of human institutions,' what chance should I have of escaping?"

Discussion

The five-decade long drama between libertarians and social purity advocates highlights an important paradox of

American society, namely the willingness of the public to support freedom of expression sometimes in theory and sometimes in practice, while at other times acceding to the demands of an often small, yet vocal, minority who stridently argue for censorship during periods of social or political strife. Because of this waxing and waning of public support for freedoms enunciated in the Bill of Rights, there are always individuals who come to the fore, compelled to singlemindedly support values they personally hold dear.

The libertarians sought to give shape and form to an abstract principle of democracy: freedom of expression. Like abolitionists, civil rights supporters, suffragists, and temperance advocates, the intellectual, social, legal, and political battles fought by these radical libertarians were fraught with long odds and frequent setbacks. Yet, the libertarians eventually saw their views adopted by the public, legislators, and judges as Victorian thinking and lifestyles gave way to a modern, pluralistic, consumer-oriented and progressive-thinking culture.

Although the U.S. Supreme Court would not address the issue of whether or not material that dealt with sexual matter was worthy of any level of First Amendment protection until 1957, this small group of libertarians promoted limited government restrictions and the value of free expression in a democratic society to a public which tacitly accepted the concept in theory and voiced it as part of popular democratic rhetoric, but rarely debated its boundaries. In the late nineteenth century, therefore, libertarians were largely alone in maintaining that the Fourteenth Amendment incorporated the provisions of the Bill of Rights to protect expression and in offering a broad interpretation of the scope of First Amendment protection. Almost fifty years would pass before the U.S. Supreme Court would concur.

The libertarians recognized that the nation's support of censorship was a product of the political, economic, social, and cultural turbulence that marked the late nineteenth century. Such changes led purity crusaders to scrutinize all printed material, including literature, medical and educational books and pamphlets. The clashes that emerged over freedom of expression, whether to repress new ideas or embrace them, were inevitable and frequently explosive.

Although purity crusaders ultimately failed to stop the tide of social change, they partially succeeded in chilling expression on a number of controversial social, religious, gender, and health topics, despite the libertarians' efforts. And, Comstock's ability to pejoratively label the liberals "friends of obscenity" and his claims they were engaged in a "conspiracy" hampered libertarians' efforts to reach as wide of an audience as they would have liked.

The questions and discussion these libertarians raised were the same ones that the U.S. Supreme Court would consider in the years following World War I. Should the basis for individuals' rights to freedom of expression rest in state constitutional guarantees? Or, should the First Amendment, via the Fourteenth Amendment, provide that protection? If so, how much protection should the First Amendment guarantee? Should all utterances be protected, or, should there be a hierarchy of protected expression with some ideas given hill protection and other ideas regulated to varying degrees? The story of these "forgotten" libertarian radicals and their accomplishments are far more complex than one paper can do justice. Hopefully historians and legal scholars will rekindle their interest and further examine a group of individuals who were so influential in defining and shaping twentieth-century views of First Amendment theory and doctrine.

Chapter 3

The Problem of Modern Writing

All students of modern literature are, presumably, familiar with Georg Lukács's analysis of naturalism and formalism in the essay "Narrate or Describe?". For Lukács, the ascendance of the descriptive over the narrating mode in fictional writing signaled the epochal aesthetic changes that had been occurring in European literature since the mid-nineteenth century. The main cause for such changes was, he writes, capitalism, which was characterized by "objective facts" such as "the domination of capitalist prose over the inner poetry of human experience, the continuous dehumanization of social life, the general debasement of humanity" .

Instead of the wholeness of composition and depth of character that one finds in the well-plotted novels of Scott, Balzac, and Tolstoy, writers of the bourgeois capitalist era, such as Zola and Flaubert, had become increasingly preoccupied with the tedious accuracy of turning minutiae into lifeless tableaux, in the face of which authors and readers alike were reduced to passive, cynical observers (rather than participants). For all its virtuosity and specialized craftsmanship, therefore, description was the sign, in writing, of a general ideological and social crisis.

It is easy to point to the ideological and aesthetic assumptions behind Lukács's analysis and criticize his readings for their seemingly elitist longing for the writing methods of a bygone era. Indeed, the examples of literary works classified by him as "great art" reveal the obvious biases in his cultural frame of reference. Once this is understood, however, his account remains thought-provoking, not least because it offers a sustained discussion about the vital connections between social necessity and the making of fiction -- in what we nowadays would call the politics of style. Embedded in Lukács's text is a crucial question that has lost none of its relevance even today: how does one see in verbal language?

The traditional manner of responding to this question has tended immediately to translate the act of visual perception into something nonperceptual, so that the question becomes "how does one understand in verbal language?" Such a translation "resolves" the problem by stripping sight and visuality of their sensuous dimensions, so that seeing becomes, in effect, a mere metaphor, a convenient stand-in for the idealist, nonperceptual vision called understanding.

This typical, metaphorical resolution effectively avoids the complexity of the historical and philosophical questions about sensory experience -- such as what is outside and inside the human organism, whether sense impressions are singular or compound, how the senses and memory interact with one another, and so forth. Yet by the same gesture, it also forecloses the possibility of coming to terms with the semiotic status of visual or sensualized descriptions -- with the fact that such descriptions are by no means natural or the same as actual physical visual perception itself.

Once we refuse this traditional practice of simply de-sensualizing seeing, questions of a different order open up: How does the sense of sight operate in a medium that is not preeminently visual? Indeed, can the sense of sight operate in a medium that is not visual, a medium such as verbal language? Conversely, how does one write visually -- how does one narrate with visual signs such as images and metaphors?

With these questions in mind, it becomes possible to rearticulate Lukács's concerns in "Narrate or Describe?" as symptomatic of an anxiety over the complicated interconnections between seeing and writing in an era in which the explosion of visual information could no longer be comfortably contained within the artificial limits of the Gutenberg leadtype technology.

As Nancy Armstrong points out, the onset of pictorialism Lukács found so deplorable in certain realist novels was the sign that a fundamental change was taking place, in mid- to late-nineteenth-century Europe, in the relationship between the codes of visuality and the codes of writing. Lukács accurately sensed that the proliferation of visible, material objects that invaded the perceptual field -- something he attributed to bourgeois capitalism -- had rendered obsolete the well-organized narrating methods that he deemed laudably characteristic of the classic realist novels.

Hence the unmistakable tone of mourning in his language: "Narration proportions, description merely levels"; "Description . . . becomes the dominant mode in composition in a period in which, for social reasons, the sense of what is primary in epic construction has been lost. Description is the writer's substitute for the epic significance that has been lost" . "The loss of the narrative interrelationship between objects and their function in concrete human experiences means a loss of artistic significance" . "With the loss of the art of narration, details cease to be transmitters of concrete aspects of the action and attain significance independent of the action and of the lives of the characters" .

We may summarize Lukács's predicament as follows: being a sensitive and well-trained reader, he discovered the insuppressibility of visual objects in literary writings of the bourgeois age; he even noticed that the narratives of certain authors had become dependent on incorporating the multiplicity of the visual as such, yet in his tone he still clung nostalgically to the idealist notion of seeing-as-understanding. When recast in the medium of vision, his arguments are iconophobic, intent as they are on the necessity to control and repress the increasingly fluid interpenetration between visual and nonvisual systems of signification.

For him, the relationship between such systems had to be a hierarchized one: if the visible world looked random and fragmented, it was the writer's responsibility to coordinate -- or subordinate -- it in such a manner as to represent a kind of moral-aesthetic order. In his mourning of epic proportions, there is a sense that visual data are potentially not only disruptive but usurpatory; their sheer abundance can easily take over the age-old practice of storytelling, turning the latter into a mere documentary produced by a mechanistic camera eye. ("When description is the dominant technique, . . . writers attempt a vain competition with the visual arts" .)

Strictly speaking, then, the practice for which Lukács was nostalgic was not simply the classic realist novel per se but more precisely a kind of writing by overlooking: it is only by appropriating and restraining visual attention, his argument implies, that a mastery of narrative perspective can be achieved. Narration, in other words, is ultimately about seeing not with the eyes but with the mind. Description, alas, has let the (seemingly) spontaneous function of seeing dominate in such a way as to paralyze the act of narrating, which is now deformed by an overload of observable information.

Inscribed in Lukács's impassioned account about fiction writing is thus, first of all, a cluster of overdetermined epistemological issues pertaining to the exact nature of the relationship between abstraction and sensuousness (seeing, in particular). These issues include the enmeshment, in philosophy and literature, of seeing with understanding, and the consequent impossibility of talking about seeing without the idealist baggage; the continual hierarchy by which the act of seeing is trivialized and considered inferior to philosophical or artistic vision; and the difficulty of assessing the precise status of visuality in narration. Add to these the historical situation of bourgeois capitalism, in which the combined forces of commerce, imperialism, technology, and urbanization mean that visuality has become and will continue to be an ever-expanding realm, and we can begin to appreciate the magnitude of the problem at hand.

Although Lukács was constrained by his specialization as a reader of philosophy and literature, the alarming and conservative conclusions he drew about the sense of sight, and the desperate attempts he made to reconjure a time when sight could still be disciplined, hidden, or eliminated are in fact not entirely distinguishable from the overall theoretical concerns over vision and modernity that are shared by other major theorists. We think here of Martin Heidegger "The Age of the World Picture", Walter Benjamin "The Work of Art in the Age of Mechanical Reproduction", and, closer to our own time, Guy Debord Society of the Spectacle and Paul Virilio War and Cinema. These theorists write about the hegemony of vision as a result of modern technology, the mechanical reproduction of art, the ubiquity of the commodified image, and the strategies of modern warfare with their techniques of precise visual targeting.

Such a hegemony has led, in turn, to a profound distrust of vision, and theorists working in advanced industrial nations have accordingly adopted critical approaches that warn about the danger, indeed the untrustworthiness, of vision as both a spontaneous and a coerced phenomenon. To this extent, there are the deconstructionist critics who seek refuge in the negative mediating work of language in order to stave off the alluring immediacy of the visible (something they relegate to the realm of phenomenology), and there are also those who, like Virilio in particular, theorize visuality in such ways as to historicize the political programming and ideological manipulation that structure the preemptive ubiquity of vision.

In this larger cultural-theoretical context, what allows Lukács's discussion to retain its germaneness is his attention to visuality (in the form of descriptive minutiae) as a problematic of writing, specifically of narration. How is one to write, his work asks, in an age dominated by the continual production of visual information, when writing can apparently no longer compete by bringing the visual field under its control? Should writing accommodate visual technologies such as photography, film, television, video, and so forth, adhere to the function of documentation, and become thus the instrument of a straightforward reflectionism? (Though a Marxist, Lukács's criticism of the propagandist tendencies of socialist realism should be remembered here as consistent with his criticism of reflectionism in general.) Does it still make sense to speak of narration; can stories still be told in light of the preemptive dominance of visuality?

Despite his claims to historical understanding, Lukács's elegiac mood made it impossible for him to see the historically transformed relationship between visuality and narration in any terms other than a tragic fall. Nor was it possible, consequently, for him to grasp that alternative manners of narration could be emerging from the ruin of the older assumptions about seeing. What unnerved him, in Nancy Armstrong's terms, was the new cultural collaboration that was taking shape between the codes of fiction and the codes of visuality in the production of knowledge itself.

The sense of loss so insisted on by Lukács in his mournful theory may, I believe, be overcome if we turn to another equally well-known argument, Roman Jakobson "Two Aspects of Language". Intended primarily as a study of the disturbance of aphasia, Jakobson's structuralist differentiation between linguistic functions offers a useful means of moving beyond the impasse left by Lukács's account of the demise of narration. According to Jakobson, each linguistic sign acquires intelligibility by two operations, both of which put the sign in relation to other signs. The two operations, which he designates by the terms metaphor and metonymy, work respectively by way of alternation and by way of combination: "A given significative unit may be replaced by other, more explicit signs of the same code, whereby its general meaning is revealed, while its contextual meaning is determined by its connection with other signs within the same sequence".

The metaphoric operation, premised as it is on an internal code of equivalence (or similarity), is usually hidden from the actual utterance, while the metonymic operation, whose principle is that of contiguity (or alignment), is usually detectable in an external or contextual relation of a sign combining with other signs. As Jakobson puts it, "the development of a discourse may take place along two different semantic lines: one topic may lead to another either through their similarity or through their contiguity. The metaphoric way would be the most appropriate term for the first case and the metonymic way for the second". Moreover, "a competition between both devices, metonymic and metaphoric, is manifest in any symbolic process, be it intrapersonal or social".

Extrapolating from Jakobson's schema, we may argue anew that the crisis of writing elaborated by Lukács is, in effect, an observable moment of historical change in the relationship between the metaphoric and metonymic functions in verbal construction. What Lukács refers to by the term narration -- namely, a mode of storytelling in which sensuously and visually perceptible details are "naturally" subsumed under or simply withheld from the actual writing so that a proportioned, commanding vision may emerge -- can now be reformulated as a particular politics of style in which the metonymic operation remains the foremost strategy of narrative organization.

What Lukács calls description, that is, the mode that packs the narrative space with one material detail after another with no end (that is, no proportioned structure) in sight, may now be understood in terms of a new politics of style in which the metaphoric operation (which establishes the equivalence among things -- which "levels," as Lukács writes of the descriptive mode) has seemingly become dominant to the point of overtaking the metonymic. The onset of pictorialism -- that is, of a repetitious detailing of visual phenomena -- in narration was disturbing, then, because (as Lukács rightly perceived it) an epochal shift in the balance of power between metaphor and metonymy had taken place.

For any novelist working in a modern urban setting, some version of these profound questions about the historically changing relationship between abstraction and sensorial perception, between the metaphoric and metonymic functions of writing, would no doubt present itself. One can only speculate that, in a metropolitan environment such as early-twentieth-centuryShanghai, in which the encounters among different cultures and peoples, and the abundance of commodities from foreign lands were daily affairs, the entire twin problematic of how to see in writing and how to narrate in visuality would only intensify exponentially. In the framework of non-Western modernity, the attempt of a Lukács to look back to tradition -- to Lessing Laocoön, for instance, and through Lessing to Homern Odyssey -- in order to trace the genealogy of narrative methods is compounded by a conscious nativizing of tradition itself, a nativizing that is typically accounted for not only by way of the rise of bourgeois capitalism (as in Lukács's case) but also by way of the invasive and unavoidable presence of the foreign, of Westerners.

If we are to follow the socio-aesthetic lead of Lukács's analysis, it would be necessary, in the case of modern non-Western writings, to supplement his classic Marxist attention to capitalist impact with an equal attention to the impact of that specter generally referred to as the West, in order to evaluate historically any politics of style. The literary author I would like next to discuss in some detail is the renowned Chinese woman writer Eileen Chang, who rose to fame in Shanghai during the first half of the 1940s, when the city was occupied by the Japanese. Writing in a culturally transitional period and being well-read not only in her ethnic literary tradition but also in European and American literatures, Chang was no stranger to the ambivalent epistemological possibilities produced by visuality in modernity.

If she participated in the fascination with visual spectacles that were generated by capitalist urbanization and commodification -- as the colorful descriptions of streets, urban living, fashion, food, and other quotidian details in her writings indicate -- she was equally aware of the destructiveness of warfare and of the ideological coercion enabled by political surveillance machines. For precisely the reason that they offer some of the most uncompromised insights into the contradictions of nationalism, patriotism, and modernist enlightenment, her works were, for a long time after 1949, considered politically incorrect, and disappeared from mainland Chinese critics' attention until the 1980s.

Outside China, her fame was restored when her works were endorsed by the male Chinese new critic C. T. Hsia in his book-length appraisal of modern Chinese fiction, the first of its kind to be published in English in the United States in the early 1960s. While Chang's reputation as a writer has since been firmly and irrevocably reestablished, at least among Chinese-reading publics, the peculiarities of her writings remain, as ever, resistant to elucidation.

There are innumerable references to sensuous pleasures in Chang's writings, especially in her autobiographical and critical essays. She loved colours, the scent of gasoline, the rattle made by trams. She contemplated experiences of reading, looking at art, listening to music, watching dancing -- activities that are specifically oriented toward aesthetic enjoyment. But the range of her foci extends considerably beyond the restrictively intellectual and aesthetic spheres to encompass entirely mundane activities such as living in an apartment building, going to the fresh market to shop for her meals, visiting fabric stores simply to admire the colours and patterns on display, and looking at old family photographs.

As well, she wrote about personal encounters in her university dormitory, in the hospital where she worked as a nurse, or on the street during wartime in Hong Kong. Meanwhile, if Chang's prose is suffused with references to the material aspects of quotidian living, it never became or attempted to become a theory of aesthetics in that the experiences of sensuousness she so relished were never distilled or abstracted to become philosophical arguments. Instead, Chang remained primarily a fiction writer whose concerns had to do with narrative strategies and constructions.

This is not to say, however, that sensuous experiences simply enter her writings in the form of themes. Rather, the point I would like to make is how the sensuous as such can be seen in Chang to bring about certain adjustments in the very conceptualization of narration itself. Obviously, this is a large point, a full-fledged demonstration of which cannot be done in the space of one essay. I will therefore raise some issues through a reading of one fictional text, the short story "Hong meigui yü bai meigui" ("Red Rose and White Rose", first published in Shanghai in 1944), in the hope that the implications, if valid, can be taken up in a longer study.

"Red Rose and White Rose" intrigues me in part because of its explicitly metaphoric associations, as the title itself indicates. It is, for instance, possible to interpret this story by elaborating on the meanings of red, white, and roses, and how they correspond to the two main female characters. What I'd like to argue, nevertheless, is that Chang's use of such metaphorical elements is indicative of a more interesting effort to juggle the mutually implicating problematics of visuality and narration, of metaphor and metonymy -- an effort that cannot, to my mind, be reduced to what the French author and critic Alain Robbe-Grillet in his essay "Nature, Humanism, Tragedy" has perceptively called the "analogical vocabulary of traditional humanism". This point will become clearer in a moment. "Red Rose and White Rose" describes some years in the life of an accomplished young man, Tong Zhenbao.

A well-educated "new youth" of the "new China" of the Republican era, Zhenbao went to Edinburgh for advanced study and has recently returned to his hometown Shanghai. He is now a skilled textile engineer at a high-level position in a company financed by foreigners. Before he has his own lodgings, Zhenbao is staying temporarily at the home of a friend, Wang Shiyuan, who has a pretty and flirtatious wife, Jiaorui. While Wang is away on business, Zhenbao and Jiaorui have a passionate affair. Jiaorui becomes so seriously in love with Zhenbao that she wants to divorce her husband, but Zhenbao, aware of the bright future that lies ahead of him, has no intention of committing himself to her.

In spite of her pleas, he abandons her and soon afterwards establishes himself with a well-educated bride from a good family, Meng Yanli, who eventually gives birth to a daughter. (The story actually begins when the daughter is nine years old and "expenses for her college education were already secured" .) Yanli is the opposite of Jiaorui. Not only is she quiet, skinny, and boring; she also has no interest in sex. If their home is, to all appearances, well-maintained and peaceful, the couple's relationship is virtually nonexistent except in the form of mutual resentment and suspicion. Zhenbao openly and regularly indulges himself with prostitutes. By chance one day, he meets Jiaorui again on the street trolley. She has remarried, aged, and put on weight, but seems contented. As she talks about her life after their separation and tells him that it was he who taught her about love, Zhenbao, overwhelmed by feelings of jealousy and melancholy, begins to cry. His relations with Yanli continue to deteriorate. One day, Zhenbao discovers that she is having an affair with her tailor. He becomes reckless in his womanizing behaviour, neglects to give Yanli housekeeping money, and gradually loses his good social reputation. But life goes on.

What are the visual images of red rose and white rose doing in Chang's narrative? They are, we are told from the beginning, the two names Zhenbao gives to the two most important women in his life: "There were two women in Zhenbao's life. He called one his White Rose and the other his Red Rose. One was the holy and chaste wife, the other was the passionate mistress" .

Rather than being endowed with their own subjectivities, the women characters are deliberately presented by Chang as objects of a man's erotic imagination. To this extent, the images serve the function of metaphorizing female sexuality, with red standing for romance, experience, licentiousness, and white standing for virginity, innocence, propriety, and so on. Yet to follow this line of inquiry would be, first of all, to adopt without questioning Zhenbao's masculinist perspective. Secondly, it would be to adopt a habit of interpretation with the assumption that narrative meanings are a matter of excavating what is hidden in some interior depth beneath the surfaces, the images.

Put in another way, it would be an analogical manner of reading because it is primarily invested in establishing corresponding or equivalent meanings that are held together within the visual metaphors. Whereas in Jakobson's account, metaphor is simply differentiated structurally as one kind of linguistic function, Alain Robbe-Grillet, paying special attention to the fact that language always produces moral value, offers a provocative critique of metaphoric reasoning in terms of its implication in humanism or anthropomorphism.

The gist of Robbe-Grillet's argument can be glimpsed in the following:

- A true bridge of souls thrown between man and things, the humanist outlook is preeminently a pledge of solidarity.
- In the literary realm, the expression of this solidarity appears chiefly as the investigation, worked up into a system, of analogical relations.
- Metaphor, as a matter of fact, is never an innocent figure of speech.

To say that the weather is "capricious" or the mountain "majestic," to speak of the "heart" of the forest, of a "pitiless" sun, of a village "huddled" in the valley, is, to a certain degree, to furnish clues as to the things themselves: shape, size, situation, etc. But the choice of an analogical vocabulary, however simple, already does something more than account for purely physical data, and what this more is can scarcely be ascribed only to the credit of belles-lettres.

The height of the mountain assumes, willy-nilly, a moral value; the heat of the sun becomes the result of an intention. . . . In almost the whole of our contemporary literature, these anthropomorphic analogies are repeated too insistently, too coherently not to reveal an entire metaphysical system. . . . Metaphor, which is supposed to express only a comparison, without any particular motive, actually introduces asubterranean communication, a movement of sympathy (or of antipathy) which is its true raison d'etre.

For Robbe-Grillet, the principle of equivalence that constitutes the functioning of metaphor is not just a structural differentiation but rather a mechanism of metaphysical value-production: metaphors work by implying that there is a hidden unity between themselves and the things they metaphorize. Because such a hidden unity can only be the result of the participation of human consciousness in the world of things -- because, in other words, metaphors are a means of endowing things with human attitudes and intentions -- metaphoric thinking is ultimately a moralizing process in which what is being affirmed remains human subjectivity. In metaphor, man remains the centre of things. Although Robbe-Grillet's examples are nonvisual ones, his thesis applies with equal pertinence to visual metaphors.

Indeed, precisely because images are conventionally theorized in terms of notions such as resemblance and likeness (to reality), Robbe-Grillet's point about the ideological assumption of analogical reasoning becomes arguably the clearest in the case of visual metaphors.

Returning to Chang's narrative, we will see that if we simply concentrate on "red rose" and "white rose" as metaphors for the women characters, something crucial will be missed. The polarization of the two terms, Red Rose and White Rose, distracts attention from the fact that the women in Zhenbao's life are parts of a series of exchangeable, replaceable objects. Early on in the narrative, we are told that Zhenbao's choice of metaphor is inspired by another woman previous to Jiaorui and Yanli, a woman called Meigui, or Rose, whom he had met while he was a student in Britain.

A Eurasian whose father was English and whose mother was Cantonese, and an easygoing, carefree girl, Rose would have let Zhenbao do whatever he wished with her sexually. While taking Rose home in his car on the day he was to leave her, he was almost aroused to the point of breaking propriety, but he restrained himself. Having been born poor, having been sent as a "new youth" of China to Britain for an education so he could serve his country, Zhenbao told himself that he had to remember and submit to his higher duty.

This episode with Rose left such a deep impression on him that her name has since become the signifier with which he conceives of the women in his life. "Rose," then, is not simply a name but an objectification of a kind of a primary, unforgettable encounter, the emotion of which is not fulfilled until later. "Rose" cannot be given up and will need to be repeated with variations.

Before Rose, there had also been the odorous prostitute in Paris to whom Zhenbao lost his virginity; after Yanli, in Shanghai, there are the "dark" and "plump" prostitutes he favours for the hot sex he cannot enjoy with his wife. Clearly, once this serializing of women is made obvious, it would no longer be sufficient to read "red rose" and "white rose" analogically, as straightforward metaphors corresponding to Jiaorui and Yanli.

If roses are metaphors, the femininity they metaphorize is itself another metaphor, one that, moreover, is being multiplied in the form of a repeated and endlessly repeatable phenomenon.

This conscious narrative strategy of proliferating metaphors and visual objects is not unlike the tendency toward degenerate pictorialism that Lukács finds alarming about the descriptive method. What is thought-provoking here is that Chang does not simply replace narration with description; rather, she reworks narration from within, using the most conventional and stereotypical of metaphors yet assigning to them a decidedly different function from that of an analogical embedding and excavation of deep meanings.

In her hands, the metaphoric fantasy attached to women from a masculinist perspective is now staged over time in a steady succession of female appearances, in the form of partial segments. Using Jakobson's terms, we may say that metaphoric substitutions and repetitions -- roses, women -- are now actively projected by Chang onto the metonymic axis, the axis of combination that constitutes the narrative movement itself.

If, in Zhenbao's perspective, rose and femininity are a unified and hence infinitely repeatable paradigm -- a paradigm that nonetheless receives its meaning from him, the new Chinese man -- the actual syntagmatic chain of the narrative, by giving us one imperfect woman after another and never with any sense of wholeness, systematically undermines that unity.

The projection of the metaphoric function (of alternation) onto the metonymic axis thus becomes a way of rendering visible, of making explicit -- at the level of formal structure -- the ideological assumptions that have been condensed in the value-producing mechanism of metaphor, the mechanism that equates rose with a particular woman, then with multiple women, and finally with all of femininity.

The scuttling of metaphoric reasoning accounts for the detailed descriptions of the material environments around the women. Topographically, the successive appearances of the women are coordinated through a number of temporary spaces and locations, which further the sense of displacement characteristic of the narration. Zhenbao's transaction with the prostitute in Paris was conducted in a cheap hotel room.

With Rose, intimate physical contact took place inside the cramped space of a car. With Jiaorui, the mutual seduction takes place within her apartment in her husband's absence (Jiaorui compares her own heart to an apartment building, only to Change it to a "newly built detached house" after she falls in love with Zhenbao .

Yanli, of course, is the only one with whom sex is conducted within the confines of a permanent home. Finally, with the Shanghai prostitutes, it is back to brothel rooms and rickshaws. The last encounter with Jiaorui happens in the public space of a street trolley.

Therefore, although Zhenbao, as the protagonist, occupies the more or less secure position of a man standing in the forefront of the new nation, the narration of his story takes us in a rather different direction. Writing with an obvious enthusiasm for the deliciously picturesque kinds of details that Lukács frowns upon, Chang participates in what may be viewed as a major shift in narrative methods, in China as elsewhere, that was the overdetermined outcome of globalist modernity in the twentieth century.

So far, I have pinpointed this shift in formal, comparative terms by drawing on the literary theories of Lukács, Jakobson, and Robbe-Grillet. While Lukács's concern with pictorialism helps lay out the problematic of modern writing, Jakobson's structuralist arguments have assisted with explaining the astute displacement of the alternating function of the metaphoric mode onto the metonymic in "Red Rose and White Rose", and Robbe-Grillet's critique of metaphor's anthropomorphic assumptions has served to foreground the satiric, anti-masculinist implications of Chang's narration. However, the nuance of Chang's text is far from being exhausted by these literary-theoretical explanations; it demands further elaboration by way of a more explicitly sociological focus.

METONYMIZED OBJECTIFICATIONS

The metonymized objectifications of the women characters in "Red Rose and White Rose" are a remarkable way of dramatizing the issue of cultural dislocation at a point in Chinese history when contacts with foreign peoples and things have made it necessary more than ever to reimagine what it means to be "Chinese." In the story, such contacts with the foreign are made explicit from the beginning.

Not only are the events located in Shanghai, which, during the first half of the twentieth century and prior to the ascendancy of Hong Kong, had been the most Westernized Chinese city; we are also told that Zhenbao once studied abroad and is now hired by a firm financed by foreigners. But although Zhenbao has, clearly, crossed cultures as a kind of cosmopolitan man, his behaviour is that of a character who has absorbed foreign wisdom in order to apply it to national self-strengthening back home.

Similarly, although sexual adventures take him in and out of his own culture (he had sex with a Paris prostitute and later with Shanghai prostitutes), and in and out of the propriety of civilized society (he had sex with a friend's wife and then with his own wife), there is never a doubt that he remains firmly Chinese -- and a respectable member of the new Chinese society at that.

Even during an age when "semen," to cite Frank Dikötter's perceptive observation about the scientific thinking on sexuality in Republican China, "was a form of capital which had to be carefully managed in the interests of the nation and future generations", Zhenbao's transcultural seminal dispersal, like his transcultural academic endeavor, is never allowed to challenge the authenticity of his cultural and national status. In more than one sense of the phrase, here is a man who is free to go in and out of places (countries, female bodies) without endangering his sense of who he is. From the beginning, he is described as "a modern Chinese person who has come closest to the ideal", and, as the ending of the novel comments, whatever has happened, "Zhenbao woke up the next morning, Changed his bad behaviour, and once again became a good man".

The West, insofar as it is a recurrent spectral presence in modern Chinese writing, appears here in the manners in which the women characters are described in contrast to Zhenbao. From his perspective, the prostitutes, of course, are beneath mention -- they are women who have long crossed the boundary of propriety to become social outcasts and untouchables. But consider Rose, a Eurasian who is also considered a huaqiao, an overseas Chinese.

In her case there is the suggestion that her sexual looseness -- her willingness to engage in sexual activities before marriage -- has something to do with the fact that she is, somehow, not genuinely Chinese. In the case of a woman, then, the crossing of one kind of boundary renders her suspect in regard to all other boundaries; sexuality, nationality, and cultural identity are thus inextricably implicated with one another -- so much so that they become ways to interpret one another. This is similar in the case of Jiaorui. A huaqiao from Singapore, she had been sent to England by her family for further studies, but really in order to find a husband.

In the scene in which Zhenbao first meets her, her attempt to show him her own name in Chinese triggers comments from her husband that are repeatedly studded with the distinction between an "us" and a "them": "Tamen huaqiao" ("They overseas Chinese") . Throughout Jiaorui's seduction of Zhenbao, multiple sensuous and material details are provided to suggest her cultural impurity-that is, her inauthenticity as a proper Chinese lady.

When she is introduced to Zhenbao, for instance, she has just emerged from a shower with her wet hair wrapped inside a towel. As she shakes his hand, he realises that hers still has soap on it. She likes peanut butter, coffee, and Western confection; she plays the piano; she has boyfriends in her husband's absence; she is experienced and passionate in bed. While such a hybridized female object is exotic and erotically exciting to be sure, she is not marriage material for our new Chinese man "poised at the threshold of the world" .

Conscious of his humble class origins and of the fragility of what he has earned through hard work , Zhenbao is determined to "create a 'correct' world which he can carry with him," and in which "he will be the absolute master" . His resolution on the sexual front is that he will marry an authentic, virginal Chinese woman, who still holds herself and, by implication, her culture, intact. Yanli's frigidity can thus be seen as a suggestion precisely of her "integrity," her refusal to let herself cross that important boundary into the terrifying reality of physical and psychological maturity. But it is not enough to portray her as a sexually frigid wife. In one of the most visually striking passages in modern Chinese fiction, Chang describes Yanli as being constipated and preoccupied with her own obstructed bowel movement:

Yanli became sick with constipation, and had to sit in the bathroom for several hours every day. Only during that time could she justifiably do nothing, say nothing, think nothing. The rest of the time she also said nothing and thought nothing, but then she was still a little anxious and would feel the need to walk about, albeit without a purpose.

Only in the bathroom during daylight did she feel secure, rooted. She lowered her head to look at her snow-white belly, so pure and so white -- sometimes it stuck out a little, sometimes it caved in. The look of the belly button kept changing too -- sometimes it was the sweet, clean, and expressionless eye of a Greek statue; sometimes it was abulging angry eye; sometimes it was the eye of some satanic idol. There was a dangerous smile in the eye, but still it was lovely, with its corners bending, giving shape to some crow's feet.

Zhenbao took Yanli to a doctor, and bought her some medication according to the newspaper advertisements. Then he saw that she was not entirely enthusiastic about getting well; it was as if she wanted to keep this sickness around for the sake of self-respect. So he no longer cared. Read against Lukács's criteria, this image of Yanli unable to defecate is a perfect example of precisely the representational mayhem triggered by the descriptive method: once the epic sense of proportions is lost, any kind of minutia, even that which used to be aesthetically off limits, becomes admissible into the frame of narration. From Lukács's standpoint, Chang's narrative resembles rather an indiscriminate camera's eye, thrusting before us in a matter-of-fact manner embarrassing pieces of information that an old-fashioned artist would for certain have suspended from view.

One way of countering Lukács, naturally, would be by arguing and reasserting the metaphorical profundity of the distasteful image. Accordingly, "White Rose" sitting on the toilet, literally holding everything inside herself and looking at herself in this lily-white condition can be seen as a visual metaphor of the ambivalence of what it means to be Chinese in modernity: Should one let go of the shit inside and become liberated, or should one hold onto that shit like a sacred treasure, one that is fiercely guarded by the eye of some mysterious idol?

Being Chinese -- is it a source of inconvenience and inferiority, or a source of pride and superiority? Significantly, this image of narcissistic excrement-retention is superimposed upon that of domestic femininity. The woman at home is thus the one who embodies or epitomizes the purity of that cultural essence called China, in contrast to the licentious ones, like Rose, Jiaorui, or the Shanghai prostitutes, who have, exactly like Zhenbao, transgressed cultural and sexual boundaries.

In this light, the final ironic twist to this tale of roses is, of course, that the constipated Chinese lady herself, too, is committing adultery right under her husband's roof, with her tailor. In the terms of our argument, however, the image of a viscerally self-contained "White Rose" does not stop at being a metaphor for a profound truth about China. Something has happened to the operation of metaphorizing itself in Chang's description.

Placed in tandem with the woman and the place that are supposed to be Zhenbao's home (with its imperative of biological reproduction and participation in national self-strengthening), this image is strapped onto the idealist, masculinist projections of a new China like an enormous prosthesis, an unexpected and vulgar extension. If, as Robbe-Grillet argues, metaphoric thinking is ultimately invested in a kind of metaphysical unity between man and things, a unity which receives its efficacy through the belief in interiority and depth rather than in surfaces, such a unity is resolutely circumvented in Chang's narration. For one thing, there is, narratologically speaking, no need for such a description of Yanli to be in the story at all, yet Chang would go on to append yet another related passage:

Under the light in the bathroom, Yanli's colour was her own pale yellow. Of course, paintings of pretty women throughout the ages had never adopted such an embarrassing theme: there she was, lifting her pants, bending, about to get up from the toilet. Her hair was falling over her face. She had already changed into her pajamas with a white background dotted with small flowers. The top was raised pretty high, with half of it tucked under her chin; the pants were heaped cumbersomely around her feet. In the middle one could see the segment of a body that looked like a white silkworm. In the United States, this sight would probably have made a fine commercial for toilet paper.

The effect of these images is not exactly that of the pathos of the ordinary. Rather, by deliberately exposing a character in such undignified moments, these images are unmistakably aggressive, making it difficult for us to be sentimental about her. In describing Yanli in these superfluous sensuous details, Chang has not, I would contend, so much made use of visual metaphors to project deeper meanings as she has made visible, through the most ungainly kind of pictorialism, the limits of metaphorizing itself -- in the form of a physical blockage, a pathological self-absorption, and a rooted resistance to change.

Strictly speaking, therefore, White Rose's constipation stands both as a metaphor and an absurdist banalizing of metaphor: the idealist vision/understanding of the ambivalence of being Chinese , arguably still the outcome of metaphoric reasoning, is in these images mercilessly materialized into the sordid sight of a married woman bored out of her mind, gazing at her own navel while sitting on the toilet, or of her in the awkward position of having just finished her business and in the process of getting up, her pants still around her ankles.

By ignoring the decorum of visual restraint and releasing the descriptive data around Yanli's bathroom rituals, Chang makes it impossible for the metaphor of "White Rose" to stay in place as metaphor. Instead, the congruence of metaphoric reasoning itself is now metonymically derailed into something quite alien from its principle of speleological equivalence. The purity of "White Rose" turns out to be no more -- and no deeper -- than a case of stopped-up interiority.

In concentrating on what they perceive to be matters of language and writing, none of the theories of Lukács, Jakobson, and Robbe-Grillet is particularly concerned with women, but read together their analyses serve to articulate a modernist problematic around visuality and writing, which can also be clarified in terms of the problematic of metaphor and metonymy. From this it is but another step to realise how women, on account of their frequently metaphoric positions in representation yet continually liminal positions in societies East and West, must somehow also be (already) present in the implications of these theories, the silence of our male theorists notwithstanding. In Chang's short story we find a salient instance of how women, by being staged narratively as the sensuous objects that seemingly stand in the way of a classical dramatic action/ vision, have brought about a revamping of the balance of power between metaphor and metonymy, and thus a reconceptualization of the practice of narration from within.

The cultural and linguistic belittling and demeaning of those who are in diaspora -- those who, for historical reasons, are compelled to leave home and whose ties with the authentic fatherland have become suspect because of contacts and couplings with foreigners -- is something familiar to diasporic communities around the world, but in "Red Rose and White Rose" this sociological fact is explored specifically in relation to the narrative descriptions of femininity and sexuality.

If the endless debates about what is authentically Chinese (value) and what is not -- debates which undoubtedly have their equivalents in other cultures -- are characteristic of the histories of diasporic populations in modern times, these debates are given a new turn in Chang's story by being linked, by being contiguously placed in relation to sexism; it is sexism, her story demonstrates, which constitutes the core of cultural authenticity, loyalty, and patriotism -- and gives them their metaphoric depths.

Such sexism makes women the visible bearers of cultural and sexual boundaries, bearers whose transgressions matter, while the equivalent transgressions of men continue to be overlooked. As in Lukács's theory about narration in classical times, the possibility of a proportioned, hierarchical vision is achieved at the expense of subordinating certain unruly, unwieldly material phenomena. In the narration that is the tale of conventional sexual mores, these often turn out to be women.

The vivid descriptions of women in Chang's fiction thus stand as a narratological device of coming to terms with the fraught relationship between seeing and writing, a relationship whose ambiguities are clearly part and parcel of the encounter between the Chinese and Western cultures. Although, even in light of Robbe-Grillet's stringent critique, readers will probably never be able to give up reading such descriptions of women metaphorically, it would seem appropriate now to redefine even the most irresistible of such metaphors in Chang instead as unfinished, untotalizable fragments of an ongoing writing of modernity, in which the proliferation of femininity in objectified forms, together with the innumerable sensuous details elsewhere in her work, is symptomatic of her subtle and original endeavor to reshape and reinvent the politics of narrative.

In Chang's narration, women are placed not exactly as metaphors but more precisely as prosthetic installments of a picture-story ever in progress. Their objectified materiality can no longer be "overlooked" and subordinated as in Lukács's theory; instead, these women-objects are now constitutive of a kind of narrative motion which specializes in the systematic unfolding of differences between, as well as within, cultures.

Chang's dislodgment of metaphors may finally also be seen as a rejection of the sympathetic reasoning that, as Robbe-Grillet writes, always refers back to human beings as the consummate subjects. Against the backdrop of the revolutionary and nation-building rhetoric of her age, she has narrated a world with bright and colorful images that turn out to be glossy, slippery surfaces that neither serve as repositories of human sympathy nor encourage any kind of humanistic solidarity.

This, a nonWestern woman author's, consistent defiance and avoiding, through writing, of the euphoric sentiments of anthropomorphism is, to say the least, evocative, and it will likely remain a point of controversy in Chang's enduring fascination for her readers. The translations of Eileen Chang's texts in this essay are my own. I would like to thank Elizabeth Weed for her helpful comments and suggestions.

Chapter 4

Communication Technology in Obtaining News

Several scholars have complained about the lack of theory concerning journalism and technology. The most substantial set of technologies that requires the development of theory is the one that journalists use for sourcing of publishable news information, outweighing news dissemination, storage, and presentation technologies, the results of which may be displayed, distributed, or stored subsequently by other technologies.

As the nature of knowledge acquired by reporters may be shaped by the manner in which they acquire it, these devices may be perceived as "epistemological technologies," the study of which could help answer key questions about the nature of journalism, such as the extent to which journalists perform activity in time or space, tend to rely on firsthand witnessing or mediate the second-hand experience of others, use technologies allowing for interrogation of sources or acceptance of source versions as is, and employ their technologies proactively or for passive reception of source-initiated materials.

This study seeks to lay the foundation for a theory of epistemological technologies, based on their actual use for sourcing in different media. To obtain a comprehensive picture, the study incorporated nonmediated contacts as well (i.e., face-to-face interviews and news-scene presence). Data were gleaned in a series of face-to-face reconstruction interviews, during which reporters described how they obtained a sample of almost 850 news items published by nine leading national Israeli news organizations in three different media: print press, radio, and online news Web sites. The fourth medium, television, was omitted because it embodies certain apparent production and visual biases and could overextend the scope of an already broad study. The three designated media were studied concurrently using the same research tool.

Data deal specifically with recollected sources of information subsequently used in published (or broadcast) stories, comprising the entire sourcing process. Although serving the core journalistic functions that yield the public news diet is probably the most significant role of communication channels, the study does not cover the whole reporting process by any means, primarily because it lacks three essential components.

First, it may overlook non-item-oriented information, such as reading newspapers or visiting news Web sites, that does not necessarily end up in specific published items, its prominent place in daily journalistic routines not with standing.

Second, even item-oriented information may leave no traceable residues if items are subsequently dismissed during the selection phase or if information possessed an auxiliary journalistic function and consequently reflected an indirect, abstract, or supplementary character, such as background information, self-updates (about a particular issue), or searches for a suitable source or a specific datum.

Third, the method is not immune to memory inadequacies and possible interviewee bias.

To mitigate the first and second shortcomings, a complementary study was conducted using traditional interviews with reporters that focused on Web uses other than sourcing. To minimize memory problems, reconstruction interviews were conducted as close as possible to the date of publication.

Generally speaking, there is no justified rationale for considering Israeli news media to be significantly different from other Western, free, modern, commercial, and competitive media. Obviously, Israel has several unique structural, politi-cal, and cultural characteristics, but any attempt at determining the precise manner in which these macro attributes-and especially their composite-are translated into micro patterns of technology use would be highly speculative. Therefore, the extent to which the Israeli case is representative may only be determined after this study is repeated in other locations and news cultures. The study follows an inductive pattern, beginning with introduction of the findings and then proceeding to generalization and the proposed theoretical framework.

TECHNOLOGY AND JOURNALISM RESEARCH

Numerous scholars have recognized the role of communication technologies in shaping newswork, as well as the information that reporters may or may not acquire by using them.

The most prominent channel types, mentioned in the literature as tools of sourcing, are new technologies such as the Internet and e-mail. The other two are non-mediated channels, such as news-scene attendance and face-to-face interviews and more traditional technologies such as landline telephony.

The importance of communication channels in journalism lies in their possible impact on news information, enhancing or limiting its scope, quality, diversity, depth, and accuracy, as well as their role in shaping the epistemological qualities of news information.

For example, the face-to-face interview is considered a channel that enables nonverbal information to be obtained, and the telephone interview is one that allows reporters to negotiate source versions and implement interview techniques. E-mail, in turn, is described as a dubious channel that strengthens a source's control over messages and invites untraceable involvement of PR practitioners.

The connection between episteme (knowledge) and techne (art) is an ancient concept, dating back to Greek philosophy and addressed by modern thinkers such as Innis and McLuhan. In this study, however, the concept of epistemological technologies is employed neither as an embodiment of scientific or practical knowledge nor as a tool for shaping the knowledge of media consumers, but rather as the means that media producers use to obtain information.

Not all scholars agree that new technologies necessarily change news practices: "Reformists," probably the largest school of thought, claim that technologies created a significant shift in the work of reporters; "Traditionalists," apparently the smallest group, identified long-range trends in news production methods that may limit the effects of the new technologies significantly; while "Selectivists" assert that journalistic work has changed dramatically for television reporters, whose speed of reaction and ability to gather information have been accelerated by new technologies.

Three shortcomings of the existing body of empirical research may thwart theory-building that would address both journalism and epistemological channels:

1. *Fragmentation*: Most studies focused on a small subset of technologies and sometimes even on one technology only. This fragmented scope limits their generalizability, inviting overestimation or underestimation of the technologies studied. Multi-technology studies were not only scarce but also limited to the public relations field. At least one study exhibited a multi-technological and multi-source perspective, but was restricted to print press reporters, who are not necessarily the most advanced among technology users. Moreover, the study was conducted before the new generation of mobile and broadband technologies became popular and possibly revolutionized newswork.
2. *Non-journalistic Theories*: Most studies applied nonjournalistic theories - such as diffusion of innovations or uses and gratifications - that are virtually blind to the specific context of the journalistic field.

3. *The Novelty Bias*: Naturally, new technologies attract extra research attention, especially when perceived as a remedy for the weaknesses of journalism. Nevertheless, exclusive focus on new technologies as "one of the biggest hopes (and hypes)" of journalism, with some studies appearing "upbeat and at times even Utopian in their conclusions," renders all but brand new conduits symbolically extinct.

The current study tries to overcome these shortcomings, supplying a comprehensive picture of old and new channels, both mediated and non-mediated, determining their actual contribution to published news and integrating the results within a broader journalism theory.

Following McManus, the present study distinguishes between two principal stages of the newsmaking process:

- News discovery, during which the reporter becomes acquainted with the existence of a potential new story.
- News gathering, in which the reporter obtains the building blocks locks of the news item, as news discovery data is often incomplete and insufficiently substantiated. Both phases were studied only regarding items that were subsequently published or aired, however.

RESEARCH QUESTIONS

In keeping with its exploratory nature, the study addresses research questions and expectations rather than formal hypotheses.

- *RQl*: What are the relative contributions of the respective communication channels to news published in the three media studied?

With some caution, based on several of the studies mentioned previously, one might expect to find that while most news information is technology-mediated, telephony is still widely used and textual channels serve primarily as news discovery conduits.

- *RQ2*: How often do reporters use the Web as a news

source? Do online reporters do so more than their counterparts in other media?

According to several prominent studies, journalists use the Web extensively. Furthermore, online reporters are expected to rely on the Web more often than their counterparts in other media, as they also use it as a vehicle for display and consequently acquire considerable Web savvy.

Method

Traditional methods might prove problematic in examining the journalistic role of technology, as surveys and interviews capture per- ceived functions of the various channels that may differ substantially from their actual use; moreover, observation alone cannot detect the full spectrum of channels operated by different reporters in different settings to obtain information from different sources. Consequently, the present study uses face-to-face recons-truction interviews, a method that has proven its ability to identify the respective contributions of different entities to the production of news.

The procedure consisted of three steps (prior to the interviews):

- Random Selection of Beats: Ten parallel print press, online, and radio news beats were chosen randomly from nine leading Israeli national news organizations.
- Identification of All Published Items within Beats: The sampling period extended over four weeks (beginning November 15, 2006), reflecting the attempt to achieve a fair balance between variety of stories and use of material still fresh in reporters' memories. News Web sites were visited four times a day.
- Random Sampling of News Items: Ten items per reporter were selected randomly (average monthly output per reporter: fifty-three items) to address the necessities of source confidentiality. The sample is thus large enough to allay any concern that stories could be matched to their descriptions but not so large as to tax reporters' focus and patience.

Further measures to maintain source confidentiality included asking reporters to describe how they obtained each of their sampled items without revealing any identifying details about them, as well as the seating arrangements: the reporter (with a pile of sampled stories) and the interviewer (with a pile of coding sheets) sat on opposite sides of a table with a screen between them.

Reconstruction interviews were conducted during the month following the sampling period, each approximately ninety minutes in duration. Although nearly all interviewees cooperated, the goal of deciphering 300 items per medium was not entirely achieved because of structural constraints applying to the organizations studied, such as insufficient number of business items for one of the radio stations and the need to avoid double-length interviews of Haaretz reporters who work for both print and online media.

To preclude the distorting effect that the missing items may exert on comparability, each medium was weighted to 300 items, maintaining the internal proportions of the sampled newsbeats. For the most part, data were displayed and analyzed as percentages, thus presenting an overall picture of the channel mix with each channel displayed in the context of other channels and other media. Because of its exploratory nature, the study uses effect size measures (D-statistic) rather than significance tests. Effect values of 0.20 through 0.49 are customarily considered small, 0.50 through 0.79 medium, and 0.80 and above large.

Obviously, no method is without its shortcomings. The current method's drawback is that data deal very specifically with recollected sources for information subsequently used in published (or broadcast) stories. To compensate for this shortcoming and study the uses of technology beyond the specific item, a supplementary personal interview was introduced.

As these interviews were conducted after the rather long reconstruction interviews, however, only 49-61 reporters out of a total of 80 agreed to respond to them (depending on the specific question).

The data display unambiguous differences between common and rare uses of the Web and as such will be used only in the Discussion as a general indicator of Web use for purposes other than news sourcing.

FINDINGS [H]

The findings supply an initial overview of the ways in which reporters in three different media operate a comprehensive set of epistemological channels to obtain their news.

Relative Contribution

The data show that channel use across media is highly homogeneous except for a few aberrations, concentrated in the discovery phase, that may be explained chiefly on organizational grounds. The greater use of landline telephones among online reporters is not really substantial, as their total use of telephony is very similar to that of their counterparts and the greater use of pager messages among radio reporters is counterbalanced by their limited use of e-mail. Furthermore, greater use of pagers may reflect the correspondence between the short and instant nature of both pager messages and radio items, as well as the mobility and urgency of radio newswork, at least in the Israeli case.

Similarities across media intensify if the data are clustered according to the three major channel types embodying the epistemological qualities of the interactions they enable:

- Non-mediated channels, involving the reporters' physical presence at news scenes and face to-face interviews, constitute the smallest group: ranging (across media) from 7% to 10% of the contacts in the discovery phase and 15% to 18% in the gathering phase. The remainder consists of technology mediated coverage.
- Oral channels, led by telephony-mediated contacts (landline + cellular), contribute the main course to the news menu: ranging from 46% to 50% in the discovery phase and 54% to 65% in the gathering phase. This cluster's share is actually even greater, as it also includes the non-mediated channels.

- Textual channels comprise a rather formidable cluster, particularly in the news discovery phase, in which it accounts for 39%-43% of the contacts, decreasing to only 18%-29% in the gathering phase.

Internet Use

RQ2 focused on the actual contribution of the World Wide Web, the most celebrated technology in journalism literature, across different media. The Web's contribution to published content as a news source was no more than 3%in both phases. Even online reporters do not use their publishing platform as a sourcing tool to any greater extent than their old-media colleagues do. The Internet's contribution rises substantially if we include e-mail: ranging from 8% to 21% in the discovery phase and 4% to 15% in the gathering phase. This increment is puzzling, however, as reporters play a proactive role when using the Web and generally adopt a passive or reactive one in e-mail use.

The way in which reporters employ communication channels to obtain news data, at least according to the nine news organizations studied here, appear to challenge common wisdom nurtured largely by a series of seemingly ubiquitous references claiming that new technologies had "revolutionized" newswork. Four aspects of reporter behaviour are particularly challenging. The discussion begins with the more general aspects, namely the surprisingly modest use of non-mediated coverage and the lack of any substantial differences among the three media. The remaining two aspects are oriented towards specific technologies: the Web's marginal role as a news source and the enduring dominance of telephony.

The image of extensive non-mediated coverage is fostered not only by scholars (who contend that such coverage prevails in conjunction with telephone interviews), but also by the traditional ethos that extols "shoe leather reporting" as the supreme news gathering method, as well as by journalists themselves, who do not go out of their way to expose the truth behind a deteriorating work pattern that still establishes their occupational legitimacy and authority. Many have even developed a set of practices to conceal their remote coverage. Although some American reporters declared that face-to-face interviews are their second choice as a newsmaking channel, the current findings indicate that, in practice, non-mediated coverage is far rarer than might be expected, or, as the legendary Jimmy Breslin observed, "in many newsrooms, the shoe-leather reporters are regarded as throwbacks or has-beens."

The overali similarity of channel use across media challenges the widespread belief that at least online reporters embody "new regimes of content creation" with a distinct media logic.

Apparently, tendencies toward journalistic "isomorphism" overshadow medium differences, at least insofar as methods used to source information are concerned, reflecting similarities in organization around newsbeats and news sources, perceived newsworthiness, and the inclination towards homogeneous news products. Two of these relatively homogenous patterns challenge common wisdom regarding specific technologies: the use of telephones and the Web for news sourcing.

THE WEB AS A NEWS SOURCE [H]

The limited use of the Web observed in this study appears to challenge findings suggesting that the Web had become a "dominant" and "indispensable" newsgathering tool that had changed the face - if not the soul - of journalism. Interestingly, the Web's contribution as a source for published news is not only marginal but also stagnant, having displayed no growth over time - at least with regard to the Israeli print press, studied in 2001 using the same method and research tools as the present study.

However, in contrast to its limited use for sourcing, the Web is widely used for more general newswork functions. Personal interviews with reporters show that they use the Web for two hours and fifty minutes a day for journalistic purposes, plus one hour and twelve minutes for personal matters - about four times more than the average Israeli citizen and about an hour less per day than American computer reporters, who are probably among the most intensive Web users.

The rich assortment of Web functions used by reporters may be categorized into three basic types:

- *Productive*: These include core journalistic functions directly involved in sourcing publishable news materials, such as discovering and gathering news information, followed by two types of auxiliary functions that exert less direct impact on news products and more on news processes and news environments.
- *Referential*: Including self-updates, monitoring other publications, fact checking, locating potential news sources, and finding background material.
- *Communicative Functions*: Communicating with different stakeholders-superiors, news sources, counterparts, and competitors, mostly via e-mail.

Functions performed routinely (i.e., on a daily basis by at least half the reporters) are mostly referential. The only exception is the highly frequent use of e-mail for receipt of press releases. This still does not guarantee an impact on publications, however, as many if not most press releases are discarded during the selection process.

The highly infrequent use of e-mail for interviews may surprise scholars who described e-mail as "the killer Internet application" for journalists. On the other hand, it will relieve those who condemn e-mail interviews as a "method of last resort for conducting anything approaching a candid interview" because it avoids real interaction and invites hoaxes and "canned" PR responses. Journalists' paradoxical use of the Web - seldom for sourcing and often for more general newswork assignments - suggests that although journalists enjoy "cutting edge gizmos," they are choosier about using them for core journalistic assignments such as sourcing.

Hence, until another study refutes the current findings by taking the exhausting route of investigating - source by source - a sample of published items outside Israel, using the current method and research tools, one cannot rule out that limited use of the Web for sourcing, together with extensive use for more general newswork assignments, extends beyond the case at hand and may even be a relatively universal phenomenon. It is definitely not an Israeli peculiarity, as shown by initial findings of another study employing the same method and research tool to study Chilean national press reporters in the summer of 2007. Those reporters used the Web for only 5% of discovery contacts and 7% of gathering contacts. There is some indication that figures for the United States, Portugal, and Greece do not differ dramatically. At least part of the difference between the current study and those claiming vast use of the Web may thus be rooted in method (reconstructions of specific published items versus general estimations of technology use in surveys and interviews) and research focus (specific uses for sourcing of published items versus more auxiliary uses for reporting). This line of reasoning is supported by current findings reflecting heavy daily use of the Web, mostly for functions other than sourcing.Some American scholars agree that the Web has not become a major news source despite its numerous advantages.

According to one observation, American newsroom adoption of computer-assisted reporting yielded mixed results. Another opinion maintains that the journalistic advantages of the Internet "are counterbalanced by a number of inherent weaknesses," some of which have already been mentioned in the relevant literature: poor quality of information; limited reliability, believability, and accuracy; as well as time constraints, lack of training and navigation and design faults.

The following drawbacks should be considered as well:

- *The Proactive Role*: While most other textual channels, including e-mail, assign reporters a passive or reactive role, the Web calls for their proactive performance in such tasks as database analysis or investigation - demands that go against the grain of mainstream news reporting, which is reactive in nature.
- *Impersonal Data*: While other channels enable and improve communication with human agents, the Web

usually bypasses them in favour of largely impersonal data. Hence those who perceived the Web as a promising news source were not wrong about the technology, only about its users. Journalists, it turns out, are not in the general information business but rather supply information originating among human agents.

- *The Extra Burden of Corroboration*: Constant suspicions concerning the trustworthiness of Web materials could have been resolved by crosschecking with additional sources. As their time frame shrinks, however, reporters may wonder why they ought to use a news source that requires additional sources a priori instead of simply contacting these sources themselves.
- *Unqualified Material*: Apparently, the Web's marginal contribution to published news (and that of other mass media) contradicts the nature of news producers as heavy news consumers above all, who start each day by reading one another's publications. Media consumption does not necessarily contribute directly to specific news items that are subsequently published, however, but rather informs reporters about current events in general and the output of competitors and counterparts. Furthermore, the Web offers "too much information or [...] too little information" and is loaded with previously published items that are useless to reporters who refrain from plagiarism unless they find their own angle or follow-up, employing an independent sourcing process.

Some of these weaknesses are the strengths of a much older technology, whose contribution to the public news menu tends to be overlooked.

THE ENDURING DOMINANCE OF THE TELEPHONE

The enduring dominance of telephony challenges the assertion that newsmaking was conquered by new technologies, especially when combined with insistence that the golden age of the telephone in journalism ended during the 1950s. Some scholars have mentioned the ongoing prominence of telephony together with face-to-face interviews but did not specify the respective contributions of each.

The continuing dominance of the telephone in the new technology-saturated news environment, after a hundred years of service and despite more sophisticated alternatives, can no longer be explained in simple terms such as the immediacy and efficiency of the given technology. At first glance, it may appear that numerous factors motivate reporter and source alike to avoid oral communication.

Why should reporters trap themselves between oral input and textual output, adding the burden of translating vocal utterances into written stories? Why would they work with loosely structured, ephemeral raw material that leaves no paper trail and is replete with redundancies, inconsistencies, and multiple, interwoven threads of thought?

And why would news sources, in turn, use channels that impede realization of a speaker's full potential and downgrade control over verbalization, precision of expression, lexical richness, and grammatical sophistication, thereby forgoing the advantage of imperceptible emendation and rendering themselves vulnerable to audible self-correction that sounds like "denial and patchwork"?

Several considerations may explain the persistence of the present situation:

- *Naturalness*: Oral channels are a "primary form of communication for humans." They are "addressed by a real, living person [. . .] at a specific time in a real setting" and are more "natural to thought and speech" than writing, more spontaneous and more dynamic and vivid, as vocal expression is itself a live event in space and time, anchored in the "life-worlds" of real people.
- *Informativeness*: Oral communication always includes "much more than mere words." Even telephone conversations retain many attributes of face-to-face

interactions, including "use of language [...] the way words are pronounced, elements of intonation or prosody, syntax and semantics [...] variations of loudness and pitch beyond that involved in intonation, tempo, resonance, pauses and nonfluencies, as well as nonlanguage sounds such as laughing and sighing."

- *Unavailability of Suitable Texts*: Journalists generally search for news within a narrow time slot once a new event or story begins to unfold and before others cover them - at least in the same news market. During this short period, texts may be unavailable, unsuitable, already published, or authored by PR professionals.
- *Participatory Role*: Oral channels are actually the only conduit through which reporters may play a participatory role in shaping the raw materials of news.

This role corresponds with four aspects of newswork:

- As a "negotiated phenomenon" (i.e., an output of bargaining between reporters and sources), news tends to flow through channels such as the telephone, that enable negotiations between the parties.
- As news constitutes a co-production by reporters and their sources, the former perceive their authorship as including mandatory participation in the formation of raw news material and not only post hoc reduction of source-initiated texts. Oral channels increase reporters' control over their raw material, whereas written versions accord their writers the advantage, giving them more leeway to hide, slant or frame information as they see fit. Oral channels enable interview techniques that may not only improve source accountability but also reinforce the status and legitimacy of reporters as trustees of the public who pose questions on its behalf.

- Competitive Advantage: While many written materials are distributed to or may be approached by numerous journalists, oral channels give reporters a chance at exclusivity. Most of the time, such exclusivity does not apply to the items as a whole, that are shared by their counterparts and competitors, but rather to certain details thereof.
- Smaller (Perceived) Risk: When leaks are involved, both sources and reporters are especially careful to avoid textual channels, as they may leave clear traces in case of investigation. Although they cannot promise full protection, oral channels are perceived as safer than others except in cases of serial leaks, such as the Pentagon Papers, in which randomly chosen pay phones were the instrument of choice.

Epistemological channels, a collection of communication technologies and non-mediated conduits of news coverage, are probably the keystone of technology and journalism theorization, thanks to their crucial role in shaping the scope and quality of information that subsequently becomes the public news diet. The current study suggests an initial theoretical outline for the role of these channels in news sourcing, based on a careful analysis of their contribution to a random sample of about 850 stories from three different media.

Just as a hierarchy of credibility prevails in the realm of sourcing, according precedence to certain informants over others, a technological hierarchy governs the world of communication channels that echo the logic of sourcing, determining which conduits are to be given priority. The subordination of these channels to a higher order of sourcing considerations is observed both in the combined tendency of the reporters studied to rely on human agents (in 87% of their contacts in the discovery phase and 92% in the gathering phase) and to communicate with them orally (57% and 75%, respectively). Heavy reliance on technology-mediated coverage suggests that reporters accord much lower priority to the demands of space than to those of time. Hence the basic role of communication technologies is to release reporters from spatial constraints, thereby enabling them to meet temporal demands. According to the findings, reporters sourcing their published news prefer various remote data excavation technologies to first-hand witnessing, and prefer reliance on human agents to technological sources such as the Web and oral communication to textual. Hence the principal role of epistemological technologies is to enable remote coverage while keeping close to human informants.

The methods journalists employ to obtain published news indicate that news is a social product, fabricated chiefly through interpersonal reporter-source contact. As such, news is more a matter of trust between humans than of independent witnessing, fact finding, or fact checking. This process is none too compliant with "foundationalist epistemology" that expects validation of facts by empirical findings or rational substantiation, but rather conforms with social epistemology that makes do with facts established by communal agreement within "specific epistemic communities."

Furthermore, news is a textual product of oral processes. This "oral culture" allows reporters to omit, edit, select excerpts, and "tidy up" quotes in a manner that often bears the seeds of tension between parties. To a certain extent, this may explain the vast quantities of journalistic errors, misunderstandings, misquotes, and source statements taken out of context. As one Wall Street Journal reporter put it, "It's your notes against their word."

This study focuses on the most substantial role of communication channels as conduits for generating the public news diet. Despite the meticulous methods employed, however, it is not free of weaknesses and blind spots, as it addresses involvement of different channels only in items that were subsequently published or aired, relying on the recollection of reporters themselves.

Hence, the current study sets a broad agenda for further studies, especially those considering other types of reporters who probably employ different patterns of channel use, particularly TV reporters, investigative reporters, citizen journalists, multimedia and multi-skilled reporters, and so on.

Subsequent studies should focus on other news cultures, especially that of the United States, testing the hypothesis of limited use of the Web as a news source and extensive use for other newswork functions. Newsroom observations may contribute another missing link by mapping the inevitable gaps between reported and actual uses of communication channels. These may also focus on the oral culture that associates reporters and sources, the patterns in which oral raw materials are transformed into final news texts and the extent to which this transformation is susceptible to errors, misunderstandings, and disputes between the parties.

Chapter 5

Pre-modern Online

Observers have frequently attributed the onset of the latest incarnation of globalization to new communication technologies, particularly the Internet. A critical property of cyber technologies is their ability to integrate several types of media and thus radically transform the communication experience into a seamless and limitless multi-media act. As a result, the conventional divides among journalism, advertising, public relations, and texts and images associated with independent media domains are being challenged.

Added to this, the volume of information available worldwide at one's fingertips, coupled with the speed of transferring information across various geopolitical and geocultural borders, has led to two broad categories of understanding the global social implications for technological convergence. On the one hand, a sense of helplessness that capital now overwhelmingly determines the social has led scholars like Viswanathan to problematize globalization in what he terms as a series of metaphors.

He asks - "Is it a juggernaut, a seduction, a genocide, a set of flows, a master narrative?" Further, "such an approach," he observes, "dissolves the possibility of play and politics" . The second broad category of understanding engages with precisely the political possibilities offered by the Internet. Convergence of information and communication technologies has led to the investment of hope in new media as a harbinger of globalization from below that (usually) consciously dissociates from capitalist globalization. For example, development anthropologist Escobar has suggested that new technological networks "reflect the emergence of new actors, identities, and practices," and thus are an important consideration for development communication . Between these two positions of endangering and enabling we can locate a space where varying degrees of negotiation occur between two broad typologies of democracy - the capitalist democracy of "cyber- financial globalization" and a defini- tion of democracy that favours distributive justice based on grassroots participation.

This research examines a case that might be located in this broad middle range as a "third way," an indicator that explores an intersection of the bottom line and the grassroots or, rather, organizational claims about such an intersection. It involves analysis of a "development corporation's" web site to understand and evaluate the corporation's claims about adopting a path to development that incorporates the interests of a for-profit company technically located in the United States (but with a public presence on the Internet that makes it a virtual company) and rural communities in various countries as joint stakeholders in the development project.

The inspiration for the term "third way" in this project originates in Giddens's recovery of the idea from the political history of many nations in the last hundred years or so, and specifically in the post-Cold War era. The concept attempts to articulate a political-social space that accommodates the globalizing tendencies of capital and the welfare and more communal politics of a social democrat, or socialist, state. The "third way" explored in this study refers more to a cultural-economic than the political-social space proposed by Giddens. The aim of this research is to understand and evaluate the corporation Greenstar's claims to having found a third ay for development on the converged media of the Internet.

Specifically, the study involves network and frame analyses of the web site of the company Greenstar, which promotes environmentally conscious, sustainable development through new information and solar energy technologies in return for local cultural products such as music, poetry, folktales, and oral histories (many in digital form) from these regions, which are sold on the Net worldwide by Greenstar. Its corporate approach to sustainable development in developing regions and its ecommerce in cultural artifacts produced by rural communities have made the company a constituent of a new global cultural economy. This study is a response to the urgency for considering new media within the domain of communication and development.

In their attempts to contend with the implications of convergence for developing regions, critics either praise or condemn these media for their one powerful connective property - global networking. Greenstar adopts a third position - the enabling rhetoric sympathetic to the rural world in developing regions, but capitalist roots that have, in the past, at least partly hindered productive and desirable social change in several regions of this world. These claims are persuasively packaged in Greenstar's self-representation on its web site; in the process, the company projects competing discourses about development and a new medium.

What are these discourses and how are they projected in the corporation's self-representation? Where might the discourses be "suspect," and where might they suggest novel modes of "doing" development? Can the participatory aspect to development and the profit motive of capitalism co-exist? Is there a possibility for the "public good" and private enterprise to meet (without collision and casualties) in virtual space or does juxtaposing the two ideas continue to signify a contradiction in terms? What are the implications of this third position for the future of developing regions? These are broad questions to which this study alone cannot provide conclusive answers.

However, as a starting point, it does provide some exploratory responses and attempts to make the following initial contributions to the literature on communication, development, and globalization:

- It explores a particular form of cultural convergence and its implications for the other side of the global digital divide.
- It employs a concept (a third way) that problematizes

the antinomies of capitalist democracy and participatory democracy.

- It expands the concept of the third way suggested mainly in a national, political context to one of a global cultural-economic context.
- Methodologically, the study employs a combination of critical modes of analysis that are responsive to the nature of text construction peculiar to the web (here, an initial exploration of network analysis) and, more generally, web content through an examination of framing strategies adopted by the authors of the site.

In the sections that follow, I first introduce the case for this study - the corporation Greenstar. I then establish the conceptual framework for the study by examining theories of development and postdevelopment, and globalization. The origins of the modern development project date to the colonial period in the nineteenth century and have morphed through two centuries into what has recently been referred to as the postdevelopment era. Tracing the entire history of development discourse is beyond the scope of this chapter, but the emergence of "postdevelopment" is examined since, in a sense, Greenstar's activities are postdevelopment activities.

The phenomenon of globalization is an equally important component of the conceptual framework for the study because along with the concept of social change, it serves as the inspiration for Greenstar. Following a discussion on various attempts to theorize globalization, I integrate globalization and development in a specific way.

Utilizing the term "convergence" associated with new media, I examine the idea of convergence from technological and cultural standpoints as applicable to this project, where the social implications of convergence could take at least three forms - pan-capitalism, empowerment, or a third way.

Following the theoretical framework, I provide a description of the method adopted for the study and conceptual explanations of the modes of analysis used to examine the data. I then analyse Greenstar's significations of development in the structure and content of its communication. Finally, I bring together the results of the network and frame analyses to summarize responses to the research questions posed for the study.

I conclude by evaluating Greenstar's discourse of development in the global era and the implications of this discourse for developing regions. Capitalism, Community, and Environmentalism: A Political Economic Profile of Greenstar as a Development Corporation Greenstar Development Worldwide, Inc., is a corporation based in Massachusetts, USA, established with private shareholders. As primarily a virtual organization, Greenstar is best understood through its web site. Established in 1998, Greenstar Corporation and Greenstar Foundation constitute the Greenstar organization.

The corporation engages with communities and the commercial aspect of its operations, while the foundation handles philanthropic activities and relations with several organizations worldwide. The company's Board of Directors is international in profile, including veteran diplomats and specialists in a host of related fields such as engineering, ecology, business, law, politics, media, medicine, and social work, to name a few.

The company's presence is more virtual than real, since business is transacted mainly on the Net, but for administrative and distribution purposes, offices in some major cities across the world have been established (especially Los Angeles, Boston, Washington, DC, Cairo in Egypt, and Hyderabad in India). Greenstar India opened recently in Hyderabad, India, with Indian companies as majority shareholders. Other organizations in various locations, such as local governmental and non-governmental organizations, private companies, and non-profit institutions work with Greenstar as partners in local operations.

Greenstar is also linked in various ways (operations, advice, fellow contractors, etc.) to departments of State in the United States, to the National Renewable Energy Laboratories, and also to organizations like the United Nations. Greenstar's goal is to "provide... an environmentally-sound way to achieve economic independence". Greenstar maintains that it consciously selects communities and seeks sites that typically do not attract other development agencies. It invests approximately USD 25,000 in each community.

The company uses a series of criteria, including geographical remoteness, size of the community, some form of institutional infrastructure, and clearly defined leadership to help set up a village cooperative. It has selected communities located in nations that generally have politically favorable relations with the United States. Communities have to be identified by Greenstar as "off the grid," meaning existing outside the global technological and financial networks - the more remote the community, the more likely it becomes a candidate for a Greenstar development site.

The company also uses the rationale that the more remote the community, the more traditional the culture, and therefore the greater the advantage for transforming it into an asset and a resource for the production of digital culture. Thus the main actors in the Greenstar enterprise are the company members and their partners in change - the rural communities. The current list of communities includes ones from the West Bank, Jamaica, Ghana, India, Brazil, and Tibet.

In its projects in locations worldwide (Asia, the Middle East, Africa, South America), Greenstar declares its mission is to provide solar energy facilities for powering various technologies, including media, in rural communities. With the help of solar energy panels and related technology, Greenstar argues, village populations are able to avail themselves of various benefits such as generating power to operate water pumps, storing vaccines in solar-power-run refrigerators, and connecting to the Internet to obtain literacy, health education, and other information.

In return, villagers produce crafts and other cultural products such as music, videos, and records of oral histories from their local traditions and cultural reservoir, which are then marketed on the Internet by Greenstar. A transaction fee, charged for all e-commerce purchases, constitutes the return on investment for Greenstar. The company is a for-profit venture; part of the profits goes to the community and the rest is divided among shareholders and future projects. The idea of a development corporation thus presents a paradox.

This paradox is central to the study in that a for-profit company plans its pricing and distribution of profits in such a way as to benefit itself as well as its partner communities in rural areas of developing regions. Converging Discourses of Development and Globalization: A Theoretical Framework In this section, I begin with a brief discussion of the origins and contours of the discourse of development and the idea of postdevelopment.

I then briefly discuss the current conceptual debates about globalization. Finally, I address the idea of convergence derived from the capabilities of new media technologies, its potential for social change, and its implications for developing regions.

DEVELOPMENT AND POSTDEVELOPMENT: ORIGINS, STATUS, AND CRITIQUE

In a brief genealogy of the modern idea of development, Saunders outlines its emergence in the nineteen forties as a critical response to the then prevailing "hegemonic liberal view" of the market as the chief instrument for establishing equilibrium in the international arena. At this time, the idea of modernization of traditional societies was theorized and programmes were launched to transform economically poor Third World societies into self-sustaining nations capable of holding their own in the international community. The media played a prominent role in both the development rhetoric and many development projects; they were purported to deliver education, health, a progressive mentality in the modernist sense, and to instill the need for democratic governance in developing regions.

After about half a century into the development project, policymakers, planners, donors, and people in developing regions gradually realized that the changes there diverged considerably from planned paths and expected outcomes, and that increasingly, the disparities between developed and developing regions were exacerbated. These unexpected (and frustrating) changes led to a collective disenchantment with the development project. Though there are multiple causes for the failure of "development" as originally conceived, the general critique has pointed to the "equation" of development with western ideas and ideals of progress and advancement.

Fissures in the development discourse emerged from a questioning of the power and knowledge complex where development served as a means for economically powerful nations to control the world. A series of activities and discourses is now cohering to challenge development from multiple constituencies such as women (gender and development), environmentalists (sustainable development), and grassroots activists (participatory development).

An important part of this ferment is the increasing prominence of information and communication technologies (ICTs) and their potential for global connectivity, a phenomenon recognized by international development agencies and communities in developing regions alike. This large-scale ferment on the whole has destabilized the discourse of development.

Researchers, governments, and development agencies have turned their attention to the potential of ICTs for developing regions, thereby producing an emergent discourse of the knowledge economy, empowerment of developing regions through ICTs, and global connectivity. This complex of critique, technology, activism, and redefinitions is referred to as postdevelopment, characterized at least in part by the converging discourses of globalization and development.

It has displaced traditional development discourse even in the agenda of traditionally development-oriented supranational agencies such as the World Bank. The development corporation Greenstar, with its capitalist framework, activist rhetoric, mission of sustainable development, strategic uses of ICTs, and global reach can be located in the era of postdevelopment. Development anthropologist Escobar has called for a joint consideration of globalization, culture, and development to grasp new trajectories that map the history of the present global order. In the process, he underscores the importance, potential, and pitfalls of new media networks for social change in parts of the world that continue to be referred to as developing regions. The Internet exemplifies the concept of the technological network that has changed to an extent, and is working to further change the development communication landscape.

Although I do not delve deeply into the spatial aspect of globalization and new technologies, I believe that Escobar's use of the concepts of space and place in relation to the global and the local are especially helpful here to understand an emerging advocacy for an important role for the Internet in development. He contends that the "technological networks and flows" are becoming central to the "creation of the social." Through global networks among concerned communities, there might exist possibilities to preserve the local (or place) in the face of the more deterritorializing global (or space).

This implies that not just transnational corporations (TNCs) but local communities also may by-pass the legal and political gateways devised by the nation-state to communicate to other parts of the globe. The same technology that has worked in favour of the TNCs could work in favour of "globalization from below" by empowering communities, as studies now indicate (for example, the work on the Chiapas uprising by Russell). The work of several grassroots organizations engaged in media activism worldwide is another example. These organizations are now gaining visibility through global associations such as OurMedia, comprising activists, media workers, and academics.

Discourses of social change have offered a variety of optics through which to consider the practices, culture, and ideology of development (see, for example, Teheranian for a review of perspectives in relation to communication, and Crush for a variety of perspectives external to communication and development). Approaches to studying development also include Rodriguez's) work with citizens' media and use of video technology in small communities, Huesca's work on the appropriation of radio in urban peripheries, Escobar's groundbreaking work on a poststructuralist approach to development as discourse, Nandy's postcolonial position on the interpretation of technologies in the contexts of former colonies, and Gupta's postcolonial approach to agricultural development in India.

If traditional notions of development privileged the state and suprastate institutions, the more recent perspectives are concerned with community ownership and operation of media, redefinitions of modern agricultural practices for and within local contexts, and so on. The idea of the development corporation inserts itself into this picture.

A dimension to postdevelopment that needs to be closely examined is the green development theory as suggested by Adams. This is especially pertinent to the study as Greenstar's plan centers around environmentally friendly and sustainable development through the use of solar energy and communications technologies.

Dividing "green" discourses of development into technocratic and radical camps, Adams demonstrates the domination of a "utilitarian view of science" in the technocratic approach to sustainable development and "ecosocialist" overtones in the radical approach. The latter paradigm, in Adams's analysis, opposed developmentalism and emphasized tenets such as endogenous development, self-reliance, and social justice.

Both positions inform Greenstar's self-representation as an ecologically-conscious development corporation. My analysis suggests that these positions constitute competing ideologies in the self-representation of the company in its web site. Postdevelopment is not without its critics, even if they do not explicitly use the term in their critique of technological convergence and implications for new forms of class, gender, and other divisions.

The social consequence of technological convergence on digital has been the creation of the digital divide. This is a new divide within developing regions, much like in the developed countries but with significantly greater disparity in numbers. On the other side of the digital divide lie nations where less than one per cent of the population might have access to the Internet. For example, in the case of India, the digital divide represents an exacerbation of the already-existing economic chasms between the urban middle class and the rural poor majority.

In addition, developing regions continue to be integrated into the global techno- and financescapes as cheap labour and as desirable sites of production depending on the incentives offered to the TNCs by the individual states-a major argument of dependency theory now resurrected. But despite critique, various constituencies are engaged in exploring new ways of "doing" development with ICTs, along with other organizational and structural facilitators.

THEORIZING GLOBAUZATION

The pervasive reach of capital and the networking capacity of ICTs are integral to the phenomenon of globalization. Other factors also, such as migratory labour and increased tourism and travel, have helped accelerate this phenomenon.

Whatever the current disputes about globalization in various circles-that it is an old or new phenomenon, that it has taken over the entire planet or not-epistemic communities of various stripes such as globalization theorists, feminist scholars, policymakers, and activists agree upon the central role media and communication play in this phenomenon. Even a brief glimpse of the literature on this subject from various fields besides media studies, such as sociology, political science, development studies, gender studies, anthropology, or cultural studies, reveals the centrality of the technology, culture, and economics of the media in relation to the globalization discourse. If it is not stated, then, as Beck has observed, "there is...a tacit assumption...that the mass media are a prerequisite of globalization".

This is clear, for example, in Fredric Jameson's analysis where globalization is essentially a "communicational concept... alternately masking or transmitfting cultural and economic meanings." Further, historically the present signifies a "third multinational stage of capitalism" and globalization is "intrinsic" to this stage. Globalization is constituted by what Tomlinson terms as different "modalities" that manifest themselves in linkages of people, goods, information, and practices. Brah points out that such an understanding of globalization makes the phenomenon seem more abstract than it actually is.

Instead, she reminds us that such processes are "thoroughly marked by human agency". Brah's observation is in line with Tomlinson's later description of globalization as "an empirical condition of the modern world." This study is one such demonstration of this empirical condition marking globalization, where technology, culture, and capital constitute recurring and convergent themes.

Schölte has pointed out that confining analyses of globalization to capitalism restricts our understanding of the phenomenon to "a narrow materialist political economy," and that globalization also entails other "causal" factors such as "identity, community, knowledge, and ecology," all of which we see coming into play in the case under consideration for this study, in the mission and operations of Greenstar.

The process of globalization has facilitated an intersection of cultures, and this dimension is also central to theorizing globalization. Such intersections have spawned new cultural and aesthetic forms that can evoke images of hybridity in Cyberspace. According to sociologists like Lash and Urry, these hybridities are acted out as an aesthetic in the global.

As with the case of Greenstar, ethnic and local cultures available for perusal in global Cyberspace also signify cultural convergence. Appadurai has suggested that the notion of the local, or locality, is "relational" and "contextual." Additionally, it is "phenomenological" in that there is a lived, experiential component to the idea of the "local."

When the local (pre-modern) enters the more global space of the Internet as a product, it enters a global consumer culture, a culture frequently identified with a postmodern global economy. The cosmopolitan global consumer seeks new aesthetic forms as a mode of self-expression and a declaration of identity, a phenomenon that Lash and Urry term as "aesthetic reflexivity". Reactions to this type of cultural convergence have taken two principal forms that coincide with Caldwell's master narratives for globalization-lamenting the loss of the local in its cooptation into the global, and celebration of this convergence as a triumph of new media technologies to enable various localities to enter the global market.

Greenstar positions itself between these narratives and claims to offer what might be interpreted as a "third way" for practicing development and demonstrates these claims by deploying the rhetoric of both pan-capitalism and empowerment. The discourses of globalization and development converge in Greenstar's self-representation on the web. Convergence and Its Social Implications: PanCapitalism, Empowerment, or a Third Way?

Concerns about convergence (an intersection of previously discrete media technologies and functions) in new media technologies and their consequences for developing regions have led to theorizing about the digital divide from a political economy perspective and about agentic potential from a cultural studies perspective. While these two responses to convergence are described sweepingly as the "totalizing cultural allegories" of our times , they nevertheless are a useful entry point for a dis- cussion on convergence in the context of social change today. I provide some possible understandings of convergence below, from the standpoints of communication technologies, economics, and culture.

Demonstrating the struggle to grapple with the change in thinking about new media, Caldwell has described convergence as a "force of unification," and as a "new master paradigm" . The power of digital has swept aside discrete functions and operations of many media technologies preceding it. Forms of the more traditional mass media (audio, video, print) and media practices (advertising, public relations, journalism) converge in the computer and on the Net to create interactive media experiences that have scrambled more traditional understandings of media and audiences. The sweep of this technology is global; it requires descriptive terms that encompass the planetary reach of new media, Appadurai supplied us with new "scapes" to help us grasp some of these lineaments of globalization. Four are especially applicable to technological convergence-technoscape, mediascape, ideoscape, and financescape-for describing the operations and effects of media convergence.

"Technoscape" suggests a panoramic sweep of the globe by new media, specifically here the Internet. By "mediascape" we can take to mean the convergence of previously disparate media (print, audio, audio- visual, television, film, computers) to form a single (new) media experience. "Ideoscape" refers to the cultural resonances of the media on a global scale. "Financescape" describes the global reach of capital as a result of its marriage with technology. It can best be understood by examining more closely the idea of pan-capitalism on a global scale.

The term convergence now becomes a metaphor - for convergence of the global and the local through the propagation of a pan-capitalist ideology, for connectivity among subaltern populations now able to link across the globe for purposes of activism and social change, and for the coming together of the discourses of capitalism and the empowerment of the dispossessed in ways that are not available through the state or the market - a third way. The metaphor of convergence implied in all these activities is important to identify and understand since Greenstar's activities and discourse point to these convergences, and finally to the discursive convergence of globalization and development.

Castells, in his work on the sociology of information technologies, claims that "for the first time in history, the whole planet is either capitalist or highly dependent on capitalist economic processes". Scholars like Castells and Schölte detail mainly what we might construe as the production side to global capitalism. Among other things, concerns about production/manufacturing, distribution, labour, capita markets, new economies of scale, and new modes of management inform their analyses. At least some of these factors clearly come into play in the operation of Greenstar.

The company "sources" materials globally (here, developing regions) to produce goods for its virtual market (production of cultural artifacts available for purchase on the Internet). The distribution is centralized in that warehouses in the United States distribute purchased products to various parts of the world.

The logic behind this decision is the availability of infrastructure that facilitates "warehousing, shipping, and credit activities". Political economists of globalization have emphasized the globalizing tendency of capital, a result of its fusion with technological convergence in the information and communication sphere.

Going by the history of media technologies, that may be conventional wisdom now, but currently the reach of both capital and technology has taken on an as yet unsurpassed magnitude. Concomitantly, the reach of capitalist culture becomes equally pervasive. Schiller has noted that "big capital" employs the Internet as a distribution channel.

Rafaeli suggests that the sense in which the Internet can be conceptualized as a distribution channel is similar to thinking of shopping malls as a distribution channel - a sophisticated space where image and window dressing (the spectacle) are as central to the consumer experience as the products and services themselves - all available to the consumer with access to the Net and the requisite purchasing power.

As Rafaeli has noted about the technological capabilities of the medium itself, its "capacity for addressing the senses," employing " text, voice, pictures, animation, video... and virtual-reality motion codes" make the virtual shopping experience more entertainment-oriented than real shopping, and more real than real - to use Baudrillard's term, "hyperreal." Practices of consumption constitute a key part of the equation of global capitalism.

Especially in the cultural realm, consumption becomes a prime activity in the global market as it is tied directly to converging technologies as well as the constant reformulation and self-identification of new markets. Taste cultures fuse, hybridize, revert, and multiply, and corporations constantly attempt to fix (at least fleetingly) these changing audiences long enough to realise sales and profits. Factors such as exponentially increased cross-border tourism, migratory labour, technological advancements that have enabled virtual malls, and a host of others that Lash and Urry have elaborated, have transformed consumer tastes in the affluent, postmodern west, and tastes have expanded to the increasing acquisition of authentic "ethnic" products to define the self and the lifestyle.

As Waters has so astutely observed, "in a globalized world we will be unable to predict social practices and preferences on the basis of geographical location." In Marxist terms, Lash and Urry explain that the sign value (previously associated more with the domain of advertising and branding) now overlays both consumption and production, practically replacing the exchange and use values of products and services. Consumers define and reinvent their tastes and identities periodically through the sign (a discussion of the social contexts for such redefinitions is beyond the scope of this study. Increasingly, producers in the postmodern global economy invest in the semiotic and the aesthetic dimensions.

What Canclini has termed "symbolic distinction"-a process of setting oneself apart from others through choices in design, thereby creating an identity-dominates both consumption and production. Arguably, the consideration of the aesthetic/ symbolic is built into the rationale and decision making behind both production and consumption. The sign value serves as a marker of difference and increases the desirability (or not) of such commodities. Translating this theoretical foray into the nature of current global capitalism for this project, we can reasonably understand that in the case of Greenstar, the Internet serves as the gateway/marketplace for indigenous cultural products to be showcased for consumption in the global market.

Besides pan-capitalism, a second position that is frequently referenced by Greenstar is the idea of empowering rural communities on the development map. Rodriguez's work on citizens' media is particularly helpful in articulating the concept of empowerment and its explanatory value to studying Greenstar's claims and statements about its community projects.

For Rodríguez, empowerment is "active participation in actions by the members of a public to reshape their own identities, the identities of others, and their social environments, thereby producing power". In relation to the media, Rodríguez holds that empowerment also means the ability to "actively intervene and transform the established mediascape", a practice in which Greenstar communities can engage.

These communities produce media material in the form of poetry, music, and oral histories on compact disc (Greenstar's phrase is "digital culture"), and also material cultural artifacts such as handicrafts, fabric, and other products that convey highly localized cultural origins. Villagers are trained to record on compact discs, and to access the Internet for various purposes as media users. With an interactive medium such as the Internet, what the village community chooses to use and the process of selection demonstrate an enactment of the community's empowerment as well. However, some limitations are evident.

Unlike citizens' media, Greenstar communities' intention is not political-that is, there is no intended participation in a dialogic power struggle with the larger social structures; the activities surrounding this medium and Greenstar's solar energy enterprise are intended to pertain to community advancement, or "development" on a local level. Greenstar's rhetoric for explaining the rationale behind the projects suggests a disengagement from the dominant discourse of development, a carving out of new forms of power and new power structures in development, where profit (made by the company) would be shared with labour (the communities producing the cultural products).

The ultimate goal is to enable self-sufficiency and self-management for these communities. Thus empowerment is achieved through global capitalism and not through fundamental changes in the social structure, and this is a third position that Greenstar has employed in its self-representation (FAQs link). The term "empowerment" in recent development rhetoric has raised some serious questions. Parpart observes that it has become a "motherhood" term used to express a gamut of meanings from "efficiency" to deep social change. It has been coopted by mainstream development agencies and used in relation to top-down programmes for social change. Parpart points out that the usage of this word does not address fundamental structural inequalities, the main concern of feminists, environmentalists, and other activists.

The debilitating effects of economic struggles at the national level on small, rural, and highly localized communities prompt us to evaluate the usage of the idea of empowerment in the discourse of a development corporation. This critique reminds us that evaluating Greenstar's rhetoric is important: Is the "empowerment" apparent in their self-representation geared toward structural changes in the larger society? If not, to what extent can micro-projects at the community level sustain in the face of larger structural problems at the national and international levels? Greenstar's answer is to present a third way that involves the direct induction of rural communities into the global market through the Internet, with the aim of making these communities self-sufficient.

Recently, sociologist Anthony Giddens reinserted the term the "third way" into academic and political circulation. Attempting to capture the new turns and complexities of recent British politics through this term, Giddens observed that the neo-liberal attitudes and policies associated with the former Thatcher regime, and the social democrats' approach to politics and public policy associated with the Labour Party in Britain, had found a tempered expression in the politics of Labour Prime Minister Tony Blair. Giddens suggested a possibility of the co-existence of the logic of global capitalism with the empowering dynamics of communitarian sociology.

Though this study does not involve the state and its position on global capitalism as such, the notion of its co-existence along with the people's or popular empowerment is important to the analysis and the understanding of this new phenomenon of a development corporation with unique features. The existence of a development corporation such as Greenstar and its discourse on moving away from the dominant ideology of development, yet empowering rural communities, suggests a third way, with concerns about profit, labour, expansion, and re-investment sitting side by side with environmental preservation and the rhetoric of rural empowerment through development.

The third way is a "globalizing philosophy" that endeavors to embrace a reflexive globalization that will constantly and carefully scrutinize the logic behind free trade and at the same time remain wary of state intervention in the management of the market. This third position has prompted critics to respond that a third way "advocates a 'politics without adversaries' that therefore ends up accepting the world as it is rather than truly seeking to transform it" . What emerges out of a rationale for the third way is the idea that there are now at least three Utopian social states, each proposed as a response to a historical condition. During the Cold War, capitalism marked by an ideal free market served as a response to state-controlled economies; socialism or any state-managed market system (or social democracy, in the context of British political ideologies) was a critical response to the vagaries of free market capitalism. Finally, in Giddens's presentation, a "third way" in the post-Cold War era hesitates to dismiss claims of socialism as a failure and yet is open to the neo-liberal ideology of global capitalism. It suggests a workable, even harmonious, co-existence of the two. Whether such a co-existence is possible remains to be seen; in suggesting these three classifications, my intention is not to compartmentalize political positions but to suggest a heuristic device that informs this study.

THE RESEARCH QUESTIONS

Based on the above discussion, I arrive at the following research questions. The first question treats the Greenstar site as a collection of networked links.

- *RQ1*: What does the structure of the Greenstar web site communicate about the designers' strategic use of web text for conveying certain meanings about its activities and managing certain images about itself as a "development corporation?"

  The rest of the questions address the content of the Greenstar site. The overarching research question to be answered by the frame analysis of the content of Greenstar's web site is as follows:
- *RQ2*: What are the predominant frames employed by Greenstar to articulate its version of a "third way" of doing development in the new global cultural economy, combining the global and the local to achieve this effect?

  Specific research questions that pertain to framing strategies in the web content include:
  - *RQ2a*: How did Greenstar frame development as a global capitalist endeavor? What indications in the frame suggest a pan-capitalist solution to development problems?
  - *RQ2b*: How was the idea of empowering rural communities framed in Greenstar's discourse of development?
  - *RQ2c*: How was the idea of a "third way" of development as a new solution to an old problem framed in the web site?
- *RQ3*: In this entire process, how was the developing world framed? What are the implications of such framing for possible current perceptions of developing regions?

Research Design

METHOD

This is a case study of a development corporation that presents itself as caring about human dignity in developing regions, environmentally friendly in its goals, and more intrinsically egalitarian-oriented than is expected of a standard corporation or business venture. The company describes itself as one of a kind. My search for other similar organizations did not yield results. By no means are the findings from this study generalized or generalizable; in fact, in this research context, given the unique nature of this corporation, it might be argued that generalization is of less relevance.

However, I believe that this case is very useful because it gives us an opportunity to examine claims to innovative ways of making capitalism work for social change in some of the poorest communities in the world through the connective capacities of new media. The case allows for an empirical exploration of a third way in the context of a global cultural economy. While persuasive calls for a return to Marxist responses to global capitalism exist , what Greenstar's rhetoric might entail also merits close examination as a possible vehicle for social change.

Additionally, this case permits exploration of a combination of critical modes of analyses that are especially helpful for "reading" web sites-network analysis of the web text structure and frame analysis that is associated with the study of more traditional mass media content. As with many corporate sites, Greenstar's efforts to constantly update its web site to reflect new programmes, additions, developments, and growth renders it difficult to "freeze" the site for analysis.

Most of the Greenstar material has remained stable; however, some changes and periodic updates have been made. For example, the domain has changed from dot com (commercial) to dot org (usually associated with non-profit organizations).

Even though this separation is becoming less relevant now in that many commercial organizations can have non-profit domains, the shift for Greenstar, considered in conjunction with its mission, places the company in a very ambivalent position that suggests a "third way" while it bills itself as a forprofit venture, part of the profits go to the respective villages, part of it to the shareholders, and the rest to fund new projects. It is reasonable to speculate that these activities might have persuaded Greenstar to shift to a nonprofit domain. For this study, I visited the web site over a period of time, between March 2002 andjune 2003 as the core time period, and periodically thereafter until 2005, and also in 2007. During this period, there were additions made to the web site, such as projects in Tibet and Brazil, and some changes to newsletters and press clips. Also, since March 2002, the segment "We Will Remember" mourning the lives lost on September 11 was subsequently removed.

The changes to date have not affected the mission and other core aspects of the corporation's self-representation in any significant way. Hence the focus of the analysis pertains mainly to the constants. The organization of the site is such that links connect to other pages, and even sites external to Greenstar, but the Universal Reference Locator (URL) remains unchanged. However, recent changes indicate that the commercial cultural web site, Amazon.com, no longer comes under the aegis of the Greenstar banner, and that the link to the 9-11 segment "We Will Remember" has been reinserted at the end of the home page.

MODES OF ANALYSIS: NETWORKS AND FRAMES

Analyse Greenstar's web site using a combination of an adapted version of structural analysis of web content proposed by Jackson and frame analysis that is used in the study of texts generated by the more traditional mass media. Both types of analyses are media communication-centered and address different aspects of web text. The term "text" here includes multiple forms of expression such as words, images, audio, and video. Network analysis recognizes the differentiating factor that sets web text apart from other forms of mediated text-the hypertext link-and treats web content as a collection of hypertext links.

Hypertext links are conceptualized by Jackson as a collection of "destinations" typically circumscribed by or contained in a larger "document" or system that we might refer to as a web site. Like the content, the structuring of links also constitutes a part of the designer's labour to "author" the text.

The more familiar frame analysis has been employed to study news discourse in various mass media and advertising (the classic study by Goffman 1979 is a standard example).

In a broad sense, textual frames work to place certain aspects of ideas and experience into the scope and perceptive field of the reader/audience/user, mainly through inclusionary (and exclusionary) strategies. Morris and Ogan conceptualize the Internet as a mass medium, arguing that this medium emphasizes the limits to traditional mass communication thinking.

They challenge us to redefine the terms "mass" (audiences) and "media" (technologies) and call for a greater "flexibility" in "research categories" to accommodate the changes in technology, delivery, and users. Jackson establishes a strong connection between the Internet and mass media by drawing our attention to a characteristic of web text that makes frame analysis particularly suited to examining web content. She argues that unlike electronic mail and computer conferencing, which are interactional modes of communication, web sites are "an extension of the presentational mode of communication," similar to television or newspaper content.

The site is under the control of an identifiable source-the designer/author; the message is designed by the author(s) for consumption by interested readers/users. We might extend this rationale to understand that web sites perform the information function associated with news and also the persuasive function associated with advertising and public relations. Web sites provide information, are designed to attract readers/users by engaging in what Fürsich and Robins term as "active image work," and incorporate intuitive navigation through the site from the user's perspective.

Given the technological convergence of various mass media, principles of design and authoring used in both print and audio-visual news and advertising find several parallels here. Hence frame analysis provides a useful method for studying web discourse. The important concepts that inform each of these modes of analysis is discussed in greater detail below. Network analysis. Jackson has adapted network analysis from sociology and early diffusion work for the study of "web-based communication" or WBC, a term preferred for its inclusion of all types of communication on the web. Network analysis takes into consideration the characteristics of the new medium of the Internet and addresses at least in part the property of convergence, and consequently, it allows us to understand and map the structure of web sites.

Jackson explains that to use this mode of analysis, it is more productive to conceptualize web sites as a series of hypertext links that create a network of texts rather than as spaces storing information. These links do not just serve as conduits for transporting the user from one location to another within a web page or within the Internet, but also constitute the communication strategically planned by the authors of the web site. That is, links "offer a new strategy for structuring communication" .

Jackson points out that while the two types of movements-related to entering a web site through its universal resource locator and scrolling down a page - can be determined by the user, movement through hypertext links within the site is mapped and ultimately controlled, to a greater or lesser extent, by the site's author/designer.

Hence the structure of web text is defined by the nature of the links-"nodes" or destinations for the links (for example, various web pages within a site), the extent of connectivity between pages as designed by the author (Jackson terms this as "relation"), and the nature of the links ("interlocking" links refer to a greater degree of connectivity among several nodes; "radial" links refer to stronger connectivity of several pages to a single node, usually the home page, but with little to no connectivity among themselves. The final concept important to this study is "dominance."

It indicates the position of a node that contains more links than others-for example, a radial structure indicates dominance of the central node. Consciousness of this aspect to authoring web texts, that "possible variations for structure are shaped by communicative ends rather than technological means", allows us to critically interrogate the intentions of the authors/designers of a web site. I use an adapted version of network analysis for a qualitative examination of WBC for this study.

Two broad adaptations have been made:

- The first is contextually dictated by the study on hand. For this study, the web site is referred to as the "system level" of analysis. Web pages are treated as nodes; other terms such as relation, linking, and dominance have been described briefly, but will be explicated in greater detail as they unfold in the analysis.
- Jackson recommends analysis of the population of links and pages within a site to enable full identification of patterns in the web site, with the rationale that use of samples will reduce the opportunity for identifying patterns of links. For this study, a selection of web pages (i.e., some key nodes) based on the critical information they carry about the company and its activities has been used for two reasons. First, Greenstar provides a map page as one of the main constituent pages of the web site; this map contains information on the links to each node within the web site; the links are listed under each main node. Examining the links in the Map page does not give us the same picture that links in individual pages under each of the sections do, but nevertheless, it provides the bigger plan (albeit in less detail) for the structure of the web site. In other words, the structure of the web site, in some form, is already available in the Map page. Secondly, the size and sprawl of the Greenstar web site necessitates selecting certain pages for closer analysis for practical reasons. The map page provides some information on linking patterns that may otherwise be lost if the analysis were to depend purely on selecting a sample of web pages.

Frame analysis: Frame analysis marks both a signature theory and method housed in media studies, and in particular, news studies (for example, Entman's article in 1993, which is now approaching "classic" status. Among others, for a compact synthesis of major developments in approaches to framing, ranging from theorizing in the media effects traditions to interpretive approaches for studying media texts). In general, any communication involves the "organization of ideas and "experience". As Pan and Kosicki point out, this is present in both the transmission and meaning-sharing conceptualizations of the communicative act.

As Ryan reminds us, the organization of ideas is, by default, value-laden, and specific organizations construct our perceptions of the world around us in certain ways. In his now classic work on frame analysis, Goffman describes frames as "guided doing" and sees their function as a "serial management of consequentially", an organizing activity located at the heart of frame construction. These descriptions might suggest that framing is created intentionally by the author/designer (I refer to the communication source as author/designer in a WBC context).

Considering the combination of news and information, entertainment, advertising, and public relations contained in corporate web sites like Greenstar's, it is reasonable to assume that the authors/designers have "planted" frames for certain intended effects. However, as Ryan has carefully noted, frames are also unconsciously constructed by both the author/designer and the reader/user .

Framing in communication is both intentional and unintentional because frames are primarily cultural constructs. Familiarity with shared meanings, codes, and cultural forms prompts the employment of specific frames in communication. Codes and cultural forms shared by the encoder and the decoder encourage the tendency to take certain frames for granted as routine meaning-making devices. Whether intentional or unintended, frames operate as sense-making devices in WBC.

According to Pan and Kosicki, frames, as interpretive devices, "encourage certain kinds of audience processing of texts". We can observe this of media texts in general. Central to this process is the selection of information and placement of emphasis on certain aspects of the message that elicit certain perceptions and responses in the reader/user. Frames are powerful and influential in that they can "diagnose, evaluate, and prescribe". Pan and Kosicki elaborate on several framing devices that structure media texts.

Devices important to this study include themes (central organizing ideas), connections (of ideas), and rhetorical devices that refer to "stylistic choices" made by the author/designer-metaphors, exemplars, catchphrases, depictions, and visual images. Thus, in the case of Greenstar, for example, the construction of capitalist, empowerment-oriented, and developmentalist frames emerge through a reading of the framing strategies contained in the web text.

Major depictions include the portrayal of Greenstar as a businessminded, yet humanistic, enterprise; of development as a cultural, technological, and environmental endeavor; of the company's actions as new and innovative, with a cutting-edge approach to development; of the rural communities as wise, intelligent, entrepreneurship-oriented, but needy of exogenous help; of the global market as both vehicle and destination; and of western society as a postmodern people needing spiritual rejuvenation that is best provided by the traditional cultural products of pre-modern communities.

In discussions of both network and frame analyses, the reader/user/audience is vital to completing the communicative act. In the case of network analysis, to an extent, the text is created in a customized fashion by the reader/user following links of interest within the parameters set by the author/designer. Jackson recommends analyzing server log files to see how close users' patterns of linking might align with the author's calculations of placing links in certain parts of each page.

While such an analysis no doubt adds to the reliability of the researcher's reading of the links, for this study, an exploration of connectivity at work takes into consideration specific web pages and limits the analysis of links to these pages. Both network and frame analyses take into account that communication occurs and "meaning" is realized by the active work of the readers/users/audiences. This research recognizes that the reader/user is important for structural and frame analyses of web texts. However, audience interaction (and reaction) is beyond the scope of this study. The central problem in this research is to examine self-representations of a development corporation on its web site, and hence the web content is the focus.

The researcher's reading of frames may or may not coincide with the designers' use of frames or the users' perceptions of frames, but nevertheless, reasonable assumptions can be made that since presentational media communications are targeted to certain publics, accordingly, the encoder employs structure, frame, and language that will resonate to the "shared cultural maps" of many if not all decoders. The textual analyses of the web site can potentially provide valuable insights into "theory at work" pan-capitalism, empowerment, or a third way.

READING A DEVELOPMENT CORPORATION: NETWORK ANALYSIS

Conceptualizing the web site as a system provides the main reference point for the network analysis, allowing us to draw some conclusions about the type of navigation the authors have designed, as well as the extent of control they exert on the user/reader's choices and paths for browsing and gathering information. We can discern where this control is exerted and what content in the site is considered to be critical by the designer/author.

The site opens with a home page that carries a banner containing the following links: Home, Introduction (a brief about Greenstar), Search (within the site), Subscribe (to the newsletter), Map (outline, table, and list formats for the main nodes and pages in the web site), and Contact (details for contacting the organization) (italics mine). This banner is present in all linked pages and also sites external to Greenstar. This group of links contained in the banner speaks to the overarching presence that the designers wish to give to

Greenstar. Besides the convenience for the reader/user, connections to commercial sites carry advantages for both the linked sites. For example, Amazon.com, when linked to the Greenstar site, benefits from a potential market for its products. Greenstar sells some of the digital culture products through Amazon.com (for example, compact discs) and, in linking to the latter, can direct potential buyers of its cultural products to an appropriate sales outlet.

The structure of Greenstar's web site from the home page reveals a complex networking system. Complexity here is a relative term, in that there is no specific number of links in a page or a site as a whole that denotes a benchmark of complexity. However, some pages within a site may carry more embedded links than others. The number and nature of links point to the complexity of the web site as well as key web pages within a site. For example, the links available in the banner on every page on the Greenstar site and links to sites outside Greenstar may be considered key web pages since practically every connection contains the provision to link to the banner items.

Approximately sixteen links were available on the home page. These links included the following destinations: digital culture product samples such as audio and video sample clips; the World Summit for Sustainable Development held in Johannesburg, South Africa, in 2002; publicity and information (press releases, press coverage of Greenstar worldwide, and the newsletter); a new products page, Greenstar Café (an outlet for selling cultural products); links to projects in the West Bank/Palestine, Ghana, India, and Jamaica; information about the mobile solar-powered community centre; a series of informational pages on e-commerce; Greenstar's organizational outlook and policy; the importance of solar energy and generally, the need for environmentally-sensitive lifestyles (products are available on this page as well); academic work by Greenstar directors; and finally, other organizations supported by Greenstar (still within the purview of sustainable development). In Jackson's terms, these numerous links define a fairly "dynamic" page that "pushes" the reader/user to explore multiple dimensions and activities in which the company engages. Thus the home page suggests a system (web site) that exhibits high connectedness (links to several locations both within and outside the site) and high dominance, which refers to a greater number of links contained within this page. Selected links from the home page lead to other pages (or nodes) that contain a fairly large number of links. This suggests a satellite system, whereby some pages are assigned a central position (given more importance) by the author/designer.

That is, when in the home page, there are numerous links that encourage the reader/user to explore various aspects of the company's activities, but within those "peripheral" or "secondary" destinations to which most of the embedded links in the home page lead, there are varied levels of connectivity to other sites. For example, the Palestinian Al-Kaabneh link from the home page leads us to other web pages and pertinent external sites. However, the destination of Patriensah, Ghana, as a link from the home page contains fewer links external to the Patriensah page. In the cases of both Al-Kaabneh and Patriensah, the banner on top leads the reader/user back to the key pages in the Greenstar site.

Upon following each link in the home page, it was discovered that most of them contain links to other pages. Typically, the links are contained within the Greenstar system (that is, they lead to other pages within the Greenstar web site); some of them lead outside the web site. The latter signals a more open system of the web text, where the designer gives the user the option of "straying away" from the web site. However, many of the outside links still come under the aegis of Greenstar since these sites open within the Greenstar site. The presence of the Greenstar banner in pages that are at extreme outlier limits along the "neural" network of the Greenstar site is designed to guide the reader/user back to the home page or to a main node of the web site at any given time.

Examples would include Amazon.com (carrying works of various musicians who have also contributed to some of the Greenstar solar communities' music recordings), Cafépress, a company dealing with design imprints on products such as mugs and tee shirts, the National Renewable Resources Laboratories (NRRL), and UNESCO. This structure suggests an encouragement for the user/reader to explore other links, but always reminds them of the source of the communication; Greenstar continuously serves as the structural réfèrent. In the few cases where certain links take the reader/user out of the Greenstar web site, there seems to be an encouragement of what Jackson has termed "associative movement"-a fundamental ideal of the creators of the hypertext. This associative movement has been interpreted as enabling a more democratic and open access to various texts on the web.

The complex of links leading to pages outside the Greenstar web site thus includes small companies, large e-commerce corporations, governmental and intergovernmental organizations, NGOs, and a variety of other organizations involved in sustainable development. Regardless of size or type (for-profit, non-profit) of organization, most links come under the Greenstar URL and the green banner. Hence, fundamentally, Greenstar maintains control over almost all the links, yet provides some room for movement and exploration both within and outside the site; the majority of links are in-site-they constitute the Greenstar web site.

Overall, it is clear from the more or less radial structure of the home page that it is a major "gatekeeping" point in the site, and hence it is designed to be more "authoritative" with the site information than other pages within the system . On the home page, therefore, Greenstar presents itself as a benign corporation that encourages much exploration within and outside the site, but always under its aegis (the banner and the URL).

There is some exertion of control over the agenda, to be expected with its clear claim as a for-profit (and not a solely philanthropic) venture, and since the home page is constructed on the assumption that it is the main portal of the site, numerous links here take us to other aspects of the site. However, the large number of links also suggests an open structure for the home page, encouraging exploration of various aspects of Greenstar and its partners. On examining nodes (web pages within the site), each emerged as fair- ly independent of the others. Not many links were designed between and among the various pages within the site. Jackson refers to such linked groups within a site as "cliques," where a clique is an identifiable collection of nodes or subgroups of pages within the larger site, identified by extensive networking among the nodes.

Each link in the banner constituted a composite of its own links, some linking back to the home page; therefore no significant clique was identified. Each node contained its own set of links that led to various destinations, with occasional overlaps. For example, the digital culture link is included in both the home and Introduction pages.

The more radial structure of the home page was reflected in each of the links contained in the banner. That is, each central node in the radial structure is more or less independent, exhibiting its own set of links. For example, the page on "What is a solar powered community" contains links to components and products such as the Suntainer - a solar-powered mobile cell housing a hospital, a school, and an office with a computer and Internet access through wireless satellite connection.

The links in this page lead to information on components and products; one can return to the main page by selecting the back option on the browser panel at the top of the screen. Another example of a more or less self-contained page is the node on housing information on the Parvatapur project in India. This page contains the following links: music (as digital culture product), a quote from Mahatma Gandhi, a printed version of the then Chief Minister Chandrababu Naidu's speech, a gallery of pictures, information on the state of Andhra Pradesh where the Greenstar village of Parvatapur is situated, artwork available for purchase through the net, and a link to the press coverage of the event (the opening of Parvatapur as the site of the first solar-powered community of this kind in India) in a national flagship newspaper, The Hindu.

The links to the digital culture products and the press coverage have connections with the main digital e-commerce and the pressroom links in the web site-two relatively rare instances of interlinking among nodes outside the home page. The Introduction page, much more detailed in its discussion of Greenstar's mission and activities than the home page, nevertheless exhibits a similar linking pattern.

Besides sharing common links with the home page (such as digital culture, community links for the various projects, and a key journal article titled "Sweatshops and Butterflies: Cultural Ecology on the Edge"), it also provides extensive background on Greenstar's business approach and philosophy, an e-philanthropy link for potential donors, and a list of criteria for the selection of villages. Links in the Introduction page are listed on a panel to the right, whereas the home page contain links embedded in the text and in locations bordering the text (top and bottom of page). The placement of some of these links common to both the home and Introduction pages varies.

Where the home page emphasizes the public relations mission of the site by placing the pressroom link very near the top of the page, it features well below on the Introduction page's links panel. Both pages privilege the actual projects, and more so the Introduction page. Thus the structure (and here, to an extent content) of the Introduction page suggests a centrality to that page in comparison with other nodes in the site. Where the home page assumes the appearance of a news magazine, with interesting information scattered throughout the page in the form of links, accompanied by many photographs and graphics, and points of visual interest such as flashing colored line drawings, the Introduction page is more text-dominated, oriented toward delivering specific and specialized information and therefore contains links selected and placed by the authors/designers accordingly.

As a final observation about the linking patterns in this web site, community projects are showcased in individual web pages. However, there is no link among the communities, as for example, between the community in Brazil and the community in Ghana. The community web pages are lihked radially from the home and Introduction pages, and they also feature in the map page. Besides the obvious reading of the centrality of the corporation to this site in such a radial structure, the placement of community web pages at the periphery prompts another reading-that the peripheral nodes have been constructed with minimum distractions to help the reader focus on the information about the community's work. In such cases, these nodes serve as repositories of information.

The linking patterns at the system level (the entire web site) suggest a careful development of the activities of Greenstar and the privileging of its role as a cutting-edge development idea, theory, and practice in partnership with the "Greenstar solar-powered communities" in its e-commerce circuit. The corporate flavor of e-commerce for digital culture products constitutes a dominant vein of pan-capitalism, especially with links to commercial cultural sites such as Amazon.com (which appears in more than one instance, through links to specific compact discs and artists in various countries). At the same time, the links to partners, some of which are non-profit, governmental, intergovernmental, or non-governmental organizations, suggest serious on-going efforts to find ways to empower rural communities in their projects worldwide to enable self-sustained and sustainable development.

A careful reading of the various external sites shows that though the ideology of sustainable development is high on the agenda for Greenstar, the opportunity structures available for the communities to help them rely on their own cultural and natural resources are limited, except for those provided by Greenstar. It is this combination of the corporate and the communitarian with Greenstar that suggests a third way in the global cultural economy. We can gain a more detailed understanding of the three underlying theoretical constructs suggested for this study-pan-capitalism, empowerment, and a third way-by examining the framing strategies apparent in the content of the web site.

READING A DEVELOPMENT CORPORATION: FRAME ANALYSIS

Structural analysis, while useful for critically examining the "material form of mediation" unique to the Internet, does not engage with the content of web text. The analytical technique of framing requires us to focus on the textual aspect of web-based communication, that is, meanings and ideas conveyed through words and images.

Frame analysis facilitates the understanding of web text as a collection of frames that convey the meanings of the communication contained in the site and the ideological inclinations thereof. While it is very likely that different frames might emerge in the reading of the same text for authors/designers, users/readers, and researchers, nevertheless an intuitive, shared recognition of frames in the acts of both authoring and reading (and hence the process of mediated communication) makes it reasonable and useful to study dominant frames identifiable in the text.

The collective recognition of frames emerges from a shared culture and language among designers/authors and users/readers. Hence the argument that interactive users/readers of web text confound textual analysis through their own understanding of the content, which is ostensibly different from the researcher's reading of the text, might disable inquiry into the meaning-making quality of web-based communication (or even other forms of mediated communication). It would be more productive to approach web text from the standpoint of shared culture and related intuitive arrangement and writing of text as a point of departure for analysis of web content.

Pan and Kosicki discuss several devices employed in the process of framing media messages. News texts constitute the focus in their analysis. Here, I apply certain strategies designed for examining news texts to study WBC. Specifically, two strategies are important for this study - thematic structure and rhetorical devices. Pan and Kosicki explain thematic structure of a news text as follows; the quote also serves to highlight the analogies in news text for web text, where both can be conceptualized as a presentational mode of communication:

A thematic structure of a news story... is a multi-layer hierarchy with a theme being the central core connecting various sub themes as the major nodes that, in turn, are connected to supporting elements. Rhetorical devices refer to what Pan and Kosicki term as the author's "stylistic choices." Stylistic choices include metaphors (using connections to ideas as an explanatory tool), exemplars (where connections to actual events, situations, or people are used as explanatory devices), catchphrases (short slogans and expressions that are at once easy to remember and associate with the frame), depictions (Gamson defines these as "characterizations"), and visual images.

Catchphrases, depictions, exemplars, and visual images are evident in many places in the Greenstar web site. For example, in the Frequently Asked Questions (FAQs) page, through its responses, Greenstar depicts itself as an organization with business interests as well as altruistic intentions and acts. Its self-representation communicates a clear, transparent, and ethically bound organization with a responsibility towards humanity, the environment, and its shareholders. Its catchphrase of "self-replicating development" appears repeatedly in the FAQs page. This catchphrase conveys the notion of empowering the rural communities to help sustain long-term ecofriendly practices leading to social change.

In the frame analysis that follows, making references to appropriate web pages within the site, I analyse the Greenstar web site using specific framing devices - themes, catchphrases, depictions, and reasoning devices such as antecendents, consequences, and appeals to principle (moral appeals). Some of these framing devices and references appear in more than one frame and thus help establish certain patterns and significations in the text.

THE COMMODITY FRAME: PAN-CAPITALISM

This frame serves to demarcate activity, strategy, and persuasion deployed for development that are fundamentally underwritten by the logic of global capitalism. It emphasizes the benefits to commoditizing pre-modern culture by framing it as a resource awaiting full exploitation. Depictions and implications range from the actual process of commodifying indigenous culture to developing a niche market for these cultural products and addressing consumption also as an important dimension of capitalism.

The commodity frame thus contains the dimensions of capital, production, and consumption. The commodifying effects emerge from the emphasis on satellite technology and the connective property of the Internet as crucial enabling agents that have the power to bring the local into the global fold. Pre-modern culture is characterized as a potential product with universal appeal and value.

As framing devices, themes, depictions, and catchphrases stand out in Greenstar's efforts to inform the reader and persuade the potential philanthropist about the unique and viable nature of highly localized entrepreneurial efforts that could directly affect the global market.

A link from the home page to a document - an article in the journal Sustainable Development International - titled "Sweatshops and Butterflies: Cultural Ecology on the Edge" (hereafter referred to as the Sweatshops and Butterflies link or page or article) depicts the cultural reservoir of rural communities in the developing world as the "unknown, unrealized asset of the disconnected," an asset that can be mobilized to create objects of "universal value," which can then be "easily exchanged worldwide" if they are integrated into the global market. Transforming this "disconnect" into a commercial asset and inserting it into the stream of global exchange would spread the benefits of ancient values, wisdom, and culture.

This depiction clearly incorporates the local into the language and economy of the global market. Traditional culture thus becomes a "hidden value" that a new medium of communication (here, the Internet) can help realise. A link from the home page to the Sustainable Development Conference of 2002 in Johannesburg, South Africa (referred to from now on as the South Africa Summit link or page), also depicts indigenous cultures and traditions as resources waiting to be tapped for the global economy, and as distinct from agricultural and industrial resources that have played a prominent role in development projects for a long time. The subhead for the South Africa Summit page, "Tools for Independence," refers to achieving economic independence through traditional culture.

The term "small global business enterprise" aptly describes these rural communities' business in digital culture, selling traditional art, music, poetry, oral history, and so on, on a small scale on the global medium of the Web. Greenstar participated in the summit by displaying a series of exhibits of its products, ventures, and projects.

The exhibit, supported in part by the U.S. Department of Interior, urged decentralization, and promoted "individual and community independence and initiative" and small business, but without the pressures of loan repayment for micro credit, as the company frequently pointed out in other pages of the site also. The contents of this page suggest a neo-liberal position on the emancipatory potential of global markets.

The Introduction page, linked at the banner on the home page, carries detailed information about Greenstar. Each major aspect of the company, in turn, is linked to its own page. Here, pan-capitalism as a frame emerges in the depiction of the nature and purpose of Greenstar - a profit-making venture, with priority given to partners in the developing world and to investors.

A link to the Greenstar Café, in the upper section of the Introduction page, leads us to products - mugs, teeshirts, caps, and bags - carrying traditional designs from the project communities. For example, the traditional Indian rangoli design, the decorative artwork on the ground made with rice flour and other materials, is imprinted on mugs and teeshirts. These designs have been incorporated into such objects commonly used in many urban areas worldwide.

This juxtaposition of a traditional design on a modern (and contemporary) product may not present a novel idea as such (museums housing material culture routinely make such adaptations and appropriations, from all parts of the world), but it is of interest here that in the context of development, pre-modern culture is incorporated seamlessly into the global consumer culture, for what the corporation presents as a new way of doing development.

In another depiction of rural areas in the developing world, Greenstar argues that peoples in these regions are forced to suppress their "entrepreneurial instincts" because of various structural constraints. By designating it to a trait that is typically associated with a pre-socialization stage, Greenstar naturalizes the "entrepreneurial spirit." The company's argument implies that the logic of marketdriven capitalism is dormant in these communities and awaiting the stimulus of modest exogenous aid (here mainly technological) for integration into the global market.

Various catchphrases are apparent across web pages within the site. They serve to project the commodity frame by repeatedly emphasizing certain qualities in traditional cultures and delineating their potential to cater to niche markets and taste cultures. At the outset, a box item on the top lefthand corner of the home page states Greenstar's objective - to bring indigenous (and it follows, unique) products to global markets. Further down the page, the short introduction to the West Bank/ Palestine project emphasizes the rarity of the music and artwork of this region, as something that has never before been available outside the geographical area.

Tradition, once a marker of underdevelopment, is now framed as an exotic object of consumption in the global market. Besides the word tradition, others like "exotic,""ancient,""rare," and "authentic" are used in several places in the site, serving as catchphrases for imagining these "other" cultures and their material expressions in the form of digital culture and other products.

The catchphrase used to describe the peripheral location of these communities, "off the grid," appears in several places in the site, most prominently in the Sweatshops and Butterflies link where the term is explained in some detail. "Off the grid" refers to communities existing outside the networked world, with minimal to no electricity and telephonic communication in rural areas, both of which are considered by Greenstar as "basic empowering tools." The company argues that by ignoring these off-the-grid areas, collectively, the world is guilty of "a tragic squandering of human capital." The link "?-merging Markets," placed in the Introduction page, suggests both the idea of an emerging new market for products of the rural communities and also the communities themselves as potential consumers since they will have access to the Internet. These connotations transform pre-modern culture into material-cultural capital in the Greenstar communities.

One of the reasoning devices employed to construct the commodity frame in the E-merging Markets page is the appeal to principle. It is the "future building" based on "cultural assets," and clearly not exploiting land or labour that makes investment in this venture morally just and convincing. Consumers participating in this e-commerce engage in socially responsible consumption. In the Introduction page and the ?-merging markets link, Greenstar claims that its efforts are intended to build a country's "intellectual capital base."

It is not clear what actually constitutes this intellectual capital, but commodification of culture and its rendering into cultural capital is intellectualized through this mode of reasoning, thereby appealing to principles of both donors and consumers (donors and consumers merge more closely in the global e-market). Further, Greenstar argues that information-based industries such as digital culture ventures are less capital-intensive. The appeal to reason and principles in the e-merging markets link then turns to "laying the groundwork for a knowledge economy" in developing regions and "teaching the transfer of intellectual capital" to rural communities.

In responses to some of the questions in the FAQs page, Greenstar employs a corporate/commodity vocabulary for explaining its operations and persuading the reader/user about its goals. For example, responding to the question about the actual functioning of e-commerce in this venture, the company explains that with some aid, communities "develop products of cultural value" which are then "translated into market value." The package is complete - it is a business venture that profits "everyone in the value chain," while keeping the partner villages debt-free. The response to another question - on solving development problems - frames Greenstar's endeavor in broad, universal terms; the company has pinpointed communications problems as the most challenging aspect of development.

This response highlights communication as the critical factor for integrating the local into the global economy. Strongly reminiscent of the opponents to a NWICO policy in the nineteen seventies and eighties, this response appeals to principle with an emphatic and persuasive statement that a fair market economy requires fair and equal communication (on the assumption that the two complement each other perfectly).

THE ACTIVIST/PRAXIS FRAME: EMPOWERING THE LOCAL

Along with the previous frame where corporate language and commodification of culture were employed, a praxis-oriented, activist frame also emerges in Greenstar's rhetoric. It declares its goal as promoting social change in ways that empower rather than drain the rural communities (which development programmes have hitherto done, for various reasons), and desires to achieve this goal through new media and digital culture. Keck and Sikkink have defined activism as a set of activities and a culture "promoting causes, principled ideas and norms", generally calling for a change in existing policies.

But unlike activist groups, Greenstar does not engage in advocating policy changes. This is clear in the company's explanation of its criteria for selection of communities worldwide in the Greenstar Business Model page . Broadly, the company works within existing policy, regulatory, technological, trade, and foreign relations (relations with the United States) frameworks to create solar-powered digital culture communities in developing countries.

However, Greenstar's activist and praxis rhetoric emerges from its engagement with environmental concerns, community empowerment, and its persuasive explanations of the reasons for its project as an ideal solution to the development problem. Several themes constitute the activist frame in this site. These themes include preserving culture and values against the adversities of the postmodern age, evoking famous political figures from developing regions in recent history and the present reputed for their approach to global problems through peaceful and productive means (such as Gandhi and Nelson Mandela), reconciling political differences (especially apparent in the West Bank link), portraying rural communities as teachers (repositories of ancient, pre-modern wisdom), and empowerment through independent self-development (for example, the South Africa summit page emphasized the attractions of community independence, small business, and "durable technology tools" that resist quick obsolescence).

The framing devices employed include depictions, key catchphrases, and two recurring exemplars - the references to famous national leaders' aspirations and visions for their respective countries, and the development project of the past half century. The empowerment frame is apparent in the opening section of the home page and links to all major community projects. A box item in the opening section of the home page describes traditional art, music, legends, and storytelling as "priceless," implying that this wealth and strength of culture and wisdom found in the remote areas of the developing world make them worthy players in the globalizing world.

Similarly, Patriensah in Ghana is depicted as the "heart of Africa," home of the Ashanti, a "people of extraordinary power and beauty." The project in Andhra Pradesh, India (the Paravatpur link), connects Greenstar's aspirations to the "memory, principles and ideas of Mahatma Gandhi." Ironically, in its solution to a development problem through technology, the company evokes the spirituality of a national leader known for his minimalist, non-technological approach to living and developing Indian society.

What we can interpret from this invocation to Gandhi is his insistence on self-reliance that serves as an inspiration for Greenstar. In the case of the Al-Kaabneh project in Palestine,

Greenstar employs a peace-making approach; its rhetoric and images here call forth a (political) peace that might place empowerment through development within the grasp of the population. The box item and link to the West Bank project titled "Speak Together" suggests a reconciliation of political differences in the region. The Digital Culture link from the home page leads to a case study of the project in Al-Kaabneh. A pencil illustration (sample artwork from the community) embedded in this page is symbolic of the desire for peace - a (male) hand with fingers forming the "V" sign for victory is superimposed over barbed wire.

The inventory of digital culture available in the web site includes pictures, photographs, music, oral histories, and video - many available for sale. The Copyright page indicates that ownership for some of these works rests with the community. That is, the intellectual property ownership or copyright rests with the actual producers of digital culture in the project villages; this decision on the part of Greenstar can be read as efforts to empower rural communities within a capitalist environment. Intellectual property rights (of which copyright is a part) in the digital age have raised fundamental questions about authors, ownership of ideas and their expression, and users of these works.

The copyright laws of the print era, originally intended to protect the author, later gave way to the "control of circulation" of copyrighted materials by corporations that has now become ever more restrictive in the era of copyrights on software. In the case of digital products of Greenstar communities, copyright for some works (especially in instances where western experts in arranging music for compact discs were not involved) are held by the communities. Monitoring the piracy of these products either by Greenstar or by the communities would be exceedingly difficult.

Though the decision to give copyright to the community suggests empowerment, the onus would fall on the community to prove piracy in the global market. Also, the issue with copyrighting indigenous cultures is its thrust to integrate the communities in the global capitalist economy by transforming the communities' cultural commons into commodities . Therefore empowerment through copyright, no doubt admirable from the point of view of the contemporary global capitalist economy, also requires critical scrutiny in this instance.

Depicting equality and partnership with the developed world is yet another strategy for empowerment apparent in Greenstar's discourse. Like the West Bank page, the Sweatshops and Butterflies page also emphasizes partnership. In the case of the former, it is a political partnership; in the case of the journal article (the Sweatshops and Butterflies link), the partnership is more economic for a growth-oriented future.

This partnership happens between populations "off the grid" and the rest of the world that is accessible through the global market. Greenstar and its communities become "partners in a positive future," where the communities and the rest of the world can learn from each other, "participate and create value," extending the cultural value of the pre-modern to monetary value through its conversion to digital format, and subsequently, sale.

The Sweatshops and Butterflies article depicted the Greenstar-community relationship as one of "enlightened partnership," with the company and the consumers of the products worldwide engaging in "respectful dialogue" with the communities, thereby placing the project communities on equal footing, culturally and economically, with the developed world. The depictions of individuals in developing communities as changing subjects - from 20th century "sweatshop laborers" to citizens and partners of the 21st century - also suggest Greenstar's investment in empowering communities from the standpoint of praxis.

At the beginning of the Introduction page, the company reasserts its commitment to "respect for and dignity of" the environment, the people, and their histories, and in this way declares its commitment toward empowering these rural communities to control their destinies and achieve social change that the communities envision as appropriate for themselves. Technology occupies competing positions in the

Greenstar web site. It is employed in the capitalist, empowerment, pragmatic, and developmentalist frames. The web, described in a catchphrase as the "New Gutenberg," is invested with the power of getting past limiting dialogues to more enabling and empowering "multilogues."

Its democratic potential ("the web cannot be managed," as the E-philanthropy link from the Introduction page of the site declares) lies in its decentralized properties, and in Greenstar's estimate, this will enable rural communities to achieve self-sufficiency and well-being (presumably without the burden of restraints and controls at the regional and national levels).

Greenstar's stated goal is to provide villages with ways to achieve economic independence without the environmental cost and without the loss of tradition or dignity. To this end, the Greenstar communities would be engaging in what the company depicts as "selffinancing" for development through e-commerce. The catchphrase often accompanying this idea in many pages on the web site is "self-replicating development," which implies that the engine and energy for growth and change would come from the community itself.

The reasoning device most apparent in this frame is the appeal to principle, especially visible in the FAQs page - communities would own key assets, "define their economic value," and have the value returned to the villages eventually in the form of a share of the profits from the sale of their cultural products. Digital culture enables a social, cultural, and economic condition that allows people to "make correct decisions about their lives," which Greenstar claims is central to its approach to development.

This picture is vastly different from the critique of traditional development approaches in the Sweatshops and Butterflies page, where the company pointed out that the older paradigm promoted "a vicious cycle of dependence and indignity." Here, Greenstar sees itself as a change agent of the development discourse itself - as removing the shackles of dependent development and liberating communities to pursue development according to their needs and plans. The powerful appeal of debt-free progress for the communities involved in this endeavor is a major empowering theme. This claim posits a bold move as part of "postdevelopment" avenues to social change.

THE PRAGMATIC FRAME: ACHIEVING DEVELOPMENT A THIRD WAY

Greenstar has encoded a strong, practical appeal in its rhetoric and operations. This frame is perhaps the most prominent one in this web site and frequently informs many of the other identified frames.

The corporation's aim is to help rural communities reach their development goals with "a mixture of human condition, dignity, and technology." This practical mix suggests a third way to development, where sustainability and "selfreplication" work together to utilize the global market in two ways - as a vehicle for development and as a final destination for the developing world. The reasoning devices most apparent in the construction of the pragmatic frame are historical antecedents and the appeal to principle.

Contrasting its approach against development efforts from earlier paradigms, Greenstar provided arguments for the viability and fairness of its enterprise from the standpoints of the rural communities, the consumers of digital products, the corporation itself, and its beneficiaries (of which the project communities are one group). Other devices that aided in the construction of the pragmatic frame included catchphrases and depictions.

Employing historical antecedent as a reasoning/framing device, the Sweatshops and Butterflies article reminds us of recent history, where the rich nations "got richer at the expense of the colonies." The consequence of this single-minded pursuit of wealth, the article argues, is the loss of "a sense of meaning" to life and living.

Greenstar's solution to the "development failures of the past" is to foster self-sufficient and sustaining growth that would disengage rural communities from dependence on aid and other forms of exogenous interventions in the name of development. Where the article appeals powerfully to principle is in its argument for the recognition of a "fast-moving cyber economy" in which traditional approaches to development requiring large industries, cheap labour, and vast tracts of natural resources become outdated because of their impractical demands and because of the standards imposed on developing regions, and consequently, their toll on the environment.

The authors of the article see in this traditional approach "vestiges of postcolonialism" and urge the integration of traditional communities into the global economy on their own terms, which would lead to development success - rural communities can sustain themselves and pursue "development" as they see fit, and also contribute to renewing and recharging the meaning of life for what Greenstar defines as an empty, postmodern (first) world, through their digital culture products.

A strong pragmatic appeal to this line of reasoning lies in the fact that communities need not migrate to urban areas that hitherto have typically lured rural populations seeking the wealth and benefits of urban modernity, only to bring them "sweatshop paychecks." The connectivity enabled by solar-powered information technology, its power to bring rural communities into the "grid," and its capacity to transform tradition from a cultural repository to an economic resource in the ecommerce world are presented as a very practical way of doing development in a globalizing world.

At the same time, Greenstar argues, it is this articulation and re-articulation of tradition through digital culture circulating in the global market that will keep pre-modeni cultures from becoming extinct under the onslaught of "McCulture." More, traditional culture would restore the sense of "human connection" that is lost in the "postmodern. ..cynical media world."

This line of reasoning suggests a third way of doing development where all parties - the developing world, the developed world, the corporation, and its partners and shareholders - stand to gain. In the Introduction page and in some of the embedded links such as the Greenstar Business Model and?-philanthropy, there is a blend of sympathy and humanitarianism and a carefully argued, hard-headed practicality.

The humanitarian side is expressed through concerns for voice, dignity, and the importance of community-driven development. The practical approach is evident in the company's explanation of the corporate rationale, the business logic, and the provisions and possibilities of solar-powered technology in developing regions. The mutual, global-local advantage is expressed as follows: ...building a network of people, skills, ideas, tools and cultural voices that will be of incalculable value to the whole world - and to the people of those villages.

The South Africa conference link clearly indicates the support for making communities independent by mobilizing indigenous culture and tradition as revenue-generating resources. The appeals of decentralization, the importance of small business and the independence it allows, and the maintenance and spread of traditional knowledge and art are combined with a shrewd business strategy to enable these things to happen.

The title of the Greenstar conference exhibit - "tools for independence" - can also be inter- preted as a catchphrase that emphasizes media for development, such as the solar and hand-crank radio or connection to the Internet through satellitephone. Greenstar's appeal to principle is evident in its argument for a means of achieving independence through technology and minimal aid - financial assistance alone encourages dependence and meets short-term needs but "does not address underlying challenges."

In such a situation, Greenstar argues, sustainable development combined with independent revenue-earning activities that depend on rich cultural resources (rather than the depletion of natural resources) is the most practical solution. The Sweatshops and Butterflies page emphasizes a "partnership" with developing regions that is markedly different from the "old" linear, unidirectional transfer of money, technology, knowledge, and standards from the developed to the developing regions. This page contains catchphrases like "enlightened partnership" and "respectful dialogue" that imply a mutual exchange between the rural communities and the world fostered by Greenstar activities.

Within this picture, Greenstar's commercial operation is strategized as both a profit-making enterprise and a development agency addressing development needs that are not typically associated with aid from western sources. Here, the company positions the sale of indigenous culture as an intervention to salvage the deteriorating social and moral values in the postmodern life of people in developed regions. The Sweatshops and Butterflies article argues that the "McCulture" that the developed world now generates can only be meaningfully challenged by indigenous cultures.

In the Al-Kaabneh (the West Bank) project link from the home page, there is a careful blending of the local and the global that suggests a third way to development through a productive encounter of pre-modern culture and a communication medium associated with global markets (the Internet). The corporation argues that rural communities in developing areas like Palestine/the West Bank embody strength in the traditional and that Internet connectivity - "gateway to the world" - embodies strength in the global.

Again, the implication here is that a coming together of these two could only mean a winning move for all. The title for this page, "Speak Together," suggests the desire for geopolitical reconciliation in the region, but also a more practical idea of joint corporate and community endeavors for development. Addressing another aspect of capitalism, Greenstar depicts profit-making as something practical that benefits all parties involved. The company's profit distribution intentions also reflect a "third way" in the context of development in that the emphasis is on profits for partners (the villages), investors, and finally the company itself, which will invest the profits in new projects and communities.

This could be interpreted as standard image-building public relations that corporations routinely engage in;

however, Greenstar's declared intention, and its transparency in explaining its activities and plans, such as the ways in which to create a debt-free development environment for its selected villages runs counter to the notion of the sole strategy of image-building. Thus the persuasive appeal to principle in the text calls our attention to rural communities' ownership of the Greenstar solar energy centers and their shareholding capacity in the company.

The ?-merging markets link highlights a "crossroads of knowledge sharing and economic development" to characterize the Greenstar project, where sharing traditional knowledge revitalizes a jaded postmodern world, and sharing technological knowledge more characteristic of the latter also empowers "off-the-grid" communities with knowledge about effective use of new technologies.

In addition, the Introduction page emphasizes the need for a practical solution, a "formula" (catchphrase) for successful development and claims to have found it - "new jobs and skills[that] strengthen local culture and language, and affirm people's independence." In the process, instead of depleting natural resources, "inherent cultural assets" will be mined. The purchase of digital products and other traditional artifacts translates to socially responsible consumption that defines consumers as participants in a "green" programme.

THE DEVELOPMENTALIST FRAME

In the last decade or so, critics have repeatedly demonstrated suprastate agencies' sole understanding of development as being built around the cornerstones of economics and technology. The economic dimension, in the context of this study, is subsumed in the commodity frame discussed earlier, where it merges with global capitalism. Greenstar's heavy reliance on technology suggests a continued investment in traditional development methods.

The Greenstar web site invites a paradoxical reading of the place of technology, specifically new media and solar power technologies, in its discourse. On the one hand, we have the former allegiance to technology as a principal deliverer from poverty, an approach aligning with an ideology that Escobar and others have termed as "developmentalism," which promoted media technologies as fundamental to social change. Further, the corporation's connection (and links in the site) to the U.S. Department of Energy's NRRL (National Renewable Resources Laboratories) and the United Nations suggests an approach to aid similar to the "developmental era."

Traditionally, the United States and international agencies such as the United Nations were partners in development programmes. By re-establishing these connections, Greenstar invites the former "developmentalists" into the fold of postdevelopment. The presence of those links on the Greenstar's web pages adds legitimacy to its claims of being a development corporation.

On the other hand, increasingly, underprivileged communities use Internet connectivity to enhance their operations, such as the Self-Employed Women's Organization (SEWA) in India. Former critics of developmentalism such as Escobar and grassroots activism scholars such as Rodríguez are now exploring the empowering and emancipatory potential of new technologies for local communities.

They are cautiously enthusiastic about such new avenues and document several grassroots efforts that now place communication technology in a wholly new light as enabling and in the hands of the people, rather than as oppressive and under control of the state. New media technology is a challenging dimension for classification in development thought at this time because of the new empowering properties at the microdevelopment level that are being experienced and theorized in various places by communities, activists, and scholars.

Arguably, Greenstar's rhetoric retains the flavor of the old ideology, while at the same time that it embraces a postdevelopment discourse of media and communication technologies. Technology constitutes a major engine for the type of development and social change proposed by Greenstar. Since technology has played a big role in earlier developmentalism, and continues to play a role today (somewhat differently), it informs what I have termed here the "developmentalist frame" in a fundamental way. Repeatedly, either explicitly or by implication, technology forms the reference point for Greenstar's rationalization of its existence and operations.

For instance, Greenstar lists technology as a basic need, and as the prime enabling agent for transforming culture into an economic resource. In the analysis that follows, I have retained the focus on technology, but have referred occasionally also to the role of economic development and diffusion as a development theory in instances where they evoke the developmentalist frame for the reader/user.

The framing devices identified in Greenstar's developmentalist discourse include catchphrases and depictions. The use of the term "grid" in the catchphrase "off the grid" signifies the technological grid, from which the majority of the world's populations are excluded. Depictions of certain practices in the present era as "information-age economics," and the web as a force mobilizing what Greenstar refers to as the "intellectual capital base" are examples of this particular framing device at work.

At the outset, in the home page, the reliance on technology as the solution to problems created by underdevelopment becomes evident. The catchphrase "off the grid," plays a salient role in the construction of the developmentalist frame. The term is used with reference to "much of the world." In large part, the grid refers to connectivity through media and some related requirements for technologies to function, such as electricity.

Telephones, computers, and Internet connectivity are classified as basic needs, along with clean water and access to healthcare and education. The relatively fewer countries within this grid represent the norm; those outside must be brought within this technological framework. Consequently the emphasis placed on the power of technology to deliver local communities from underdevelopment and connect them to the global market is strongly reminiscent of the earlier developmentalist discourse. In its efforts to argue for connectivity and its advantages for participating in the global market, Greenstar implicitly uses the logic of comparative advantage in international trade in the context of the global market - that of each nation participating in trade (here, it would be e-commerce) in terms of its strengths. According to this argument, these rural communities possess an invaluable asset - traditional culture.

In Greenstar's analysis, this asset will save the postmodern world from going off the grid (to invert their catchphrase) in a spiritual and values-in-life sense, and restore a human connection that has been lost in the scramble for material wealth. In return (by implication), the Greenstar project communities have access to the material advantages that the postmodern world has to offer.

One of the most interesting analyses of the Web the company has presented is located in the ?-philanthropy link from the Introduction page. The revolutionary power of the Web has been likened to that of the printing press. The Web is depicted as "the most significant transformation in human affairs" and a "second Gutenberg."

Although Greenstar recognizes the change from "industrial-age economics" to "information-age economics," it does not see a diminishing need for aid and hence its appeal for "ephilanthropy" to help rural communities enter the communication technology grid.

With quotes from the then Vice President of the United States, Al Gore, the U.S. Department of Commerce, and figures from the World Bank, Greenstar framed new information technologies as the most effective answer to development problems.

The corporation emphasized the Web as the catalyst for "unleashing" incredible human power and persuaded donors to realise the magnitude of implications for mobilizing the "intellectual capital base" in rural areas, and bring villagers into the fold of the knowledge economy.

Even though the idea of self-sufficiency is frequently raised in the web site, developmentalist measures in cultural intervention are apparent. For example, musicians from the

West (in places such as Los Angeles, a thriving capital for the world's music industry) would help rural communities shape their work (music, delivery of oral histories, poetry, etc.) to convert to digital form.

Thus western experts helped to adapt local cultures for digital forms and eventually for global consumption. Depictions of such adaptations, such as "shaping music into a clean, professional format," and "assembling stories into a coherent collection" denote external intervention in the production of local culture.

That such intervention could alter what Greenstar characterizes as the pristine quality of these cultural forms does not seem to be acknowledged in the text. Rather, this technological intervention (here, in the form of "know-how") was seen as improving the traditional and preparing it for sale worldwide.

Containing performances on disc, using traditional designs on products such as mugs, tee-shirts, and caps (the Greenstar Café link), and photographing panoramic views and vistas (pictures are posted on the site), arguably, could change the experience through the mediated version of the culture that is unique to this era of media-cultural globalization. Equally, such activities could also affect site users' experience of these cultural artifacts that are purported to act as a compensation for a loss of values and humanism characterizing postmodern societies.

Other depictions that support the centrality of technology and economics are also apparent. For example, in the FAQs page, the company's selfpresentation suggests that Greenstar could be considered a change agent for development at the local level. Phrases such as "providing a start on... basic human needs" and making conditions hospitable for "providing a connection to the web" suggest Greenstar's role as a diffuser of innovative technologies in a development context. This role places the company, again, in the traditional discourse of development.

Arguments that "symmetrical market economies" need "symmetrical communications" evoke a sense of déjà vu since they were present at the time of the New World Information and Communication Order debates, where development and democracy were tied closely to the ideology of free and open markets and information flow.

THE ENVIRONMENTALIST FRAME: CULTURE AS NATURE

The Greenstar logo suggests a new postdevelopment theme of environment conservation. The name "Greenstar" evokes greening land (rather than appropriating from it) and also the biggest star in the solar system - the sun and Greenstar's use of solar energy.

As a development corporation, Greenstar uses solar energy technology that will aid in creating both selfsufficient, sustained local development as well as products for the global market. Paradoxical to this postdevelopment theme is a frame that is more in keeping with earlier views of traditional cultures as "pure,""uncontaminated," and "natural."

Through reasoning devices such as appeals to principle (aimed at consumers and philanthropists alike) and framing devices such as depictions and catchphrases, it is apparent that the company evokes traditional culture as nature to persuade the reader/user of the importance and viability of its projects.

A theme recurrent in the web site is the actual identification of traditional culture with nature. Tradition, a spiritual resource for the postmodern world, is depicted as becoming extinct, similar to many ecological species. Depictions in the Free Digital Videos link from the home page, such as "traditional,""remote,""roots" (for example, captioning pictures of Jamaica as "roots of reggae"), are equated with authentic expressions of human life that are fast becoming extinct in the noise of "McCulture."

The Sweatshops and Butterflies link argues that the more remote a village, the more likely its traditions' connections to the earth. It merges the culture into history, legends, traditional herbal knowledge and "ways of living that are of supreme value." In this section of the article, an image of a Mayan icon has been placed with an excerpt from a Mayan prayer below it. The antiquity of this motif is connected to authenticity, which in turn could evoke an authenticity typically associated with nature. The catchphrase of "cultural ecology" constitutes part of the article title, "Sweatshops and Butterflies: Cultural Ecology on the Edge.""The edge" can connote the periphery of the global economy, and also as being on the brink of extinction. Both these connotations are evoked to depict the plight of the rural communities. Traditional culture is depicted as "dying," and on the verge of "becoming extinct."

The article draws a parallel between culture and nature by arguing that diversity in social cultures is as vital as diversity in biocultures. The equivalences are clearly drawn - just as industrialization had "endangered butterflies, the whale, and the hummingbird," McCulture is endangering cultures that are ancient, traditional, authentic, and pure. The Sweatshops and Butterflies article further argues that just as the ecosystem developed over millenia, so too did oral traditions - "cultures which took thousands of years to refine will become extinct."

Another phrase used in relation to the onslaught of McCulture is the "great spasm of cultural extinction." By integrating these communities into e-commerce, the article states, "our global culture could be enriched with vivid, ancient energies" and e-commerce could ensure the continued existence of pre-modern culture. The article Sweatshops and Butterflies appeals to principle by attributing traditional cultures with the power to give life a "sense of meaning" that is lost in postmodern society. The authors of the article ask whether, indeed, this sense of meaning could be the "most precious resource of the new century."

The Introduction page refers to "inherent cultural assets" that are mined, are renewable and renewed in their continued articulation and circulation, and contrasts these assets against natural resources that, once mined, are lost forever in many cases, a state of affairs at which the world is arriving after prolonged environmental depletion. Traditional cultures are thus essentialized as inherently pure and authentic, and by implication, natural. They see these "traditional voices" as being endangered, "just as much as the ozone layer and the harp seal. Oral traditions are fragile, like an ecosystem." The authors of the article believe that these ancient cultural expressions can be preserved and transmitted in pure form through digital culture. In return, these rural communities will gain access to basic amenities that are now taken for granted by populations within the "grid."Cultures formed over millennia, in their estimate, could become extinct, and it is this cultural milieu and diversity that the article refers to as cultural ecology, an ecology in inherent danger of being extinguished by a homogenizing and homogenized artificial global culture.

Another mode of framing culture as nature is closely connected to the culture of capitalism. The authors of Sweatshops and Butterflies argue that suppression of the entrepreneurial instinct by global forces and traditional development approaches has only served to perpetuate poverty. Greenstar portrays traditional culture and populations as resources that are waiting to be tapped, housing enormous entrepreneurial "instinct." In the company's framing of this instinct, liberating it and bringing it into the flow of global capitalism is a natural (almost evolutionary biological)) development of human and cultural resources.

COMPETING SIGNIFICATIONS IN NETWORKS AND FRAMES

The two modes of analysis used for this study, network analysis and frame analysis, work in conjunction with each other to communicate the web site owners and authors' (Greenstar's) self-representation to a global audience. The network analysis employed for this study draws from Jackson's proposal of this method, and is a tentative and exploratory venture as a critical, qualitative analysis of web text that interrogates the authors/designers' intentions behind the creation of this site as a collection of linked documents (a network).

The frame analysis used in this study responds to the traditional media attributes apparent in web text - the informative newspaper, the persuasive advertisement, and the attempts at accountability and transparency typically associated with an ideal practice of public relations. Additionally, the audio-visual elements contained in the site in the form of illustrations, photographs, and video samples parallel corresponding mass media (in particular, magazines). Utilizing the results of both forms of analysis, we can summarize the responses generated for each research question.

Analysis of the structure helps us answer the first research question:

- *RQ*1. What does the structure of the Greenstar web site communicate about the designers' strategic use of web text for conveying certain meanings about its activities and managing certain images about itself as a "development corporation?"

We can answer this question by starting, first, with a summary of the network analysis. The network structure suggests that the "central core" of the text constitutes the home page, with this document occupying the principal position in the hierarchy of links.

This is a fairly intuitive placement of the home page in most web sites; however, in cases where the sites are completely open and "democratic" in the way that the creators of the networking system envisaged it or cyber theorists hoped for it, the home page need not necessarily serve as anchor for the site, but can serve as an entry point and as a space for organizing content of the site. Hence the explicit acknowledgment here that the home page serves as the central core of the Greenstar site.

Each of the nodes (or pages, with clusters of links within) that link from the home page address sub-themes of the activities and contributions of Greenstar, and in turn these nodes occupy a higher position in the hierarchy of the web structure in comparison with other links contained in these documents that serve as more peripheral, "supporting elements."

These supporting elements constitute pages within the site, as well as sites external to Greenstar. The links to various destinations outside Greenstar include US governmental agencies (for example, the NRRL), several nongovernmental environment conservation organizations, commercial sites, and more academic and informational sites (such as the ones on Palestinian heritage and Middle Eastern politics).

These external sites can be opened within the Greenstar website, with the banner including Home, Introduction, Map, and Contact information links appearing in each of the external sites. As Jackson has pointed out, this extensive linking encourages users to "meander" and "explore" and "get lost" within the site, and thus "increasees their contact with the site's content."

The overall structure of Greenstar's web site roughly coincides with Jackson's identification of a satellite structure, where the Greenstar site as a whole is central but is connected extensively with numerous external sites. Within the internal architecture of the site, the home page, with the most important pages indicated in a banner on top, constitutes the centre. The structure suggests mass communication functions and user expectations for the corporation's web site.

Information and persuasion seem to be key goals for Greenstar. The satellite structure, according to Jackson , is evident in "online news products." The linking suggests that Greenstar would like to inform users/readers and works to convince them of the venture's viability and principles - links to several non-governmental and non-profit organizations, governmental sites, research laboratories, and commercial organizations frame Greenstar as trustworthy in its transparency. The pages in the periphery of the site (with the provision to link back to the main areas in the banner, but with few to no links among themselves) serve as repositories of extensive and useful information.

The large number of links both within the web site and external to it are designed to demonstrate Greenstar's range of capabilities, connectedness in the general picture of development, and communication between highly educated authors and highly educated, intellectually-inclined users who not only shop online and exercise reflexive consumption but also "give" online (?-philanthropy). The centre of gravity for the web site, however, remains with the Greenstar home page, and within the large picture of Greenstar's web presence, ultimately suggests a radial structure. The final effect is that of signifying Greenstar as a development corporation that has invented a third way to material and social progress in the rural Third World, combining the profit motive, environmental conservation, and community concerns.

The frame analysis attempted to answer an overarching research question about the content of the Greenstar web site:

- *RQ2*: What are the predominant frames employed by Greenstar to articulate its version of a "third way" of doing development in the new global cultural economy, combining the global and the local to achieve this effect?

Five frames were identified, using themes and framing devices (such as depictions, catchphrases, exemplars, and reasoning devices). The predominant frames apparent in Greenstar's web site included the commodity frame, emphasizing the commodification of pre-modern culture in new media (the Internet), the activist frame - engaging with empowerment of rural communities, the pragmatic frame - building a third way to development, the developmentalist frame - resonating to traditional development discourse, and the environmentalist frame that constructs a "cultural ecology" of near-extinct cultures.

Competing significations of Greenstar (besides being an organization, as an idea that combines empowerment with the profit motive), the Third World (as safeguarding sanity in the excesses of the postmodern world and as a region needing external aid for development), and development (redefined in the information age, exploiting cultural rather than natural resources) are apparent in these frames.

Specific research questions that pertain to these frames in the web text included:

- *RQ2a*: How did Greenstar frame development as a global capitalist endeavor? What indications in the frame suggest a pan-capitalist solution to development problems?

The commodity frame employs corporate balance sheet language and emphasizes, in Marxist terms, the exchange value of pre-modern culture where earlier, such culture has typically been assigned more use value by its participants. This frame brackets out a purely local existence and instead asserts that integration of the local into the global market is the key to sustaining the local economy.

The user/reader is presented with a scopic vision that conceptualizes unexploited cultural resources as a waste at both the local and global levels. Traditional culture is seen as containing the panacea for the jaded postmodern spirit, as much as it is seen as a resource to be mined for local prosperity. The advertised commodities in the web site such as compact discs, videos, paintings, textiles, and so on have encoded premodern culture in a pan-capitalism that is both the engine and result of the globalization process. The commodity frame worked to reinforce the idea of the free flow of goods and the market as the vehicle for development.

In keeping with Greenstar's claim about safeguarding communities' interests in retaining control over their definitions of and actions toward social change, the second research question addressed the notion of empowering communities, and the corresponding research question was as follows:

- *RQ2b*: How was the idea of empowering rural communities framed in Greenstar's discourse of development?

Greenstar demonstrates its vision for bringing the local, off-the-grid communities within the grid, on their (the local communities') terms. An action and activist orientation given to praxis for social change is apparent in Greenstar's representations of its motives and aspirations.

Communities could remain debt- and obligation-free while building their own economies in the global market with some exogenous help. Essentially, empowering communities would emerge through an alternative mode of integration into the global economy. But the activism does not carry through entirely, since there is no "alternative politics" accompanying this drive towards empowerment. Thus Greenstar's self-representation is perhaps "activism-like" rather than activist, the difference lying in the absence of a political agenda.

The separation of the economic from its political consequences aligns Greenstar with a neo-liberal orientation that has, historically, proven to be detrimental to developing regions. The interesting twist to Greenstar's rhetoric lies in its "pragmatic" approach to development, where the activist language merges with capitalist language to produce a third way to development, and this is addressed in the following research question:

- *RQ2c*: How was the idea of a "third way" of development as a new solution to an old problem framed in the web site?

In its self-representation as an innovative and cutting-edge development organization, Greenstar works to convince the reader/user (and potential philanthropist) that its approach to helping regions achieve social change is beneficial to every party involved. The "benefits" discourse renders the company's idea highly persuasive - debt-free economic advancement for villages, on their own terms and with their dignity in tact, profits for shareholders and the villages, conservation of the environment by using solar power and information technology, a new category of goods available in the global market, and for those who purchase Greenstar villages' cultural products, the satisfaction of engaging in responsible consumption.

Juxtaposing each of these benefits against older models of development, Greenstar is careful to point out that earlier development models steeped the developing regions in debt, and donors dictated plans, materials, and action for development. Further, the company argues, based on the industrial age model of development, the earth's resources were being systematically depleted, and global "McCulture" was forcing traditional culture to extinction.

Therefore the company attempts to bring together the profit motive of capitalism, the advocacy of environment conservation, and an approach to social change that, in the contemporary era, has been referred to as "postdevelopment." Paradoxically, however, certain pictures of the developing world emerge in Greenstar's site that are in keeping with developmentalism, and the frames pertaining to these depictions were examined in the following research question:

- *RQ3*: In this entire process, how was the developing world framed? What are the implications of such framing for possible current perceptions of developing regions?

Two frames emerged from a reading of the developing world in the web site. Both frames contradict the previous frames, in particular, the activist and empowerment frames. The paradox is apparent when juxtaposing them against the developmentalist and environmentalist frames. In the former, the developing world is framed in "developmentalist" terms with the emphasis on technology and economics; the latter frames pre-modern culture in these regions as being in inherent danger of extinction, very similar to near-extinct animal and plant species.

These frames suggest a continued investment in the earlier, dominant discourse of development, and serve to reinforce former images about the developing world in current perceptions. Indigenous culture is romanticized and environmentalism is also harnessed to persuade readers of the web site worldwide to save a "dying" species.

Communities are cast as pre-modern in the environmentalist frame, and pre-modern is considered to be close to extinction, which with a little exogenous help, can be rescued by converting that culture to a resource. Greenstar argues that when this resource appears in the global market stream, two types of extinction can be averted - the extinction of traditional cultures, and the extinction of human and moral values in the postmodern world.

This study has attempted to understand, through the analysis of web text as both a network and a collection of frames, a third way of doing development in the era of global capitalism. The development corporation Greenstar has encoded discourses of progress and change from environmental, economic, technological, and praxis positions. The presentation of its positions and activities on its web site reveals several interesting parallels to informative and persuasive mass media texts. Clearly, the material is located in a particular culture, with its appeals to academics, highly educated and reflexive consumers, and those possessing a cultural familiarity with this media form. The "cognitive shortcuts" characteristic of frames in media texts have been carefully designed in many ways to strike a responsive chord in this type of reader/user.

The network analysis of the Greenstar site has revealed a clearly identifiable locus of control (the company, the home page), but also shows a highly complex and sophisticated networking to allow users to "meander" and get acquainted with the many dimensions to this company's claims, initiatives, and activities.

The networking includes artists' sites, commercial sites, governmental sites, and non-governmental sites. The corporate, activist, pragmatic, developmentalist, and environmentalist frames demonstrate Greenstar's negotiations among at least three ideological positions - pan-capitalism, empowerment, and a third way that the company has attempted to define and spearhead.

Two especially relevant components of globalization for this study:

- New media technologies and their role in facilitating opportunities and at the same time creating new forms of difference (such as the digital divide).
- Hybridity (a mixture of the global and the local, the capitalist and the pre-capitalist, in cultural form and material practice) - have affected development practice and discourse.

Recently Elyachar , writing on development in Egypt, has observed that the critique of development has been "given a discursive burial". This does not seem to be the case with this corporation since both critique of former paths to development and at the same time, reliance on earlier signifiers of development such as technology and economics, constitute the backbone of Greenstar's self-representation on the web. This study has attempted to demonstrate the efforts of a development corporation fo reconcile discourses that are intuitively inconsistent with each other - pan-capitalism and community empowerment from the grassroots level.

Greenstar has displayed a reflexive awareness in its shift in emphasis from traditional development discourses to engaging in ways of achieving social change in what many now consider a postdevelopment era, where community, culture, identity, and voice are foregrounded. In trying to bring together two ends of a continuum, Greenstar has placed itself in a paradoxical position - a third way (for which, in a political context, Giddens's work has proved to be controversial) as removing the political edge necessary for true social change at the level of the larger social structure.

It is clear that Greenstar speaks to an audience well able to comprehend the dilemmas and ethics of neo-colonial economies and post-colonial societies and the pitfalls of traditional developmental aid. The company recognizes "village voice" as part of the popular landscape; however, while this landscape has been theorized at least from the time of Granisci to the present as a terrain where political consciousness is cultivated and multiple oppressions are contested, in the case of the Greenstar communities, the political aspect of the struggle towards social change is consciously kept out of the picture; Greenstar mostly seeks politically conciliatory communities for its projects. Political power does not become a part of the analysis of empowerment in this sense.

What Greenstar does make clear is the power that derives from a debt-free, economically independent existence that is within reach of these communities, built on and enabled by technology - solar power technology for modernization, and new media technology for integration into the global market. The term "empowerment" in this study refers at least partly to this power. At the same time, there is a curious dissociation of empowerment from popular politics, and this makes for critique about Greenstar's venture as developmentalism as much as its dependence on technology and capitalism - the underlying paradigm of modernization is visible.

The paradoxical third way is also apparent in Greenstar's attempt to transform the laborer into entrepreneur and subject to "citizen." While solar technology constitutes the main source of power for operating various energy-driven devices including computers in the Greenstar communities, the company believes it is the connective property of the Internet that will save both these communities and the postmodern world. On a concrete level, where the sales of digital and other products stand at the moment, and to what extent the plans for profit distribution have been implemented (from lower profit shares for communities at the beginning, to gradually increasing returns, and concomitantly decreasing the share for the company and non-village shareholders, per the web site) remain to be seen.

The focus of this inquiry is the analysis of the web pages of the Greenstar site; profit margins, percentages of the profit shared with rural communities, and other information that might help evaluate the effectiveness of the Greenstar's approach is not available and hence the conclusions of the study are confined to those relating to the analyses of its web site. The unavailability of this information makes it impossible to assess whether the proposed third way has really worked in practice. The addition of new Greenstar communities is one indication of its success, but the exact nature of empowerment in monetary and financial terms is difficult to gauge without figures on actual performance.

However, the site is the critical portal toward communicating a new way of doing development, and it merits close examination. The real object of this study was to examine the web-based communication claims and discourses of Greenstar. The idealism present in the Greenstar web site is similar to the idealism in previous theories of development. The findings reveal a novel and persuasive approach to social change in developing societies. Simultaneously, they also suggest that such a path may not be able to avoid privileging and hierarchizing key aspects of global capitalist over local indigenous cultures. The implications for representations of the developing regions in this web site are noteworthy. Respect for these communities' potential contributions to global culture is apparent, as is the recognition of the importance of returning the dignity to these regions that traditional development aid has succeeded in taking away, in many instances. But there is also cause for concern in portrayals of the developing regions in this light. Through the narratives of progress, the village communities are constructed as ancient, romantically traditional, and perhaps most of all, static.

The Sweatshops and Butterflies article claims that "global culture could be enriched with vivid, ancient energies," which would otherwise give way to "a great spasm of cultural extinction... [and] priceless histories that reach back into pre-history [will] vanish." Gupta's cautionary note is especially relevant here, that "indigenousness is a conjunctural location rather than an essential identity". In essentializing the pre-modern, conceptually, traditional culture is romanticized and conferred with ancient, mystical, and healing qualities able to help the rudderless postmodern soul. Besides the fact that indigenous cultures are as much subject to change as modern and postmodern cultures, there is the important aspect of mediation of indigenous cultures.

Mediation itself has been theorized as transforming the content. Therefore attempts to convey the indigenous on the Internet, such as a traditional textile design, may be unable to fully deliver the context in which that textile is used in its own setting, as cool cotton cloth in dusty hot villages that routinely experience water shortages, and in treeless desert areas (tactile experience), or traditional festival clothing worn by almost every member of the community, or even familiarity with the traditional designs and the reasons for sequencing patterns in certain ways (cultural or religious experiences).

Similarly, experiencing musical performances in digital form such as compact discs is, at least to some extent, a result of shepherding indigenous culture into formats and structures and shaping them into consumables for a market unfamiliar with the cultural context. On a final note, this study remains a tentative, exploratory attempt to understand development claims and self-representations of a new entity, the development corporation. The case study of Greenstar has revealed some interesting and paradoxical representations of development and various ways of achieving it-through new media, environmentalist!!, and global capitalism. Many dimensions to the approach to development by this corporation merit further analysis.

For example, the gender question has not been addressed in this study. Recognizing the importance of the role of women in development, Greenstar has placed a link to its work on gender and development in its FAQs page. Women appear in images throughout the Greenstar site, but their absence is particularly noticeable on certain pages (for example, the Al-Kaabneh, the West Bank page). In other pages, especially those pertaining to India, Ghana, Brazil, and Tibet, images of women demonstrate their engagement with labour, celebration, and the everyday. However, it is interesting to note that photographs with individuals near solar power plants and other locations involving modern technology, positions of power (for example an individual standing on a hill close to a water plant), and tasks involving the control of resources depict males (for example, the AlKaabneh, Palestine link).

This brief analysis points to another dimension that needs to be examined more fully-the gender question apparent in this site. This study raises other theoretical questions related to gender, new media, and development also. For example, if oral culture and products based on local religious practices and the like, enacted more in the private and non-transactional domains of the home and community, are conceptualized as part of the larger informal sector of the economy that is an important concern for feminist economists like Carr, Chen, and Tate, what are the implications of their integration into the transactional global economy, or as Jameson puts it, the "electronic trade routes?"

Yet another dimension that could benefit from close study here is Greenstar's attempts to bring environmental conservation from the margin to the centre through the media.

This dimension is integrated closely with the communication technology promoted by Greenstar - solar-powered computers in the communities. The use of media is more than instrumental here-in Greenstar's presentation, the media claim an almost organic role in sustainable development. Since neither the discourse of development nor efforts to find the best ways to social change in regions "off the grid" is going to cease at this point, new ventures such as the one presented in this case study constitute rich grounds for further inquiry.

Chapter 6

Theorizing the Flip Side of Civic Journalism

The responsibilities of citizens in a democracy regarding their use of the newspaper have evolved slowly over the past 150 years. In Democracy in America, Alexis de Tocqueville asserted that the fully functioning citizen was one who kept abreast of the news as it appeared in print. The good citizen read for her or his personal edification so that, during times of official political involvement such as elections, she or he could deliberate well, in addition to engaging others in partisan discussion.

Several studies conducted during the waning years of the 20th century have demonstrated the endurance of the maxim, "The good citizen is an informed citizen". Good citizenship, however, involves more than simply being informed about yesterday's events so that one can make wise decisions today. Jtirgen Habermas has suggested, by implication in The Theory of Communicative Action and more explicitly in The Structural Transformation of the Public Sphere, that appropriate citizen action involves knowing the content of the news and applying that knowledge in constructive interactions with others in democratic regimes.

Reading and interpreting the news, as well as interacting with others, contribute to the constitution of an individual's lifeworld and allows one to form and take steps to maintain connections among the lifeworlds of others. It also helps the citizen apprehend the "system" of modern democratic bureaucracy more fully. "The formation of will that takes place via communication between parties" in the public sphere, asserts Habermas in volume 2 of TCA, "is a result of . . . the pull of communication process in which norms and values are shaped, on the one hand, and the push of organizational performances by the political system, on the other".

The good citizen, then, uses print news as an impetus for adding to the lives of others and for fostering the well-being of those living in her or his democratic community. This occurs through a person's participation in activities such as voting and debating public policy, of course, but it also happens on less formal levels, such as when one makes an interpersonal contribution to the public "omnilogue" on living well in civil society. Recent work in communication studies has gravitated increasingly toward interactive, "public" theories of communicative citizenship, like the one elaborated by Habermas. In the body of literature variously termed "public" or "civic journalism" especially, media theorists, critics, and practitioners have proposed ways to use the news media to stimulate citizen interaction and reinvigorate democratic life.

The set of theories comprising civic journalism has been founded on one fundamental idea: During the present time of citizen disgust with politics, if the news media perform their jobs better, readers likely will execute their citizenship duties with more interest and with more effectiveness. Altering the way journalism is "done" in a democratic society is a necessary, though by no means sufficient, condition for democratic renewal.

Other institutions must be reconfigured as well, either externally by citizens or internally, for democratic political renewal to take place. Until that happens, though, journalists face an important task. In James Carey's words, citizens hopefully will "reawaken when they are addressed as a conversational partner and are encouraged," by the news media, "to join the talk rather than sit passively as spectators before a discussion conducted by journalists and political experts". Several key theorists exemplify Carey's call to action by advocating a "dialogic" and a "conversational" conception of journalism -- a mode of journalistic communication intended to spark reader interaction at a multiplicity of levels. Others have sought to make the press into a more easily accessible "forum" for public discourse. In each case though, the suggestions for normative change have tended to focus more on what journalists should do than on the role of readers in renewing democratic life.

To be sure, theorists and practitioners working toward a more civic journalism have suggested many constructive changes to the way the press should fit into democratic society. Journalists, however, cannot accomplish the task of normative change alone. A direct discussion on reader activity is necessary if any enduring democratic renewal is going to come about. Such a discussion would cover the procedure and substance of ethical readership, both in theory and in practice. Toward that end, several important questions remain for consideration: What types of "awakened" activities can news readers engage in? If a reader were to "join the talk," what could she or he say? What should be said?

Michael Schudson has argued that the trope "conversation" has only so much salience to the conduct of democratic politics and communicative citizenship. To borrow his language, conversation is not the soul of democracy. I believe Schudson is wholly correct in pressing that argument. However, conversation is a powerful and leveling mode of communication in democratic settings: Conversations allow citizens to bridge vistas of democratic life and to articulate the communicative spaces that exist in between rhetorical interchanges and among mediated interactions. So, at some point, examinations of the communicative dimension of democracy must include detailed analyses of the place and significance of conversation, particularly with respect to the ways that conversations can animate the gaps between citizens and the press in the push for a reinvigorated democracy.

This chapter originates from an intersection of media ethics, rhetorical theory, and contemporary political philosophy. My purpose is to sketch a theory on ethical newspaper readership that begins to answer questions like those posed above; it is intended to: (a) complement recent civic-minded theories of media ethics, (b) serve as a possible heuristic for reader action. In the following pages, I examine and analyse ways that newspaper readers, living in democratic communities, can do their part to help foster the continued existence of their democratic system. The first section is a critical exegesis of the public journalism project. In it, I contend that although several dominant theoretical statements on civic journalism hint at reader activity, responsible readership ultimately is conceptualized too narrowly.

The second section then explicates ways in which readership can be joined with concepts of active, ethical citizenship. Drawing from recent work in liberal political philosophy, I argue for a broader perspective on responsible readership, one founded on moral obligations of citizenship. I propose a standpoint from which a person could ethically read, interpret, and use the news for the betterment of her or his community. This chapter concludes with a focused discussion on implications of the citizen-reader construct for the practice of readership and for normative press theory.

THE ROLE OF THE NEWSPAPER READER IN CONTEMPORARY MEDIA ETHICS

In his germinal article, "Making Journalism More Public", Jay Rosen asserted that the practice of print journalism becomes public when newspapers become "more supportive of a realm of meaningful public discussion," rather than remaining elite information sources that limit the range, depth, and diversity of voices that could contribute to the perpetuation of a democratic way of life. This founding definition has warranted the normative claim that the press in the U.S. should alter its practice in order to promote and sustain democratic ideals among the American public. In a review essay published 3 years later, Rosen pressed his argument further, stating that public news practices can occur only when journalists actively work to create communal knowledge, when news professionals take steps in their writing routines to ensure that "communities can 'know in common' what their" individual community "members cannot know alone". Rosen's focus on using the press to change the terrain of political life underwrites most civic journalism initiatives. In this respect, his assertion resonates with several key trends in polling and political science. In particular, Rosen's call is consonant with James Fishkin's arguments concerning the usefulness of "deliberative opinion polling" -- a strategy for stipulating and verifying collective perceptions of political values -- for sustained democratic engagement, and Daniel Yankelovich's call to help citizens formulate "strong public judgments" about what it means to live a valued, democratic life.

At newspapers in Charlotte, North Carolina; Columbus, Georgia; and Wichita, Kansas, then, as well as in several smaller "experiments" that have occurred across the United States, advocates of civic journalism have devised strategies for journalists to bear the burden of supporting democratic life and stimulating citizen interest in politics. For example, Rosen has illustrated ways for newspapers to convene and communicate with highly motivated registered voters so that those people can become well informed about legislative and executive political issues.

Davis "Buzz" Merritt also has suggested ways that practicing journalists can write news stories differently in order to encourage greater voter participation at election time. Arthur Charity's Doing Public Journalism is a guidebook for practicing journalists and journalism students to consult when they want their reporting to reflect the demographic diversity of the readership more accurately, thus producing more reader-friendly news articles.

Although each of these treatments pushes the boundaries of print journalism orthodoxy in important ways and challenges traditional conceptions of social responsibility theory, each omits explicit discussion of how readers can make substantive contributions to political life. This is not to say that one cannot, through close reading, discern who the ideal reader is for each writer. Rosen advances a relational version of public journalism, arguing that journalists should stress the interconnectedness of communal decision-making and people's daily lives. Columnists can do this in part by writing stories in softer narrative styles, but mostly by inviting people to gather at common places to discuss and share solutions to community problems.

His ideal reader is an active reader. She or he is well informed of events and issues, cares greatly about communal matters, and shares such tightly woven ties to other people in the given community that she or he is willing and able to sacrifice personal and family time, on a regular basis, to attend group meetings hosted by the local newspaper: She or he is "community connected". For Rosen then, the theory and practice of journalism must be reconfigured to stimulate such active readers further so that they can function to their fullest capacities, and outlets must be created to afford people the opportunity to participate in civic life.

Charity ideal reader is prima facie similar to the one postulated by Rosen. She or he actively discusses issues with other interested citizens on a regular basis, but she or he possesses a commitment to communal issues that runs deeper than relational connection.

Charity idealizes a reader who "would be eager to organize deliberative forums if only they could get a little training". It is for this reason that he provides a host of practical tips and accessible resources useful for one wishing to plan and facilitate a meeting among similarly engaged citizens. Such readers do more than act -- they initiate actions. Charity contends that news organizations must recognize this and take steps to write deeper, more textured columns. Also they must strive to facilitate more intellectually stimulating public forums because readers are better educated, more perceptive, and more discerning than ever before.

Whereas Rosen and Charity warrant their calls for civic journalism on relationally connected readers, Merritt renders a prescription for civic journalism on grounds internal to his career as a practicing journalist and as an editor. Merritt suggests that news story formats should be altered in order to more clearly demonstrate the relevance of news events to the lives of readers: Current journalism must become consistently "good journalism," which is journalism that "reengages people" to politics. Such a change is necessary because traditional, objective-style journalism doesn't convey as much social-political thrust as well-written feature columns that take explicit "steps" to facilitate reader political action.

Beyond these prescriptions, Merritt seems to pin his hope for democratic renewal on readers willing, when convenient, to speak with acquaintances or to write the editor about how the press can help people make better sense of the world. For all intents, though, Merritt never really needs an ideal reader. He supports his calls to action with his personal reasons for converting from the malaise of "straight" journalism to engaged, civic journalism. That readers benefit from his journalistic rebirth is a very welcome, though ancillary consequence of that change.

Whereas each contribution -- that by Rosen, by Charity, and by Merritt -- goes a long way toward a concrete rethinking of the press's function in democratic society, each theorist conceptualizes the ideal reader too stringently, if one is considered at all. Merritt's treatment is the least tenable because he minimizes any explicit consideration of readership: It seems as though he maintains the position that civic journalism will be practiced regardless of reader involvement or interest because it is the right thing for civic-minded journalists to do.

What remains then are Rosen and Charity's prototypical readers. The idea of a community-connected reader explicated in more or less theoretical terms is appealing because that person possesses the virtue of seeking to meld collective goals and personal agendas. Moreover, because people possess and maintain profound differences in value, or what John Rawls calls differences in "comprehensive views of the world," Rosen's community-connected reader seems especially attuned to bridging such gaps.

Rosen's construct has one significant drawback, though: She or he seems to exist only insofar as the press commands her or his presence and interaction at public meetings. If there is no pressing community dilemma reported in the newspaper, no town hall meeting called by the newspaper, Rosen's ideal reader does not appear to have any genuine motivation to cultivate and tend the communal bonds that he describes.

The implied argument is this: If there is no pressing issue, then politics must be going okay, so why come together in the first place? If Rosen's reader is deficient in this manner, Charity's reader can be seen to overcorrect the fault.

In addition to possessing the virtue of inquiring into the intersection of personal and collective goals, Charity's reader stimulates inquiry on the part of others. As I shall argue at length in the discussion section below, however, few people actually can transcend their complex lived conditions to initiate action, much less do it on a regular basis.

Furthermore, citizen-readers must be articulate in identifying the points of inequality that exist and often drive community problems. Community-connected citizen-readers must be able to maintain their connections and continue to interact even though the tenor of discourse is conflict laden, and there is every reason to want to sever one's ties .

In the next section I substantiate Rosen and Charity's notion of an interactive reader on two separate levels -- that of action and that of warrant for action. I connect ethical principles associated with democratic citizenship to an ethics of reading in order to explicate the citizenreader.

The reading standpoint that I suggest is an interactive citizen who, like the readers elucidated by Rosen and Charity, finds particular ways to contribute to her or his community's omnilogue on living well. However, such a reader fundamentally must be fashioned independent of any actual civic journalism initiative.

The normative thrust of civic journalism must be kept fully in sight, though. It is crucial to step away from the work of Rosen, Charity, and Merritt, and others for a time because, for as admirable and necessary as the goals of civic journalism are, civic journalism still is in "project" phase.

Relatively few newspapers practice civic journalism as routine, except for a small number who have routinized civic journalism-inspired norms in reporting local news. So, although civic-minded journalists, editors, and publishers continue to work at reformulating journalistic practice with some citizen groups at pilot sites, other citizens must use the news ethically and democratically, on their own initiative, where civic journalism projects and routines do not yet exist.

Ethics, Authority, and Activity of the Citizen-Reader

What should the readers and users of the news be expected to contribute to the enterprise of easing democracy's discontent? One strong and obvious response is vigorous action with an eye toward supporting collective rule. This response begs the question of how readers should act, however, and on what authority can they rest their claim to act as individuals for the sake of communal betterment.

If newspaper readers are to bear any responsibility for using the news to improve democratic life -- independent of the work done by civic journalism proponents, either in theory or in journalistic practice -- then that responsibility most plausibly should stem from the ethical dimension of active democratic citizenship.

Although the literature on civic journalism implies that readers are competent and ethical agents capable of making substantive contributions to the lives of others in democratic society -- and I would argue that civic theories of the press actually depend on such a presumption even though it often is unstated -- this point is crucial to the concept of the citizen-reader.

In many ways, the citizen-reader construct that I postulate could be read as the silent partner of civic journalist advocates who have written to date. However, I believe it is unwise to continue encouraging silence on the part of the reader, as the power imbalance inherent in such a communicative relationship subverts the whole notion of civic journalism.

An explicit discussion of reader activity and reader contributions cannot remain suppressed for long without detrimental effects to civic journalism and to the practice of democratic citizenship in mediated society. The silent partner, as it were, must be brought to full-partner status; the citizen-reader construct explicated in the remaining space is one step toward that goal.

ETHICS OF DEMOCRATIC CITIZENSHIP

Democratic citizenship consists of a wide range of constructive behaviours that one engages in while interacting with others under the rules of the same political system, on a daily basis, regardless of whether each person shares the same birth nationality or membership in the same partisan political party. More than voting and holding office or being a member of a civic association, citizenship entails a fundamental decency and respect that is enacted toward others in daily interactions.

Two basic obligations underlie minimal citizen action:

1. One's willful recognition that she or he is a member of a greater social-political entity -- e.g., a community or a nationstate -- the existence of which depends on the constructive melding of individual interests
2. Some measure of subordinating personal or group interests in order to perpetuate the existence of the larger organization of people, both in thought and action.

Both obligations stem from what John Rawls identifies as the "duty of civility," whereby people are obliged in any political society, and in a democracy especially, not to "exploit" others or social-political "loopholes" for unfair personal advantage. In his Political Liberalism, Rawls refined his discussion of the duty of civility to include a person's "willingness to listen to others and a fairmindedness in deciding when accommodations" to one's worldview "should reasonably be made".

These obligations are considered ethical insofar as they ask a person, regardless of her or his social-political standing, to widen her or his perspective on social and political happenings and to commit herself or himself to the betterment of others, in addition to self-betterment. Furthermore, these obligations ask that one respect and promote other people's interests and human development, even though such support may mean sacrificing the pursuit and attainment of one's own concerns, at least for a time. This is particularly important when conflict is manifest and the inequalities and perceived injustices that underwrite a community problem are under debate. To move from being simply a newspaper reader interested in public affairs to being a citizen-reader, the concept of readership must be coupled with the duty of civility. A discussion of the constructive intersections between readership and citizenship comprises the remainder of this section.

THE POWER OF THE PRESS AND THE CITIZEN-READER

Newspapers recount happenings in the immediate past, outline political agendas for the future, advance the level of social thought in a community, and give readers insight into the experiences of others. All this is to say that newspapers carry and convey communicative power. As such, "news" is more than simply the communication of "facts" as they are observed and recorded by human reporters in situ.

The news is a mode of discourse imbued with ideological and epistemological power that variously is considered -- at least among many nonjournalists -- to consist of the whole, factual, objective truth of an event and -- often among journalists and some nonjournalists -- to be a more-or-less neutral method of recording observations.

A newspaper's power rests in its ability to admit or refuse voices into the realm of publicity. Broadly understood, publicity is the intersubjective social-political sphere where people, ideas, and actions are appraised, granted legitimacy and reproduced, or pushed aside as being unacceptable. Newspapers also have the potential power to help citizens articulate their interests by providing them with necessary context for understanding political issues and by making connections among issues clearer.

By the very fact that reporters, columnists, and editors engage in purposive, rhetorical communication -- selecting which topics and stories to cover, at what time, expressed in what style, at what intellectual level, and placed in what location in the newspaper -- newspapers possess the power to fire people's imaginations and structure readers' thinking about and responses to social and political issues. Newspapers enact communicative power each time a story is written, edited, and published. More subtly, every time a news story is read, the press's communicative power is shared with readers. It is here that the ethical space occupied by newspaper readers can be found. If the press's power is the power of stimulation, then the reader assumes an ethical load when she or he reads and processes a newspaper's purposive communication, thereby opening herself or himself to the press's power. Readers gain knowledge from newspapers, as well as the opportunity to examine and judge events, people, and ideas to which they are not regularly or directly exposed. Moreover, readers learn vicariously from the interactions of others who are removed spatially and temporally from them and then filter these distanced interactions through their experiential and ideological screens.

Richard Means has argued that as humans, by nature and without regard to context of action, we make value judgments in our daily interactions. Newspaper reading certainly is no exception to his precept of inevitable evaluation. Snippets of the events that comprise human existence are represented in print and through photographs and tendered for a reader's review and judgment. Readers' evaluations may take the form of statements like "that is a good story" or "this is a terrible feature," as well as going further to include specific appraisals of the topic covered, estimations of people's roles in the news story and judgments of the choices people made in order to precipitate the event covered in the article. Without ever being there to see what the lives of other people are actually like for oneself, the newspaper reader has the opportunity to place or withhold value on the actions of others whom she or he will very likely never meet, talk to, or ever read about again.

TEXTUAL EVALUATION AND THE AUTHORITY OF THE CITIZEN-READER

Talk of readers making value judgments and being responsible for acting on them in constructive ways necessitates a brief discussion of readers' interpretations of the newspaper text. Theoretical work on the relationship between readers and texts has undergone a good deal of revision in recent years.

Although much has been written in cognitive psychology on the acts of reading, I confine my remarks to the debates that have emerged in literary studies. Two primary schools of thought concerning textual interpretation are germane to the present discussion. First, there are those who would argue that texts "open" themselves to interpretation and readers, living inherently evaluative lives, take advantage of those interpretative opportunities whenever and wherever the text makes them available.

Advocates in this camp focus on the fractured, polysemous character of the text. As Northrop Frye wrote in his Anatomy of Criticism, calling a text "polysemous" is to say that there are "manifold meanings" embedded in the text. The denotative meaning of a text refers to the legitimated, dictionary definition ascribed to any individual sentence, portion of the text, or to the text as a whole.

There are also the connotative meanings in a text, which refer to the idiomatic or subjective meanings locatable in a text. Connotative meanings can arise from the author's use of literary devices such as allegory, irony, metaphor or any other literary license that allows the factual statements of a text to be deciphered as having alternative meanings.

As one reads, one notices textual "seams" and applies her or his critical faculties to determining how those accessible spots in the text can be put to use. When focusing on the polysemous character of the text, readers may interpret and assign value to any given text differently. The 'Variances in interpretation and evaluation occur, however, because the text's structure allows for this kind of response. Differences in readers' reactions are not simply expected, they are predictable?

In the second school of thought, others write about textual interpretation from the opposite viewpoint, arguing that human readers are keen and discerning creatures who approach texts for their own special reasons and take what they want from the text, regardless of what openings do or do not exist in the text. Proponents from this second camp stress the active, polyvalent nature of reading. Whereas the term polysemous refers to the interpretability of texts, polyvalence describes the activity of interpretation, or "the fact that audiences routinely evaluate texts differently, assigning different value to different portions of a text and hence to the text itself".

The refocus on reader agency has assumed many guises in academe. Some critics, such as Freund.have advocated theories of reader-response criticism. Others, including Stanley Fish and Janice Radway , have argued for the ubiquity and legitimacy of "interpretative communities." In a similar vein, Umberto Eco has explored the semiotic "limits" of a person's ability to interpret texts .

Overall, each of these critics has shown that interpretation and evaluation take place at the discretion of the reader. No seam is needed for the ascription of meaning, and no access point is required for the assignation of value to a text. The reader's intrinsic agency is authority enough for interpretative acts to occur.Each line of thought that contributes to the polysemous-or-polyvalent question has its own virtues, and each camp has much to add to one's understanding of the reading enterprise, whether it be the reading of literature or the newspaper.

To phrase the question in terms of a bifurcation, though, as done above for didactic purposes, is to confuse the issue of interpretation unnecessarily in the debate over constructive versus deconstructive approaches to textual criticism. To be blunt: Texts do have openings that lend themselves to certain degrees of interpretation, and readers do possess significant levels of subjectivity and autonomy that allow them to overcome the structural openings of texts or to use them to their advantage.

Such recognition takes on added significance when one considers the activity of newspaper reading in a democratic society. Making this move turns the question from "how do readers act?" when reading the newspaper toward "how should the reader act?" An answer to this latter question follows.

CODUCTION: THE INTERACTIVE CITIZEN-READER

Reading does not occur in a vacuum. The act of reading is -- and readers are -- situated. The populated communities to which the reader belongs and the intersubjectively shared values that constitute the reader's worldview make their impressions on the reader and guide her or his action accordingly. This point is especially relevant to newspaper reading in a democratic society.

Historically, news readers have used newspapers actively to support procommunity initiatives. Neighborhoods have become more cohesive and members of large, loosely affiliated, sharedvalue communities have become closer, due in part to communication initiated among and propagated by community members about stories in the newspaper. In recent years, this tendency toward procommunity action has been interpreted as being the "conversational" dimension of journalism. Rob Anderson, Robert Dardenne, and George Killenberg provide one of the most compelling treatments of this idea in The Conversation of Journalism, illustrating how the press's approach to "doing the news" must change if the level of public conversation about news stories and issues of civic importance is going to rise. They postulate three levels at which the institution of journalism must be conversationally reconfigured. *Journalists must* :

- "Promote conversation among people about their own common involvement in public affairs,"
- Enact better "interpersonal conversation" skills when interacting with citizens and readers,
- Become "involved" as an "institutional conversation" partner with individuals.

They take it as a given that people talk about the news; I have presumed the same point throughout this chapter. However, talking about the news and engaging news stories fully and ethically with others are not necessarily synonymous activities. Ethically grappling with a story involves the practical interplay of several human processes. When one reads someone else's purposive communication, one filters the ideas seen in print through one's own fund of experiences and then extends this processed information into her or his daily life and interactions with others. These processes are practical insofar as the information that has been obtained is used to facilitate one's life and to foster good relationships with others. Wayne Booth calls this process coduction -- the ethical dimension of reading.

In The Company We Keep: An Ethics of Fiction, Booth defines coduction as "how we come to the act of judging" a text ethically. When one reads a text, one first sifts the content and apparent intent of the text through her or his experiences and presuppositions. These experiences may be derived from direct participation in events, from vicarious experiences, or even from the social knowledge that a person gains simply from being a member of a particular community.

If one were to halt the reading experience at this point, the evaluation made about the text would be "deductive," asserts Booth, as the ideas about other people contained in the text are scrutinized only against "the backdrop of [one's] long personal history of untraceably complex experiences of other stories and persons". As a one-dimensional behaviour, deductive reading neither penetrates deeply nor ranges broadly, except as allowed by one's life experiences.

One's personal reaction to the writer, topic, characters, subjects, themes, or quality of the text -- for example, enmity or revulsion, affection or uncritical acceptance -- could run untempered and inhibit one's ability to form a considered judgment concerning what has been read and how that reading might be used to promote ethical civic life. Booth therefore advocates taking an additional step, a move necessary if reading is going to have an ethical dimension: He calls for readers to share their deductive responses to a text in conversation with others. This is when coduction occurs. The coductive reader does more than merely share her or his personal reaction to the ideas communicated in a text, or simply respond to the qualities of the text itself. Coductive readers seek to substantiate the process used in coming to a judgment of a text, asking, in essence, "am I testing my reactions adequately?" and "in my reading and sharing, am I taking others' perceptions into account appropriately and sensitively?" Of the coductive process, Booth writes, "the term . . . implies a communal enterprise rather than a private, 'personal' calculation logically coercive on all who hear it". He continues:

the neologism coduction, derives from co ("together") and ducere ("to lead, draw out, bring, bring out"). Coduction will be what we do whenever we say to the world: "Of the works of this general kind that I have experienced, comparing my experience with other more or less qualified observers, this one seems to me among the better (or weaker) ones, the best (or worst). Here are my reasons." Every such statement implicitly calls for continuing conversation: "How does my coduction compare with yours?"

Although he never had an activity so routine as news reading in mind when he propounded his theory on ethical reading, several lessons can be gleaned from Booth's argument. First, when cast in light of the general desire for political renewal and civic journalism's call for greater involvement in democratic life, the idea of coduction is vital. News stories on political issues, candidates, and legislative and community agendas would be fodder for active use by citizen-readers in their daily interactions with others.

In concrete ways, reading citizens could use the news as a way to broach conversations about the process and product of political life. Second, such ethical conversations stemming from newspaper content would be scrutinized by readers situated on an equal plane -- on the level of citizenship. I return to this point in the discussion and conclusions sections below. Third, coducing the news would occur during more than official times of political choice. People are not immune to the ethical obligations of citizenship during nonelection years, so citizen-readers ought to be available, at all times, to interpret and evaluate as many stories in the newspaper as possible, not just those about partisan politics and not just when it is convenient. Using the News Coductively: Topoi for Citizen-Reader Interactions. At this point I draw together my arguments by addressing how one's civic obligation to the continued existence of her or his larger political community and one's subordination of her or his personal agendas can find expression in specific topoi for ethical interaction.

I extend my claim that ethical engagement of the news occurs through conversation by examining specific points at which one could engage the news with others. Posed as general questions for readers to consider, the following points are neither a set of rigid guidelines to be followed dogmatically when attempting to use the news interactively, nor a cheat sheet for amateur textual criticism.

They are starting points for possible conversations-intellectual places a citizen-reader could look, while reading the newspaper, to render considered judgments about supporting collective life and the good lives of others in democratic society. These topoi are important to consider if readers are going to actualize the expressed and implicit purpose of civic journalism.Following from his exposition of coduction, Booth contends that the person wanting to render an ethical reading of a text should address five fundamental questions if she or he is going to make any substantive contribution to her or his community.

Although all five of Booth's queries concerning the reading of fiction fit the context of reading print journalism, I abstract only three here:

- What is the reader's responsibility to her or his own self?
- What is the reader's responsibility to other flesh-and-blood readers?
- What is the reader's responsibility to society, beyond the honest expression of critical judgment?

In pursuing answers these questions, the citizen-reader would critically engage the story, discern potential meanings embedded in the text and consider different ways of interpreting the story in order to broach conversations with the spectrum of peoples one might encounter. The citizen-reader would, in other words, attend both to the polysemic and polyvalent aspects of reading. These topoi exemplify ethical obligations of democratic citizenship because they ask the newspaper reader to expand her or his worldview, temporarily subordinate personal interests for the sake of others, and look for ways to discuss and bring about the continuation of the larger social-political entity.

READER'S RESPONSIBILITY TO SELF

Looking at oneself before appraising other considerations or the implication a news story has for other citizens is a useful starting point for making ethical judgments about a text's content. From a self-directed stance, a citizen-reader can discern the immediate and potential relevance of the text, first, for her or his own life and then for the lives of others.

This position involves something deeper than self-preservation, though. Looking inward and seeking to protect oneself indicates something fundamental about democratic citizenship: Self-examination begins to indicate some of the boundaries of harm or benefit that could come to other citizens. In the spirit of Walt Whitman's epigram, this first stance asks the reading citizen to see herself or himself as a microcosm of the democratic whole.

READER'S RESPONSIBILITY TO OTHER READERS

Attempting to determine the salience of a news story to oneself certainly is an expedient task. It also is necessary if a community is going to retain its population of citizens. This second point of view serves to foster a "culture" of interactive responsibility in which people use their personal faculties to safeguard and perpetuate the well-being of others. It is incumbent on citizen-readers at this point to shift their self-directed actions into other-oriented sentiments. In line with the very definition of coduction, citizen-readers would ethically check their responses to the hypothetical questions posed above against the responses of others. In the process, they would seek confirmation about their interpretation of the news from other readers. Inasmuch as reading is taking place in a democracy, coductive citizen-readers would be obliged to act with similar regard to the life-interests of nonreaders as well. In addition to the actual protection of one's community, the citizen-reader might use the content of a given story to initiate conversations about the democratic process of communal life. She or he would engage others in an effort to highlight paradigms or breaches of democratic protocol, and then formulate some method of reasserting citizen control over public interest deliberations.

READER'S RESPONSIBILITY TO SOCIETY

Coducing the relevance and meaning of news stories also has implications for the local level of democratic life. Of all the details in the world, the only one about which a citizen-reader could be certain is that her or his interactions had a material effect in her or his community. This could be perceived and verified in the process or product of communal political rule. It is important to note that any knowledge a citizen-reader might gain from her or his interactions with a text and with other citizens would be highly particular. What works well in one town or one city's version of democratic decision-making may not be appropriate for another town or city. It may be even less applicable at a broader level, such as that of a nation-state, like the United States.

This is not to say that there is no possibility for the broad canvas of American-style democracy to be influenced, however. Civic renewal has more to do with the way citizens act collectively than it does with the finalized conclusions citizens draw individually, or even the way social and economic institutions reconfigure themselves in order to ensure their own preservation. It therefore is necessary to recognize that the precise conditions reported in any given news story might not occur anywhere else in the United States. One should also keep in mind that the composition of appointed leaders and bureaucratic workers might not have a parallel anywhere else either. There will probably never be a substantive change in American democracy such that the people rule the nation like the residents in a small town. However, through social intercourse and the existence of mediating groups in a democratic community, such as social, political, and professional associations, ideas are shared, can grow, and can gain a relatively wide consideration. It is the idea of coduction for the sake of collective betterment and the plausibility of imminent citizen-reader interaction that is crucial.

Booth observed of fiction reading in academic circles that "one critic's tentatively embraced norms will strike another critic as dangerous ideology; my self-evident standards may seem to you mere dogma". In a like manner, any reading, interpretation, and evaluation of a given news text will be partial. More likely than not, furthermore, any single deduction of a given text will differ substantially from others. In coduction with me, for instance, you might think I am too liberal philosophically and politically, and perhaps too laissez-faire economically. I would hope that you tell me. If I were a glib citizen-reader, I might say in response, "Fine, let's have a talk about your reactions." A more judicious response would be, "I'm not surprised that you disagree with me.

Which portion of my reading do you find misguided?" Through our interaction, perhaps I will learn that you approach the story from a narrative stance, that you are concerned with the sense of drama, or irony, or tragedy communicated by the writer. Perhaps I will learn that you wish the writer employed the word "we" and took ownership of the ideas communicated in the story rather than hiding behind the veil of objective-style writing.

Furthermore, perhaps our coductive interaction will lead you to think that my reading is unoriginal or so structured by the conventions of journalism that I miss the broader significance of the text. As such, you might therefore ask me to extend myself and to try to read the story from your point of view. The content of our interaction and the persona from which either you or I speak notwithstanding, notice that I have advocated that each citizen-reader should accept the burden of rejoinder. Rejoinder sets in motion the process of coduction. The interactions that would follow would be intended to draw reading citizens together as members of the same democratic community, rather than divide them. Coductive interactions thus have the potential, not only to substantiate the manifest and latent content of news stories and writing conventions, but also to give substance to the duty of civility.

Whether it is with other readers knowledgeable of the news content, nonreaders temporarily uninformed of the news, or even with nonreaders, the citizen-reader has the opportunity to question and help advance the interpretation and use of collective reason and rule that is endemic to democratic life. Following Rawls, elaboration of the public omnilogue̒, coduction would be a concrete step toward reaching the fundamental "point of view of civil society . . . There are no experts" when it comes to actually making democracy work and work well: Ultimately, "a philosopher has no more authority than other citizens," and at that ultimate moment, media theorists have no more authority than others either.

Philosophers, theorists, and critics of the media ought only guide debate and interaction, not settle it. I close by addressing, first, the implications the citizen-reader construct has for readership generally and, second, the implications it has for normative theories of the press. At some point, the concept of the citizenreader must pass theoretical muster concerning its heuristic value. Whereas only time and the revised practices of coduction will tell whether there is any utility to this concept, several arguments can be made in support of its practical use. At this point, two assertions stand out for immediate discussion.

First, following Rawls observation noted in the discussion above, no "expert" clause has been built into the schema. To borrow a phrase from Clifford Christians, "it is only cheap moralism to demand obligation unfairly" of the public, such as requiring people to strive for an ethical standard that can never be reached in practice. I have therefore tried at all turns to be "fair" in my prescription of active citizen-readership.

Although my main argument is ideal, however, it is neither unreachable nor unreasonable: One's commitment to democratic society and one's temporary suspension of differences with others is the challenge required of those who would seriously consider becoming a citizen-reader, not an unfair requirement of citizenship.

The epigram by Walt Whitman speaks clearly to this point. Well over a century ago, Whitman rightly pointed out that living well democratically requires a certain degree of reciprocity among citizens. That state of being is measured not only in terms of equality of interaction and equivalent expectations of others, but also in terms of one's equality of expectations for others. Following Whitman's poetic advice, not only does the democratic citizen expect others to give the democratic signs of civility so that she or he can live well, but the democratic citizen must demand other citizens be afforded commensurate consideration. This type of "enlarged thought" likely may be difficult for citizens to engage in, but it is necessary nevertheless.

Second, there has been no minimum standard of living presupposed for citizen-readers. Many suggestions for community revitalization bearing the name civic journalism ask for significant commitments of time on the part of "the citizen." Only those with more than modest amounts of leisure, though, can participate in public meetings, forums, or salons. Furthermore, there is no one-to-one correspondence between nonattendance at a meeting and a lack of commitment to democratic renewal. The citizen-reader construct thus has been built upon a foundation of broad duties first and plausible, particular activities second.

Although some might want it to be otherwise, no arena in which coduction should take place has been specified -- it can occur during breaks from the assembly line just as easily as trips to the mall. Furthermore, no time frame for how long coductions should last has been stipulated, and no goal for coduction other than the constructive advancement of collective life has been identified. By focusing on an everyday activity like conversation, I have attempted to distance this theory on readership from privilege wherever possible: It is possible for nonreaders to engage in coduction; it also is possible for people who are destitute and who cannot afford to buy newspapers but who read them secondhand to engage in coduction.

I do not mean to imply that this is secondhand coduction or even "second class citizenship." For many, picking up the newspaper that someone else has bought and discarded is the only way that they can gain access to the news; such actions ought not be denigrated. Furthermore, insofar as my sketch of ethical readership draws its thrust from duties of democratic citizenship, the formal behavioral manifestations of citizenship -- voting and ritualistic community membership activities -- have been bracketed-off in favour of individual dispositions toward the continued existence of democratic initiatives in one's community and individually defined and executed interactions.

In addition to these general arguments in support of the practicability of citizen-readership, two more points concerning the relation of citizen-readership to normative press theory stand for consideration. Both regard the philosophical underpinning of civic journalism.

First, citizens and readers living in democratic communities do far more than watch debates, learn about issues and candidates, vote, and worry about the formality of partisan politics. That is to say, people's lives intersect with politics during times other than those marked by significant electoral decisions. Normative theories of the press purporting to revamp political life must account for this situation. The communities that host newspapers are complex places, and the people who live in those communities live complex lives. Their customs and habits are unique, as are people's daily concerns.

The events that comprise their collective existence, while being similar to the events of people in other places, ultimately are common only to the people who engage in them. As a theory, citizen-readership is rendered in an attempt to account for some of the complexity of democratic life in a relatively simple set of human capacities. Represented in the citizen-reader are people's capacity for purposive interaction and the capacity to willfully subordinate their interests, at some time or another, for a common good. It is toward these general capabilities that normative press theorists should direct their work.

Those who write in support of "community" in many ways collapse the interests and abilities of the people that comprise the community into a single, seemingly univocal push for civic revitalization. In the process, distinct interests and individual needs often are not fully considered. Although it is indeed important to find ways to use the press to bolster the mechanisms of democratic life, the abilities of the individuals who operate those mechanisms require attention.

Second, on a related point, insofar as it is crucial for theorists to suggest ways to revitalize "public spheres," it must be noted that there are multiple layers of discourse that keep such a "place" viable. Not only do the news media, local patricians, and the politically powerful contribute to and maintain the level of public communication through press releases and speeches, but individuals interacting in less formal settings -- in doughnut shops, around dinner tables, at hair-styling salons, at work, at the bus stop, in line at the post office, and so on-contribute to the viability of the public sphere as well. In part, such an observation derives from a shift in political philosophy.

Many writers on civic journalism look to communitarian philosophy generally, and Habermas's civic-republican contribution to the liberalcommunitarian debate specifically, to provide warrant and backing for their claims. Further, although that vein of political philosophy does provide a useful guide for revitalizing discourse in the public sphere, it tends to do so at the expense of the individual and her or his possible contribution to the public good.

The good of the whole, as it were, is prized to the minimization of the good for individuals in public spheres. John Rawls's liberal philosophy, from which I have drawn several ideas in this essay, provides an important and clear indication of who populates the public sphere, who is addressed by journalistic communication, and who literally would benefit from normative press reform.

It is vital to keep in mind that individuals living complex lives -- lives that are too filled with family and business obligations to regularly attend civic functions, if they are attended at all -- compose the public sphere. These people often hold the status of citizen, as well. Such people interact at work, at home, during recreation, and in other nonpublic social settings, and often the topic of interaction is politics and the news. Sometimes, though, citizens do belong to some association that concerns itself with the discussion of and deliberation about civic matters. If a partnership in civic renewal is going to take place, it needs to be formed with individuals who act for the public good in concrete ways, in the ways that they can, regardless of how formal or informal, public or nonpublic their interactions happen to be.

Across the board, advocates of civic journalism are correct to suggest that the press be used to revitalize public life. In part, that means the press should reaffirm and act in support of the political mechanisms of democratic life. Journalism practitioners can do only so much, however, and academicians can make theoretical inroads only so far without a forthright consideration of how readers and citizens can become fully articulate partners in that revitalization effort. Theorizing the flip side of civic journalism means taking fundamental citizenship capacities of individuals seriously. Bridging the ethical dimensions of democratic citizenship with newspaper readership is one constructive step toward a joint effort of political renewal.

On 20 June 1949, the noted columnist Walter Lippmann visited Des Moines, Iowa, to help the Register and Tribune commemorate its centennial anniversary. Speaking to an audience of 400 of the state's editors and publishers, Lippmann praised American newspapers as bastions of freedom in the current Cold War. The strength of the country's press system, he said, was its local ownership: "American newspapers, large and small, and without exception, belong to a town, a city, at the most to a region." Decentralized ownership and management had made the nation's newspapers accountable not to parties or the government but to the communities "where they are written, where they are edited, and where they are read." Economically and socially rooted in their local communities, American newspapers had protected democracy against baleful, distant influences.

Lippmann's speech invoked one of professional journalism's deepest mythologies-the belief that newspapers are most true, pure, real, and authentic when they honour their responsibility to "the local." Curiously, he himself had not always subscribed to that myth. Indeed, his 1922 book Public Opinion had mercilessly critiqued Americans' faith in local knowledge. A younger Lippmann had complained that "the democratic tradition is . . . always trying to see a world where people are exclusively concerned with affairs of which the causes and effects all operate within the region they inhabit." He thought that newspapers' fixation on the local limited their value.

Citizens needed to understand distant, complex events, but the quest for circulation encouraged local items in which "enough people see their own names in the paper often enough, can read about their weddings, funerals, sociables, foreign travels, lodge meetings, school prizes, their fiftieth birthdays, their sixtieth birthdays, their silver weddings, their outings, and clambakes."

Juxtaposed, these two sets of comments suggest something of Lippmann's own mythic transformation. Books like Drift and Mastery and Public Opinion had won him notice. His editorials for the New York World in the 1920s established his clout. By the 1930s, he had made himself into a new type of journalist-the well-educated, cosmopolitan public intellectual.

Not everyone admired this new professional type, of course. Journalists committed to an older tradition of partisan crusading sometimes complained about Lippmann's effete, metaphysical style. Nonetheless, by the 1950s he was widely considered the dean of his profession. He earned that reputation not for his praise of the local, or for his defence of the virtues of community journalism, or for his service to his hometown, but for his devotion to the arts of influence. By mid-- century Lippmann had become the very model of the well-connected pundit, shuffling quietly through the corridors of power. Thus the significance of his 1949 comments. When a cosmopolitan cynic as well traveled as Lippmann praises "the local" in such fulsome terms, we should suspect that we are in the presence of myth.

We want to analyse that myth of "the local" as it informs American journalism's discourse about itself. At first glance, the local might seem a minor element in the profession's mythology. For example, the American Society of Newspaper Editors' 1922 Canons of Journalism and 1975 Statement of Principles both specify standards of independence, accuracy, impartiality, fairness, and decency, but neither mentions anything about journalists being accountable to their local communities. The Society of Professional Journalists' Code of Ethics, last revised in 1996, encourages journalists to "invite dialogue with the public over journalistic conduct," but does not specify that public as local. Indeed, the SPJ code cautions journalists to "remain free of associations and activities that may compromise integrity or damage credibility," an injunction that many journalists interpret as discouraging involvement in community organizations.

Scholars, for their part, have thoroughly studied other keywords that journalism uses to describe itself, most notably independence, objectivity, and public, but the local has escaped similar scrutiny. Yet, the evidence suggests that the myth of the local has been equally rich and potent. Like the terms independence and public, the local inscribes the contradictions of a commercial press in a democratic society.

Just as independence can refer to both economic wherewithal and editorial autonomy, and public to both consumers and citizens, so does the local refer both to the merchandising strategy that sustains a newspaper and the editorial philosophy that defines its mission. Recent circumstances such as media conglomeration, the emerging global economy, and changing forms of social consciousness have made references to the local more urgent, dense, and difficult. Our paper begins by identifying the myth of the local in the behaviour of news organizations and the discourse of American journalists.

By myth, we mean widely told stories that dramatize deeply held habits of mind, group beliefs, and styles of action. We focus mostly on the daily newspaper because its decline in status and popularity has inspired print journalists to embrace the myth of the local. After documenting the historical, economic, social, and political reasons that this myth figures so prominently in the discourse of contemporary American journalism, we argue that journalism's insistent invocation of the local masks the collapse of the social worlds that this term purports to describe.

We conclude by suggesting that journalism's myth of the local persists because it speaks to genuine and intractable dilemmas of the profession. Talk of the local should be understood as poignant rather than false, misguided, or naive. The local, as myth, articulates the experience of newspaper journalists-their increasing subservience to media conglomerates, their diminished cultural authority, their yearning to connect with actual rather than merely theoretical readers, their collective sadness that a profession that they love seemingly matters so little to their fellow citizens. In a sense, praising the local has become American journalism's way of whistling in the dark.

The United States is not the only country with a tradition of the local. Rod Pilling has described English journalists' romantic fondness for the "parish pump" papers of the countryside (the rough equivalent of small-town weeklies in the United States). Pilling argues that "a belief in the efficacy of the local is an enduring faith of [English] journalists." In both countries, the myth of the local sentimentally recalls the comfy immediacy of the village. In the United States, however, that myth also celebrates the role newspapers have played in the founding and development (not merely the remembrance) of American towns and cities. Long before printers made themselves firebrands of the Revolution, they were solid citizens serving the needs of their seaport towns, supplying the local government with legal forms, the business community with trade notices, and the citizenry with miscellaneous information.

Their turn to local news-to "the worldly concerns that were common to shops and counting houses, taverns and clubs, wharves and garrisons, legislative halls and council chambers"-helped create an American sense of identity. In the nineteenth century, newspapers boosted the new towns of the West, in order to attract settlers and investors. Historian Daniel Boorstin has observed, "The pioneer newspaper of the upstart city, like the western railroad, had to call into being the very population it aimed to serve."

City life established the local as an important and popular news genre. New penny dailies in New York, Boston, Philadelphia, and Baltimore soon featured columns labeled "City Intelligence,""City Affairs," or "City Items." By the 1870s, small-town papers, facing new competition from country editions of city papers, countered with similar columns like "Local Matters,""Local Intelligence,""Town Talk," and "Home News." By the end of the nineteenth century, the urban daily had established itself as the very emblem of city life. In the twentieth century, the newspaper prospered from urban growth, as real estate development expanded the circulation area. Even today, as Phyllis Kaniss has argued in her study of local news, cities occupy centre stage in much news coverage, despite the larger economic and political role played by suburbs. The death of an urban daily can still powerfully signify loss of a city's identity and heritage.

For two centuries, the newspaper had helped create and sustain Americans' sense of local community. After World War II, however, economic and demographic forces would transform the social landscape. Marketers began to notice dramatic changes in how consumers imagined themselves. By the 1980s, Bogart would observe that the traditional definition of a market as "a place where people live and buy" no longer applied. With personal identity more fluid, location mattered less. Marketers looked instead for "a common state of mind, a common set of interests or a common position in the lifecycle." The implications for the newspaper were profound. Consider, for example, the consequences of the population shift from city to suburbs.

"Suburbanization radically transformed the structure of local retail markets," Kaniss writes, "and with it the demand by advertisers for target audiences." Loss of population, jobs, and retail sales created a more decentralized metropolis, as well as technological, economic, and social problems for urban dailies. It became nearly impossible to ship an up-to-date afternoon paper to suburban readers through rush-hour traffic. The migration of retail stores to the suburbs redefined the local advertising base and encouraged new competitors such as free shoppers and weeklies and dailies in satellite towns.

These demographic and economic shifts, in turn, challenged the newspaper's ability to imagine the city as a socially coherent place. What interests or commitments might suburban and city readers share? With dozens of municipalities but no overarching regional government, coordinated political deliberation proved nearly impossible. Nor have cities and suburbs discovered a common social identity to unite them; indeed, the move to the suburbs has often been fueled by social, especially racial, differences. In the absence of an effective political response, marketing solutions and corporate management filled the void. Long--established independent newspapers, vexed by financial difficulties and family strife, sold themselves to newspaper chains, which introduced newsroom efficiencies, emphasized marketing, and demanded new loyalties to the corporation. If MBAs have come to rule the newsroom, in Underwood's apt phrase, it is partly because elected officials, journalists, and citizens never found an adequate political response to the challenge of suburbanization.

Faced with lower household penetration rates and a declining share of the advertising market, newspapers have turned to marketing research over the last two decades. Professional and trade organizations such as the American

Newspaper Publishers Association, American Society of Newspaper Editors, Newspaper Advertising Bureau, and the Newspaper Association of America have sponsored reports analyzing the industry's readership problems. These reports have been widely interpreted as justifying the turn to local news. One of the first was the Newspaper Research Project, launched in 1977 by the ANPA, ASNE, and NAB.

The most influential outcome of that $4 million project was Ruth Clark's report "Changing Needs of Changing Readers." Clark recommended a now-familiar series of changes to make news more brief, upbeat, relevant, and well-organized. A series of similar reports followed-the 1987 ASNE report Love Us and Leave Us: New Subscribers One Year Later, the 1988 ASNE Future of Newspaper Committee report The Next Newspapers, the 1991 ASNE national readership study Keys to Our Survival, a 1996 NAA survey by Washington Post polling director Richard Morin, and in 1998 the ASNE report Leveraging Newspaper Assets and NAA report So Many Choices, So Little Time. Wisconsin State Journal editor Frank Denton argues that these studies have convincingly demonstrated that readers "want more, and more-local, local news." They want "information and help to live better, they want to know what is going on around them and they want to be part of a community."

Yet these survey results may be less decisive than Denton thinks. As we will discuss, neither the newspaper nor the reader exactly knows what makes a paper "local." And readers may not actually read the news they call for. Their responses may speak to their own myths of community. Nor have all marketing researchers agreed that adding local news would attract more readers. Bogart has argued that readers' expressed interest in local news mostly reflects their demographic traits. His data from 1961, for example, showed that the preference for local news was stronger among women, older citizens, and rural readers than among men, younger citizens, and urban readers. His later data showed an apparent increase in readers' preference for local news, but that difference largely disappeared when readers were asked to rate specific news items as "very interesting" or "very important." They rated national and international news as well as local items as interesting. Bogart concluded that the local/national/ international news distinction was somewhat "unrealistic and arbitrary." Indeed, the ASNE Readership Committee's report inadvertently demonstrates this very point. Denton concludes that readers are interested in ten dimensions of local news--proximity, safety, utility, government, education, spirituality, support, identity, recognition, and empowerment.

But these dimensions share no underlying conceptual structure or essence. "Local" comes to mean whatever content interests readers. It may denote position in space (proximity), but it can also reference citizenship, social status, religious belief, or economic situation. What is surely true is that journalists prefer local news because they write it themselves. As Bogart observes, journalists believe that "a good paper reflects the work and effort of its own staff and is produced for its own community with a minimum of canned or boilerplate material."

From journalists' perspective, a paper truly devoted to local news hires a dozen enterprising reporters. Their recent work experience has been quite opposite, of course. For more than a decade, closings, corporate takeovers, and staffing cutbacks have been the rule. Thus reporters' call for more local news probably implies a critique of corporate newspapering. Journalists understand readership research as a moral fable about how their profession might still redeem itself.

Geneva Overholser, for example, has argued that if newspapers are to survive, they must understand that their franchise is "local, local, local." She recommends that newspapers develop "a powerful local identity, a characteristic personality, deep roots in the community." For Overholser, as for many journalists today, the local has become the mantra of a lost profession.

Publishers invoke the local for different purposes. For them, local news responds to readers' preferences-news that readers can use. They employ readership research to point the language of community in the same direction as the economic imperatives of the marketplace. Thus, national chains like Gannett and Knight-Ridder proudly proclaim commitment to their local communities.

Gannett's much-promoted News 2000 programme, begun in 1991, aimed to encourage responsiveness to readers' tastes, closer ties to the community, and stronger local coverage. Knight-Ridder has been countering the negative publicity that accompanied the resignation of Jay Harris, publisher of the chain's San Jose Mercury News, by running an ad on the inside front cover of the Columbia Journalism Review that boasts that "we have more people covering more local news now than we ever did." Yet, the Harris controversy also illustrates the tensions between journalists and publishers' interpretations of the local.

In March 2001 Steve Rossi, president of Knight-Ridder's newspaper division, asked Harris, among other things, to look at research indicating that readers wanted more local news, and to consider cutting back on foreign news. Harris responded that the diversity of the San Jose community made foreign news a priority, and that Rossi's financial goals (increasing the 22-29 per cent profit margins of the 1990s) could be met only through layoffs. Harris refused and resigned in protest. Knight-Ridder's conception of local news prevailed.

The national journalism reviews have similarly celebrated the profession's faith in the redemptive powers of the local. They criticize mergers that undermine newsroom autonomy, arguing that a local owner knows the community better than an outside owner could. The American Journalism Review, in particular, has sponsored an ambitious series of long stories on "The State of the American Newspaper." Each article catalogues a representative set of woes. The June 1998 installment, for instance, mourned the declining number of independent dailies, which it called "an endangered species."

The article profiled six papers that remain independent-the Anniston Star, Eugene Register-Guard, Oklahoman, St. Petersburg Times, Palo Alto Daily News, and Pittsburgh Tribune-Review. Another installment documented the San Francisco Chronicle's efforts to make itself more competitive in a complex metropolitan market. Yet another told of the Spokane Spokesman-Review's introduction of a "Connections" page-an imaginative if difficult attempt to hook every international news story in the paper to a local news peg. For its part, the Columbia Journalism Review has critiqued the changes introduced by Gannett at the Des Moines Register and Louisville Courier-Journal-two papers with long and distinguished histories as family-owned newspapers. All these articles celebrate the virtues of local autonomy and community values.

The myth of the local also shows up in journalists' everyday talk about their occupation. Journalists tell stories for a living, an occupation that at first sounds rather dreamy and abstract. They make their work less so (and more socially important) by grounding their stories in ways that readers will take to be factual, immediate, commonsensical, and authentic. One of their most common strategies is to talk about journalism as a "shoe-leather" profession.

Though many journalists drive to work, begin the day by reading their competitors' and colleagues' stories, conduct much of their research on the phone and Internet, invest their pensions in global equity funds, and dream of the day when they can move to a more prestigious paper in a larger market, they insist that one can only know life directly, on the street. "Newspapers knew more about what was going on when old-line beat reporters and politically conscious editors were more prevalent," complains Reese Cleghorn.

"If you hoofed it out there, you learned who did know what was going on." Television news has developed an iconography of the local that literally puts journalists on the street. Satellite up-links allow reporters to broadcast live and on location. Even studio shots typically feature background photographs of the local skyline or montages of identifiably local monuments. Stories told on location are not better or more accurate than stories told in the studio; they are often more hurried and incomplete. Yet news producers believe that local images help establish the authority of the news report for viewers. Journalists often stress the importance of being personally connected to their communities. Overholser argues there is no substitute for journalists' living in the communities on which they report: "No amount of planning, no level of market research, can make up for ten years of living in a town-not to mention growing up there, putting your kids through school there, watching your folks grow old there." Newspapers ought to be written, she says, "by people who feel the city's pulse, who've long walked its streets, who love its quirks, know its history, and care deeply about its future."

A related version of this story features the local journalist who left for the big city but later returned to edit a small-town newspaper. Michael Gartner is the most famous recent exemplar of this myth. Gartner had served as editor of the Des Moines Register, briefly as editor of the Louisville Courier-Journal, and for five years as president of NBC News. But in 1993 he returned to Iowa to become editor and co-- owner of the Ames Daily Tribune. What makes the story even better, from the perspective of journalists, is that Gartner has retained his big city edge. A blunt and opinionated man, he encouraged aggressive reporting of formerly sacrosanct Ames institutions, such as Iowa State University. The journalists in such tales resemble the mythic Greek figure Antaeus, who renewed his strength each time he returned to Mother Earth. Journalists hope that if they return to their roots they will be able to practice their craft in its purest form.

References to the local often resonate at several levels. When Ellen Soeteber was named editor of the St. Louis Post-Dispatch in December 2000, the paper's headline declared that "a native of East St. Louis" had been chosen. Soeteber portrayed her appointment as a homecoming: "The Post-Dispatch is not only the paper I grew up with, it's also the paper that inspired me to become a journalist." The implication in this and similar stories is that someone who grew up in the community knows what it is really like. But the assertiveness with which the Post-Dispatch publicized Soeteber's appointment suggested other subtexts. Her return could plausibly be interpreted as a peace offering to the African-American community. During the past few years, the Post-Dispatch's coverage has sometimes put the paper crosswise with blacks. It has been criticized, among other things, for its aggressive reporting of corruption in the administration of St. Louis's first black mayor; for a controversial and unsuccessful attempt to use the African-American journalist Chuck Stone as an ombudsman during that mayor's unsuccessful re-election campaign; and for its attention to the unending educational, financial, and political crises that plague East St. Louis. The fact that Soeteber, who is white, attended East St. Louis Senior High School, a district now almost entirely black, signaled that the new editor knew firsthand about local race relations.

Her appointment in December 2000 also presented reporters with yet another occasion to debate the meaning of the public journalism movement. Soeteber succeeded Cole Campbell, a nationally known advocate of public journalism who had edited the paper for four years. Campbell's efforts at reform had encountered resistance in the newsroom and strident criticism from the St. Louis Journalism Review.

When he remodeled the Sunday editorial section as a community forum, critics accused him of abandoning real news for "deliberative conversations" about "benign subject matter." When he assigned reporters to teams, some complained that the paper was ignoring breaking news. In such debates, appeals to the local figured in the arguments of both critics and defenders. Campbell justified his reforms as an attempt to reconnect the paper to the community. For example, early on he insisted that news photographs represent a broader array of citizens' faces.

Critics claimed he was out of touch with local newsroom customs and the St. Louis community. When it came time to replace him, Terry Egger, the publisher, announced that the paper wanted a new editor "who really understands journalism.""There is no substitute for the hard-breaking news the community relies on the paper for," Egger told the St. Louis Journalism Review.

"We want someone to continue to make sure reporters cover their beats, feature writers understand their subjects and columnists are in touch with the community." Hiring someone who had grown up in the St. Louis area signified an emphatic rejection of Campbell's ideas. The Post-Dispatch had chosen one of the community's own as editor, and she, at least, would not impose any fancy, out-of-town theories on her neighbors. Public journalism has stirred a similar national debate about how journalism represents the local.

Public journalism proponents say: Invite citizens into the newsroom. Critics say: Put more resources into local news coverage. In general, the movement urges editors and reporters to reconnect themselves to their fellow citizens. Public journalism takes community to be something immediate, substantial, and palpable. Proponents ground their sense of the local in their conversations with everyday people rather than with experts and official sources. They have even devised their own community rituals.

The public forums, pizza parties, and focus groups create an alternative social drama in which citizens play the leading roles and journalists serve as the audience. In short, the movement has made the local its dominant rhetorical motif. Its staunchest critics have dismissed it as an alien theory-as a form of evangelism that radically challenges the profession's traditions. Understood as a mythic narrative, however, public journalism looks anything but radical. In fact, it speaks a familiar language. Like all conversion narratives, it calls upon its followers to return to the faith of their fathers.

In so many ways, then, the myth of the local reverberates in American journalism. No matter how large or complicated the world gets, the local remains. It promises a haven in a heartless world, where journalists can discover their true and ultimate ground of being. The local world that calls to journalists is vivid and compelling. It will yield endless riches to anyone who takes the time to explore it. The local always leaves its door open, inviting the prodigal reporter or publisher to return. It can even work magic. News organizations that embrace it will be enriched. Publishers who honour it will be forgiven. Journalists who dwell in it will be saved.

Would that it were so simple. The historical forces that have made "the local" mythically potent have also thoroughly confused its referents. As the examples above suggest, it is now nearly impossible to specify what local means. The Oxford English Dictionary traces its earliest usages, in the sixteenth century, as a term for "something nearby"-- especially a neighborhood, village, town, country, district, or parish.

The local designated the here as a place that stood apart from the there. The local was a spatial construct. It assumed the physical isolation of one place from another. The idea of the local has persisted, in part, because humans' isolation from one another disappeared rather late in human history (although it can still be found in some parts of the world today). In the United States, for example, even after the transportation revolutions of the early nineteenth century, many communities continued to think of themselves as separate and autonomous up until the Civil War.

Historian Robert Wiebe has described these small antebellum towns as "island communities," locales not yet integrated into the national system. The new science of sociology, born at that moment, devised a theoretical vocabulary to capture the momentousness of these changes. Its great mythic binary-gemeinschaft and gesellschaft-made the local a taken-for-granted part of modern society's talk about itself. Community and society, the local and the national, the here and there, became the before and after of modern life. The theoretical problem of the local can be briefly summarized: there may no longer be a here here.

The local has lost much of its traditional meaning as a unit of social analysis. Carey has argued that while we often call this state of affairs postmodernism, the present dislocation actually continues trends that had become obvious by the end of the nineteenth century. "Cultural fragmentation and postmodernist homogenization," he writes, "are not opposing views of what is happening but two constitutive trends of a single global reality."Contemporary social theorists would agree. The rise of what we have come to call the global has complicated the old categories of social theory.

In the words of the British sociologist Martin Albrow, "If social relations are regularly maintained at a distance then concepts of locality, community and even citizenship are strained to accommodate them." Albrow suggests that we need less static categories, something like Arjun Appadurai's "scape," to capture the rhythms and flows of global culture. Albrow writes: "Appadurai uses 'ethnoscape' for the landscape of persons and moving groups like tourists and refugees who constitute a shifting world. He contrasts this with the relatively stable communities and networks through which these people and groups move."

Many observers believe that digital technologies like the Internet are enabling and accelerating these changes. In some ways, this is nothing new. The term local has always implicitly marked the limits of human technology-the impossibility of getting from here to there, the horizon imposed by geography, fear, cultural inertia, and happenstance.

New communication technologies always release and redefine humans' sense of the local-a point powerfully made, over the years, by Carey. Yet, the new technologies seem to be working unanticipated variations on this familiar tale. An economy driven by information feels increasingly weightless and ephemeral, radically unbound, less tied to place, less observant of traditional mores. Joel Kotkin has recently argued that the digital economy is creating a new social geography.

"By its very nature," he writes, "the emerging postindustrial economy-based primarily on information flows in an increasingly seamless net-frees location from the tyranny of past associations.... Increasingly, companies and people now locate not where they must but where they will." Kotkin, a public policy analyst, describes the forms of social inequality characteristic of that new economy. Highly educated workers have recolonized desirable locations such as Boulder, Colorado; Austin, Texas; and Irvine, California; and turned them into "nerdistans"-"self-contained high-end suburbs that have grown up to service the needs of both the burgeoning high-technology industries and their workers." Older cities-Kotkin mentions Newark, Detroit, and St.

Louis-find themselves increasingly marginalized. Within large cities such as New York, Chicago, and Los Angeles, some neighborhoods prosper while others wither. No single concept of the local can encompass all these instances. For the well-to-do, the local is a lifestyle; for the poor, a ghetto. The new global order has not erased the local, but re-instantiated it in radically diverse forms.

This new social geography has profound implications for our theories and practice of journalism. Journalism's local references a stable, geographically distinct world. But the global and local now interpenetrate in numberless ways. Members of the local community work for international corporations, and buy goods and services from outlets of national franchise stores. They spend their free time watching television programmes and movies, listening to music, and reading stories that are produced and distributed all over the world. Professionals of many sorts-lawyers, physicians, writers, professors, city managers, school superintendents, actors, corporate executives, and, yes, journalists and publishers-now think of the local as one rung on a national career ladder.

Our image of the homogeneous urban neighborhood, experienced in a similar way by all its members, has dissolved. New forms of multicultural living have sprouted all around us. "People inhabit co-- existing social spheres," Albrow writes, "coeval and overlapping space, but with fundamentally different horizons and time-spans." Even smaller cities in the United States now recognize how fully they are tied to a global economy and culture, as the Spokesman-Review discovered. Religious persecution in the former Soviet Union sent a wave of immigrants to Spokane.

U.S. sanctions on Pakistan hurt wheat exports from Eastern Washington. A local company started selling China grass seed for lawns. A Spokane man was one of six Western tourists kidnapped in Kashmir. In a world such as this, movement seemingly matters more than position.

Journalists lack a vocabulary with which to describe these emerging socioscapes, but they are increasingly aware of their existence. The newspaper business has paid immense attention to diversity and multiculturalism for a decade now, implicitly recognizing, perhaps, that the "local community" is less simple than it used to be. A few even admit that the concept of the local is changing. "'Local' is no longer where you live," notes Michael Conniff, president of Interactive Sports in an Editor and Publisher column. "'Local' is who you are, and what you care about. It can have very little to do with where you happen to live." Conniff questions newspapers' decision to become "hyperlocal," a strategy that translates into a "bottomless news hole." Nor is Conniff's criticism entirely new. Carl Lindstrom's 1960 book The Fading American Newspaper argued that newspaper publishers had retreated to the "citadel of local news" because they were unable to compete with television and magazines.

Lindstrom, who was executive editor of the Hartford Times and later a journalism professor at the University of Michigan, knew about these issues firsthand. In 1930 Gannett had purchased the Times, with assurances that its company policy was to respect "local autonomy." In the 1950s, Lindstrom wrote, "the last vestiges of local decision-making disappeared." Then as now, Gannett wanted local news but not local control. Lindstrom thought that all the new emphasis on the local signaled surrender: "Bravely the publisher has retreated to the citadel of local news, a noble fortress which may save his life-yet awhile; but this at the cost of having made the American press the most parochial in the world, at a time when the United States is in a position of free world leadership."

Kaniss shrewdly recognizes the contradictions in the way American journalists use the term local. In her account of Philadelphia news, the term local never designates a single unit of analysis. At different times she uses the term to refer to the city, suburban municipalities, and the metropolitan region that encompasses both. The fuzziness of her usage necessarily mirrors the instability of news organizations' understandings. For them, the most powerful force defining the local is marketing. Ultimately, the local is the audience that the news organization hopes to sell to advertisers.

Kaniss's account reveals other anomalies of the local as well. She notes, quite rightly, that chain ownership has changed the publishers' social position. Once a prominent member of the local elite, publishers who work for chains now answer first to the demands of their conglomerate organizations (rather than to the social values of their golf partners). In the end, Kaniss argues, the newspaper realises its most powerful role, as a local medium, when it covers development stories that create a fiction of social coherence. A local role, to be sure, but not quite the one for which journalists had rehearsed.

Finally, we need to recognize the darker side of professional journalism's talk about the local. The local remains contested terrain. News organizations invoke the local, in part, to lay claim to it, to control the meanings that others might attribute to it. The daily newspaper's conception of the local articulates a system of exclusions and prejudices. For the most part, professional journalists have accepted these exclusions as economically unavoidable. One of the worst is the decision to shrink an urban newspaper's circulation in poor neighborhoods, in order to create a more demographically focused and desirable buy for advertisers. Journalists' conception of the local does not oblige them to include everyone in the community. For television as well as newspapers, local means coverage, not access.

Newspapers want to be perceived as responding to local needs, but do not wish to yield influence to neighborhood groups, unions, churches, community activists, or press councils. In its most insidious form, journalism's myth of the local functions as an ideology by which media corporations co-opt and diminish other groups' claims to represent the people. This conception of the local has no place for the shared work of activists who meet at taverns, church basements, union halls, and public rallies.

When these groups speak of the local, they mean grassroots (admittedly, a mythic term in its own right). Local media, for them, are low-power radio stations, video cooperatives, alternative papers, and independent websites. For such media to survive, Clemencia Rodriguez has argued, they must answer to the language and culture of their audience: "The capacity to articulate the local constitutes a crucial component of the political potential of citizens' media."

Where does this leave us? No matter how unstable its meanings, the term local remains emotionally resonant, for both journalists and their fellow citizens. We invoke it in order to signify our sense of connectedness. How, then, might we honour this worthy, humane impulse? We propose three strategies for recovering the political possibilities of the local. First, we should abjure simple, fixed notions of the local, as something to be captured and domesticated. Our personal attachment to particular places does not require us to theorize the local as a spatial concept. Second, our studies of the local should explore its range of reference, rather than its essence.

As we have tried to show, Americans' talk about "the local" has been dense and contradictory. t only makes sense if interpreted as a discourse. Finally, we believe that democratic societies have a special stake in the term local. Democracy originated as a theory of politics grounded in place. Over time it has evolved into a system of relations governed by more general principles of representation and responsiveness. Thus Americans' talk about "the local" often references, obliquely, the state of their nation. If we imagined the local as a relational (rather than a spatial) construct, we would better understand such talk.

For example, we might then reconceive journalism's devotion to the local as a commitment to conversation rather than to coverage. Carey has urged journalists to make their work "accessible to people who, in fact, don't do it professionally but as part of an ordinary civic life-an ordinary civic life being the most important life we have." Here is one last meaning of the local that we should consider-the local as a word for those realms of everyday life shared by a politically conscious society committed to equality, responsive governance, and conviviality.

The local journalism of a democratic society would attend closely to the ordinary, common, pedestrian, vernacular life that makes such a society possible. The question it would pose is not where do we live, but how.

Chapter 7

Harassment of Journalists

In the summer of 1991, the St. Petersburg (Florida) Times broke a significant local story about charges of sexual harassment and sex discrimination at one of the city's larger employers. Women at the company charged that less qualified men were paid more, promoted sooner, and given better assignments.

Subtle and even blatant sexual harassment was tolerated. What made the story particularly significant was that the company in question was the St. Petersburg Times itself, and many of the women who had crowded into Chief Executive Andrew Barnes' office to voice their complaints were reporters, editors, and photographers.

Some of the stories the women told Barnes in that meeting and in a written report would have competed for sheer rudeness with the comments Anita Hill claimed Supreme Court Justice Clarence Thomas had made to her. One man had said to a pregnant female staffer, "Your breasts are really getting huge." Another, a senior editor, had been talking with other editors about a company called TMS and the problems it was causing the newspaper.

He turned to the female editor in the group and explained that TMS should "not be confused with PMS, which is worse for the company." The story attracted attention from other newspapers statewide, as well as national trade journals, and demonstrated that sexual harassment and sex discrimination are issues newspaper managers must be prepared to deal with within the newsroom, not just in stories about other organizations' problems. The term "sexual harassment" is a relatively recent addition to our vocabulary. Psychologist Julia Wood suggests that such harassment has existed for most of history but remained unnamed; the absence of visibility, which resulted from the fact that harassment had no negative effects on the men who held power, made it difficult to recognize, think about, or stop.

Today courts have recognized two categories of sexual harassment, known as "quid pro quo" ("something for something") and "hostile environment" discrimination. The former refers to situations in which an individual promises a subordinate employee some sort of tangible job benefit, such as a raise, in exchange for sexual favours.

This category also likely would include more negatively stated interactions, such as a supervisor's threat that the victim will lose her job if she refuses the supervisor's request for sexual favours.

The latter, "hostile environment" discrimination, reflects circumstances in which an employee is subjected to a pattern of behaviour - such as unwanted sexual advances, degrading sexual comments about the employee, or similar problems-that interferes unreasonably with an employee's ability to perform his or her job or makes the workplace environment inhospitable, intimidating, or offensive.

Many scholars argue that sexual harassment of women is widespread throughout academia and the workplace; however, a review of the communications and journalism literature suggests that relatively little research has been done on sexual harassment as a problem facing women journalists. Most earlier studies of women journalists focused almost entirely on sex discrimination and the likelihood of women achieving rank and pay equity with men. A review of that list also suggests that not much attention has been paid recently to studies of either discrimination against or harassment of women journalists.

One exception, the Associated Press Managing Editors Association harassment study in 1992, opened some eyes, according to Pam Johnson, managing editor of the Phoenix Gazette and chairwoman of the APME Newsroom

Management Committee. Some of the major discoveries from the survey of 640 male and female journalists from nineteen U.S. newsrooms:

- Only 30 per cent of the respondents said their newspaper had clear guidelines for filing internal complaints about sexual harassment;
- 95 per cent of the victims of sexual harassment were women;
- 2 per cent of the men and 11 per cent of the women said sexual harassment or the fear of harassment had affected their daily work habits;

While the most prevalent form of harassment was annoying or degrading comments about sex, followed by offensive pictures or posters and annoying or degrading comments about women's bodies, the APME study found that women also reported having male associates grab their breasts and buttocks or make "jokes" to them about rape.

Evidence of the female journalists' frustration came in the form of numerous vehement comments handwritten on the back of the survey form. Although most men surveyed tended to say there was no sexual harassment problem at their newspapers, women said it is a potential, if not specific, problem, and that it is neither reported nor punished in most instances.

Johnson, in writing about the study, observed: "Women in our newsrooms are impatient. They don't want to get ogled. They don't want to receive sex-related messages in their computers, they don't want to be put in the place of laughing off a sexual joke or challenging it and then having to pay for being forthright. And they definitely don't want to be fondled. But it's clear many feel vulnerable to any or all of these situations."

Flatow found that more than two-thirds of women working in the newsrooms of Indiana daily newspapers had indeed found themselves "vulnerable" to sexual harassment. In her survey of full-time editorial employees working at twenty-six Indiana dailies, Flatow found that 22.4% of the women and 6.6% of the men had experienced physical sexual harassment at some point during their careers. The same percentage of men, but nearly three times the percentage of women (61.8%) reported experiencing verbal sexual harassment, and nearly a third of the women reported "nonverbal" sexual harassment.

One recent study of women journalists in Washington, D.C., showed that 60% of the women accredited to the Capitol press gallery had been sexually harassed. The researchers, Katherine McAdams and Maurine Beasley, surveyed 273 women journalists and received responses from 37%. Of those who responded, 80% said they believe sexual harassment is a problem for women journalists.

McAdams and Beasley argue that the issue of sexual harassment among women journalists needs to be investigated and brought into the open so that individual women no longer have to deal with the problem alone. At the time of their study, Beasley and McAdams noted finding only one previous newsroom survey about sexual harassment. That study, conducted for the newspaper trade publication NewsInc., showed that 44% of the 199 newsroom women surveyed had experienced sexual harassment on the job. That figure was twice the number of women in all fields reporting harassment in a 1991 Newsweek/Gallup Poll.

More recently, Bowen and Laurion studied sexual harassment among mass communication professionals. Among their sample of 52 female and 44 male respondents, the authors found that 32% had experienced sexual harassment as students, 49% had experienced sexual harassment as interns in a mass communication organization, and 65% had experienced sexual harassment during their professional careers.

To most women, the importance of discovering the extent of sexual harassment among any group of women workers may seem obvious, and the threat of legal action by a harassed employee should be enough to get the attention of even the most old-fashioned newsroom managers. In addition, it seems particularly appropriate to examine sexual harassment among journalists because journalists have devoted considerable time in recent years to examining sexual harassment in other types of workplaces, including the federal government, the U.S. military services, and corporations. But the research also indicates that there are bottom-line considerations that make understanding and attempting to solve the problem of sexual harassment more pressing.

In short, the research indicates that sexual harassment has negative effects on women's work performance, as well as career advancement. In fact, the federal report Sexual Harassment in the Federal Government: An Update estimated that harassment cost the federal government $267 million over two years, including $76.3 million in lost individual productivity, and a recent analysis of sexual harassment in Fortune 500 companies concluded that sexual harassment costs each firm approximately $6.7 million annually.

Newspapers may not be able to figure the monetary costs of sexual harassment so conclusively, but there must be costs- in lost concentration on the stories, photos, or graphics assignments harassment victims would rather be working on. Indeed, many of Flatow's respondents reported that sexual harassment creates an environment of fear and intimidation at worst and even at best produces distractions that keep women from performing at the top of their ability.

Another major potential source of costs of which newspapers must be wary is lawsuits filed by women journalists who've been sexually harassed at work. Bunker concluded from a review of legal cases involving sexual harassment that media organizations should work to eliminate sexual harassment for their employees for selfish as well as noble reasons. He noted that: "Media organizations, like other employers, are subject to strict liability for quid pro quo harassment by supervisors.

In cases of hostile environment harassment, whether the harassment originates from supervisors, co-workers or non-employees, media organizations can be held vicariously liable if they know or should have known of the harassment and do not take immediate and effective steps to remedy it." Previous research and anecdotes like those reported by the female staffers of the St. Petersburg Times leave little doubt that sexual harassment is likely a problem for women newspaper journalists in the 1990s, despite all the effort those newspapers may put into coverage of and editorial outcry against sexual harassment in other fields. The study this paper discusses was designed to provide data about the extent and sources of sexual harassment that women journalists face.

We hoped to address a number of research questions, including the following:

- What percentage of women have experienced sexual harassment during their careers as reporters, photographers, editors, and newspaper graphic artists?
- Who harasses women journalists- supervisors, peers, subordinates, news sources?
- What percentage of newspapers have written policy statements about sexual harassment, and to what extent are all employees aware of these policies?
- Are there personal or work environment characteristics that increase or decrease the likelihood that women will experience sexual harassment as journalists?
- What do women do about the instances of sexual harassment they encounter? Method

Female reporters, photographers, editors, and graphic artists were randomly selected for participation in the survey using a multilevel stratified sampling procedure. First, the researchers drew separate samples of small, medium, and large newspapers (seventy-two small, thirty-two medium, and sixteen large newspapers).

We then contacted a newsroom manager (usually the managing editor) at each newspaper included in the samples and asked him or her to send us a list of all the female reporters, editors, photographers, and graphic artists on the newspaper's staff, including those working at bureaus.

After obtaining these lists, the lists were arranged in random order, and we then randomly selected names from the lists. This procedure ultimately produced a final sample of 208 women from small newspapers (daily circulation less than 25,000),184 women from mid-sized newspapers (daily circulation of 25,001-100,000) and 190 women from large newspapers (daily circulation greater than 100,000). After all the names had been chosen, we sent each sample member a letter describing our project and requesting her cooperation. The letter also informed sample members that only female students or faculty members would be conducting the study interviews.

Interviewers first called each sample member to arrange an appropriate time and place to complete the interview; any woman who did not feel comfortable discussing the subject in her work environment was asked for a home telephone number and called at home.

The first part of each interview was conducted using a computerassisted telephone interviewing programme; interviewers subsequently asked each participant for more details about her experiences, using a schedule of open-ended questions. The data from the interviews were analysed using SPSS for Windows.

Measures

Evaluation of Sexual Harassment as a Problem. For this section of the survey, respondents were told that "(f)or the purposes of the survey, sexual harassment is defined as any physical or verbal contacts that make the workplace inhospitable for women because of their gender."

Each respondent then was asked to say whether, in her opinion, sexual harassment was "no problem at all, not much of a problem, somewhat of a problem, a significant problem, or a very serious problem" for women as newspaper reporters, editors, photographers, or graphic artists. Each respondent used the same scale to indicate how much of a problem sexual harassment had been for her personally in her own career as a journalist.

Experience with Sexual Harassment. Each respondent was asked how often she had been "subjected to sexual harassment that did not involve physical contact, such as inappropriate sexual comments, suggestions, or gestures" made to her or in her presence by the following types of individuals: supervisors or others in positions of authority at the newspaper, other coworkers at her same level, other coworkers at levels lower than hers, news sources, employees of news sources, or in any other professional setting.

For each potential source of harassment, the respondent was asked whether nonphysical harassment had occurred never, rarely, sometimes, often, or nearly always/always. The interviewers then used the same scale (never, rarely, etc.) and the same series of potential harassers (supervisors, same-level coworkers, etc.) to determine how often the respondent had been subjected to "physical sexual harassment - that is, unwanted physical contact."

Definitions of Sexual Harassment. The respondents were asked whether they strongly agreed, agreed, neither agreed nor disagreed, disagreed, or strongly disagreed that the following behaviours constituted sexual harassment:

- When a man frequently makes uninvited and unnecessary physical contact with a woman who works with him
- When a man tells sexual jokes to a woman who has never told the same kind of jokes to him
- When a man pressures a woman who works with him to go out on a date with him
- When a man frequently makes uninvited remarks that have sexual references or double meanings to a woman who works with him
- When a man flirts with a female coworker who has never flirted with him
- When a man displays sexually oriented pictures or calendars in places where women also work.

Sexual Harassment Policies. Respondents were asked whether their newspaper has a written policy statement dealing with sexual harassment. Those who said the newspaper had such a policy were asked: "Are all employees equally aware of this policy, are women more likely to be aware of it or are men more likely to be aware of the policy?"

Demographic and Work-EnvironmentInformation. Each respondent was asked for her year of birth, marital status, job title, how many years she had worked as a journalist, how many people worked in the newsroom where she worked, what percentage of those people were women, whether her immediate supervisor was a man or a woman, and whether news employees at her newspaper were members of a union.

Results

Our goal had been to include about 100 women from each size of newspapers in the final survey, and we had anticipated that we would need approximately twice as many women in the initial sample to account for refusals to participate, ineligible respondents, and sample members who never could be reached. The most serious difficulty we encountered turned out to be contacting sample members, particularly those from the large and midsized newspapers, before they left their jobs, often for employment outside newspapers.

Once we had contacted sample members, refusals to participate in the survey were quite rare. Of the 582 women included in the original sample, we ultimately made some type of contact with 396, although in 85 cases, we only learned that the woman no longer worked at that newspaper. Of the 311 women our interviewers did speak with, only 33 refused to participate, for an unusually low refusal rate of 10.6%. Eighty-four other women were contacted and agreed to participate, but could not be interviewed because of scheduling difficulties or some other problem.

Not surprisingly, the largest number of respondents were reporters (39%). Eleven per cent of the respondents were copy editors, 15% were section editors (i.e., editors of features, business, or sports sections), and 4% were city editors or assistant city editors.

Fourteen respondents (6.2%) were news editors, and an equal number described themselves as editors. Six of the repondents (2.6%) held managing editor or assistant managing editor positions, and another six were photographers. The remainder of the sample was graphic artists, photo editors, editorial writers or columnists, held some other position, or gave no title. The women ranged in age from 23 to 74, and their experience as journalists ran from less than one year to forty-five years. The smallest newsroom had only three employees; the largest an estimated 400 employees.

The percentage of newsroom employees who were women ranged from 4 to 90 per cent. About two-thirds (67%) of the women had males as their immediate supervisors, about 31% had female immediate supervisors, and five women reported having one or more supervisors of each gender. Nearly half of the women (47.6%) were married.

The women were asked to indicate whether sexual harassment was no problem, not much of a problem, somewhat a problem, a significant problem, or a very serious problem for women journalists in general and in their own careers specifically. About 60% of the women said sexual harassment is at least somewhat a problem for women as reporters, photographers, editors, and graphic artists, and more than one in 10 (11.5%) said sexual harassment is a significant or very serious problem for women journalists.

Lower percentages reported having substantial trouble with sexual harassment in their own careers; nonetheless, more than one-third (36.1%) said sexual harassment had been at least somewhat a problem for them personally, and 17 women (7.5%) reported having had significant or serious problems with sexual harassment during their careers.

Cross-tabulation analysis determined that there was a significant relationship between beliefs about the seriousness of sexual harassment as a problem for women journalists and age. Older women (4174 years old) were three times as likely as the youngest women (23-30 years old) or the middle age group (31-40) to say that sexual harassment was no problem at all for women journalists.

Women in the 23-30 age group were twice as likely as those in the middle group and more than three times as likely as the oldest women to regard sexual harassment as a significant or very serious problem for women journalists. Women's ratings of sexual harassment as a problem for women journalists also were related to the percentage of women in their newsrooms. Women working in newsrooms in which more than half of the employees were female were far more likely to say that sexual harassment was little or no problem for women journalists; these women were more than four times as likely as women in the least-female-populated newsrooms to say that sexual harassment was no problem at all for women journalists. None of the demographic or work environment variables showed any significant relationship with women's views of sexual harassment as a problem in their own careers.

EXPERIENCE WITH SEXUAL HARASSMENT

Respondents also were asked to indicate how often they personally had been subjected to two types of sexual harassment - harassment that did not involve physical contact (sexual comments, jokes, etc.) and harassment that did involve physical contact (unwanted touching, etc.) - from a variety of professional contacts. The results indicate that news sources were the most likely to harass women journalists both physically and without making physical contact. More than 44% of the women reported that sources at least sometimes subjected them to nonphysical sexual harassment, and about 6% reported physical sexual harassment by sources at least sometimes. More than one-fourth of the women had at some time experienced physical sexual harassment by a news source, and more than 70% of the women had experienced nonphysical sexual harassment by a source.

Overall, at least one-fourth of the women said they experienced nonphysical sexual harassment at least sometimes from their supervisors or others in positions of authority over them (25.1%) and from coworkers at their same level (29.1%), and nearly one-fourth experienced such harassment from subordinates (23.6%) or in other professional settings (22.5%). Almost 5% had been physically harassed at least sometimes by their supervisors and same-level peers. Because the results shown do not indicate whether the same women were experiencing harassment from a variety of professional contacts, we created two new variables that indicated whether the respondents had been subjected to nonphysical or physical sexual harassment at least sometimes from any source. In other words, had the women experienced physical sexual harassment at least sometimes, regardless of the person engaging in the harassment. More than two-thirds of the women (67.4%) had experienced nonphysical harassment at least sometimes by someone in their work environments, and 16.7% of the women had been physically sexually harassed at least sometimes, regardless of the identity of the harasser.

In addition, nearly one in four women had experienced nonphysical harassment by three or more professional contacts, and about 6% had been physically harassed by two or more professional contacts. These results suggest that sexual harassment is occurring among women journalists in a relatively widespread manner; it isn't just a few women who are being affected by harassment from multiple professional contacts. Cross tabulations were conducted to determine whether a woman's chances of being subjected to either nonphysical or physical sexual harassment were related to her job title, age, immediate supervisor's gender, the size of the newspaper for which she worked, her years of experience as a journalist, or the percentage of women in the newsroom.

Analyses revealed no significant effects for any of these variables for the measures of combined experience with nonphysical or physical sexual harassment. However, some significant differences did exist in measures of nonphysical harassment by specific types of work contacts. The percentage of women in the newsroom was significantly related to a respondent's likelihood of being sexually harassed by coworkers at her same level; women whose newsrooms were one-third female or less were more likely to experience nonphysical harassment at least sometimes.

This may simply reflect the fact that women are less likely to be harassed by their same-gender peers, so more women in the newsroom means fewer coworkers who're likely to harass them. It also may be, however, that predominantly male newsrooms create a more sympathetic environment for employees inclined to subject their peers to verbal or visual sexual harassment. Reporters and photographers-women who spend more time outside the newsroom itself-were less likely to report having been harassed by subordinates than were copy editors, graphic artists, and others who spend all or nearly all of their work hours in the newsroom.

Again, this may reflect a simple difference in opportunities; reporters and photographers may spend less time around subordinates and therefore have fewer chances to be sexually harassed. A more likely explanation may be that reporters and photographers are less likely to feel that they have any lower-level coworkers. On this question, women did not have the option of saying the question did not apply to them.

On the other hand, reporters and photographers' time outside the newsroom makes them more vulnerable to being sexually harassed by news sources. Nearly 60% of reporters and photographers said sources had sexually harassed them at least sometimes, compared to more than one-third of copy editors, graphic artists, and others working primarily inside the newsroom.

Responses to the open-ended questions at the end of each interview indicated that the types of sexual harassment the women journalists experienced ranged from the merely irritating-being called "honey" and "sweetie" or "that little girl" - to the downright dangerous. One political reporter from a small Midwest newspaper said she deals with condescending name-calling by simply returning the favour: "After I treat them the way they treat me, by calling them 'sweetie' or something like that, it doesn't happen after that."

Other women, however, reported having to deal with much more disturbing instances of sexual harassment by sources. For instance, one police beat reporter from a small newspaper in a Mid-Atlantic state recounted two instances in which she went to a district attorney's office to conduct interviews and found him playing confiscated X-rated videotapes.

He continued to watch them during the interviews, telling her, "We just got these tapes in, and I have to look at them." Not surprisingly, the woman found the experience unnerving:

"It just didn't make sense that he would put them in the tape player. They're (videotape characters) having sex, totally nude, on TV. It was disturbing and uncomfortable, and I was trying to ask him questions. I just ignored it. I probably should have asked him to turn it off, but I didn't. He's a pretty intimidating man anyway."

Another woman, who works for a large Midwestern newspaper, was equally unnerved by the behaviour of a bond trader she interviewed at his office. She noticed that, while showing her a computer programme he used, he kept brushing his knee against her; she also noted that, as staff members left the office about 5 p.m., each seemed to make a point of letting her know they were leaving.

Uncomfortable being left alone with the man, the woman got up to leave; as she did, the source brushed her long hair back behind her shoulder. "From your father, it might be endearing," the woman recalled, "but coming from someone like that, I found it very offensive."

Many of the respondents who work or have worked as reporters reported that sources often suggested going to a bar or to a motel to conduct interviews or that sources would joke with each other about whether the reporter was having sex with one of them or might be willing to do so. Other respondents described instances of blatant physical sexual harassment by sources.

One reporter had a source who was a doctor approach her from behind and give her a "full body press." Startled, she responded by saying, "Rape," softly but loud enough for him to hear. The doctor left the room and had no contact with the reporter for the next few months.

One woman from a small Northeastern newspaper recalled being propositioned by a source whose house she had gone to. "He propositioned me, tried to force himself on me. I got out of it by talking fast. I had gone to his house to do the interview, so he considered it OK, I guess."

Unfortunately, sources were not the only perpetrators of sexual harassment. One woman recounted an incident during a news meeting in which the managing editor asked another female staffer, who was wearing a mini-skirt, to turn around so the group could appreciate her outfit and suggested that she ought to wear mini-skirts more often.

A photographer/photo editor who works for a midsized Southwestern paper reported that both sources and coworkers frequently make comments about her breasts. Once, during an assignment in Central America, she contracted a water-borne illness that resulted in significant weight loss. When she returned to the newsroom, a manager noted how much weight she had lost and said, "It's too bad it all came out of your boobs."

A night editor from a small paper reported that the newspaper's sports editor regularly comes by her desk and rubs her shoulders and touches her hair. When she finishes her work, she said, she sometimes asks if there's anything she can help him with because he has to deal with more latebreaking news. Her offer to help is greeted with more harassment: "He always- every single day- says, 'Yes, there is something you can do,' and then laughs."

A journalist from a Southeastern newspaper reported that her manager once had called her at home and asked her to meet him at a lounge to discuss something work-related. "When I got there, he was really drunk, and he said, `You want it, and you know you do.' I went out the fire escape to get out of there. When I left, I was fearful I had lost my job. But I think he was so drunk he didn't even remember doing it."

A reporter from a midsized newspaper in the Northeast had a similar experience with her newspaper's former chief editor. The editor had invited her and a male friend to a party at his apartment and then offered to let the reporter drive his expensive sports car to the apartment, while her friend followed in his own car. "This man had always been very kind to me," she recalled.

"I had no reason to expect anything." But after she got into the driver's seat, the editor began telling her that "the things he would like to do with me and to me would make him lose his job. He kept saying he was disturbed about the thoughts he was having about me." She got out of the car and left with her friend. Another of this woman's coworkers circulated throughout the newsroom a list of all the women in the newsroom, ranked according to how much he wanted to have sex with each one.

DEFINITIONS OF SEXUAL HARASSMENT

In addition to learning about the extent of physical and nonphysical sexual harassment among women journalists, we also were interested in determining how women in the newsroom define sexual harassment. Thus, the women's responses to questions about whether a variety of types of behaviour constitute sexual harassment. Specifically, we asked the women to use a five-point scale to indicate the extent to which they would define it as sexual harassment if a man:

- Made repeated, unwanted physical contact with a female coworker,
- Told sexual jokes to a female coworker who had never told him similar jokes,
- Pressured a female coworker for a date,
- Repeatedly made remarks with sexual meanings or double entendres to a female coworker,
- Flirted with a female coworker who had not previously flirted with him,
- Displayed sexually oriented posters or calendars in areas where female coworkers would have to see them.

There was strong agreement that a man who makes repeated, unwanted physical contact with a female coworker is engaging in sexual harassment; 98.7% of the women either agreed or strongly agreed with this statement. Almost as high a percentage (92.5%) said pressuring a female coworker for a date constitutes sexual harassment, and 87.7% either agreed or strongly agreed that making sexual comments or double entendres to a female coworker constituted sexual harassment.

The great majority of respondents (86.3%) also agreed or strongly agreed that displaying sexy posters or calendars was sexual harassment, and about 81% agreed that telling sexual jokes to a female coworker who never had told the same kind of jokes to the man constituted harassment. The behaviour least likely to be defined as sexual harassment was flirting with a female coworker who hadn't flirted with the man before; 37.9% of the respondents agreed or strongly agreed, but more than a third (33.9%) disagreed or strongly disagreed.

Cross tabulations were conducted to determine whether demographic or newspaper characteristics (age, years of experience, circulation size) were related to respondents' likelihood of defining each of the behaviours as sexual harassment. Age was significantly related to one measure - whether the respondent agreed that displaying sexually oriented pictures was sexual harassment; the oldest women (41-74 years old) were nearly twice as likely to strongly agree (59.3%) as were the youngest group, 23- to 30year-olds (31.1%). The relationship between age group and agreement that telling sexual jokes constituted harassment approached significance (p=.11), and the trend reflected the same pattern.

Women in the oldest group were more likely than those in either of the two younger groups to agree that a man was sexually harassing a female coworker if he told sexual jokes when she never had told him the same kind of joke. The only other relationship that approached significance was between circulation size and the likelihood that respondents defined flirting as sexual harassment. In this case, women at the midsized newspapers (25,001-100,000 circulation) appeared to be least likely to consider flirting to be sexual harassment.

Finally, the six specific questions about definitions of sexual harassment were combined into a moderately reliable scale, and this scale was tested for correlations with the respondents' age, years of journalism experience, and the extent to which she had experienced both physical and nonphysical sexual harassment throughout her career. Only age was significantly correlated with this scale, and the correlation, though significant, was quite low.

Sexual Harassment Policies

Each respondent also was asked whether her newspaper had a written policy regarding sexual harassment and if so, whether there were gender differences in awareness of the policy. About 71% of the women said their newspapers do have a formal, written sexual harassment policy. About 13% of the women said the newspaper did not have such a policy, and another 16% were not sure whether or not a sexual harassment policy existed.

Of the respondents whose newspapers did have a formal policy, the majority (70%) said male and female employees were equally likely to be aware of the policy. About 19% thought women were more likely to be aware of the policy, and 4% thought men were more aware of it. The respondents included in this survey were randomly selected, so these results should reflect fairly accurately the experiences and opinions of female journalists working at newspapers throughout the United States.

However, one significant concern arises from the fact that the surveys have taken a relatively long time to complete. Interviewing began during the summer of 1993, and the last of the respondents whose data are included in this report were interviewed in February 1995. It's possible that events occurring during the intervening months may have increased the later respondents' awareness of sexual harassment issues. For instance, there was a fairly widely publicized fall 1993 case in which the Supreme Court ruled in favour of a woman who had sued her employer for sexual harassment under the "hostile environment" rule. Newswomen certainly would have been likely to have been exposed to at least wire service coverage of this case, which could have increased the likelihood that they would begin to redefine as harassment behaviour that does not include unwanted physical contact.

Another concern is the relatively large number of women who had left their jobs at the sample newspapers by the time we attempted to contact them. We have no way of knowing whether their experiences differed significantly from those of the women we interviewed. It is possible, for instance, that problems with sexual harassment contributed to their decisions to leave their newspapers, which would mean that our results underestimate the extent of sexual harassment newspaperwomen are encountering. Despite these limitations, however, the results strongly suggest that sexual harassment is a significant problem for women working in America's daily newspapers. More than one-third of these women said sexual harassment has been at least somewhat a problem in their own careers as journalists, and three of every five respondents believe sexual harassment is a problem for women journalists in general.

The difference in those two figures is interesting and may be explained, in part, by the fact that even women who have not themselves experienced blatant sexual harassment are aware when other women in their newsrooms have such experiences. During the openended questions at the end of our interviews, we found that many respondents who had not experienced harassment much themselves were deeply concerned about incidents involving other women with whom they worked.

While knowing about someone else's experience with harassment may not be as stressful as being harassed oneself, it almost certainly produces a less-thanideal working atmosphere. Another important finding of this study was that, in comparison to the APME survey, we found a much higher percentage of women who said they experienced sexual harassment at least sometimes. Among our respondents, more than two-thirds experienced nonphysical sexual harassment at least sometimes, when all possible perpetrators of harassment were considered, and about 17% experienced physical sexual harassment at least sometimes.

Only about 38% of the APME survey's female respondents said they had ever been subjected to sexual harassment at their newspapers. Some of the difference may be explained by the wording of questions. We asked respondents about their experiences throughout their careers, while the wording of the APME survey question may have limited women's responses to those involving their present newspaper. Thus, the women in our survey may have been reflecting experiences over a broader span of time and more newspapers. It also is possible, however, that the APME's respondents were working for more enlightened employers; the papers involved in the APME study, after all, had volunteered to participate. Another contrast with the APME study appears in the identity of persons doing the harassing.

Among our respondents, problems with sexual harassment were most common in women's interactions with news sources, who were more likely than any category of coworkers to harass women journalists in either physical or non-physical ways. In the APME survey, on the other hand, 67% of women who had been harassed said the harasser was a coworker, compared to 20% who had been harassed by a source or client. This harassment by sources may be especially troubling to women journalists because many seem to feel powerless to do anything about it.

In response to the open-ended questions, many women expressed the view that there was no effective way to prevent harassment by sources because the journalist must depend on these sources for information. One woman from a small Southeastern newspaper said, for instance, that most women reporters simply put up with harassment from sources rather than alienating them. This woman, who had had a police detective ask what colour panties she was wearing and throw a pair of underwear in her face during an interview, said she did not confront him about it. "I continued to work with him as a news source. To report it would have made it worse." Another woman said she wouldn't know what to do about a source's harassment because "in our case the person you would have to go to is the one person who makes women most uncomfortable in the newsroom."

Other women dealt with the harassment more aggressively. The business reporter who was sexually harassed by the bond trader reported the incident to her supervisor, who backed her in her decision to stop using the man as a source and to tell him specifically why she no longer would seek his opinions for stories. Another woman, who now works for a midsized paper in a North-Central state, reported that while working as a police beat reporter in Florida, she had been called out on a dark, rainy night to cover a wreck. The officer who had called her about the wreck suggested that she get into his car to write down the names of those involved, and when she did, he "attacked" her. She slapped him, got out of his car, and later reported the incident to her supervisors. "Luckily when I slapped him, he backed off. I think he was stunned -he was certainly way stronger than I was," she recalled. "It was part of what led him to be canned (fired)."

Harassment by sources may be most common, but the women we talked to also were, in many cases, deeply disturbed by harassment they experienced from coworkers and supervisors. In at least some cases, this harassment has had significant effects on women's careers, spurring them to leave the newspaper to get away from a harassing situation or even, in one case, to turn down a promotion that would have put the woman in more frequent contact with a harassing publisher.

This woman, who works now at a newspaper in the Northwest, said the publisher had a habit of touching women employees on the buttocks and rubbing their shoulders. "It just never ended - and continual comments," the woman said. "The funny part is, I was offered the job of news editor, but I didn't take it because of his habits. So he was willing to offer a woman the job because he wanted to make money, and he wanted the experience I had. But he still had these other habits." Again, women who dealt aggressively with their harassers seemed most likely to get positive results. A woman from a midsized New England newspaper reported that her male coworkers once put up a poster showing a woman surrounded by ten men, with the headline, "Put an end to rape. Say Yes." She said, "The poster was up for about five seconds, and I marched into the managing editor's office and asked him if he had seen it.

He went back and took one look at it and immediately told them to take it down. In dealing with this stuff, the best thing to do is just go get a man with a brain in his head, as opposed to one of the ones with his brain between his legs." Not surprisingly, the respondents in this survey were most likely to define as sexual harassment behaviours involving unwanted physical contact and a coworker pressuring a woman for a date. However, there also was substantial agreement that sexual remarks and comments with double meanings, displaying sex-oriented posters or calendars and telling sexual jokes to a woman who hadn't told the man similar jokes constituted sexual harassment. The only behaviour we asked about that wasn't defined as sexual harassment by at least 50% of our respondents was flirting with a female coworker who hadn't previously flirted with the man.

We also found that about 71% of the women worked at newspapers where there was a written policy regarding sexual harassment (16% weren't sure whether the newspaper had a policy), and 70% of those women said male and female employees were equally aware of the policy. The fact that harassment still is going on may suggest that male journalists, regardless of newspaper policy, simply aren't concerned about negative repercussions they might face if accused of sexual harassment.

More likely, perhaps, is that male journalists do not understand that some of the more ambiguous behaviours, such as telling jokes or posting sexy photos, offend their female coworkers. Some studies also have indicated that male managers in certain kinds of workplaces - including police stations, law firms, advertising agencies, and newspapers - view their workplaces as "unique environments, where sexual harassment can be excused."

Women who want to work in these traditionally male environments are expected to play by the boys' rules or not play at all, and this may be particularly true in newsrooms still dominated by men. The finding that women working in newsrooms with higher percentages of male employees were more likely to experience sexual harassment is consistent with findings from other types of workplaces.

On the other hand, it's important to note that many of our more veteran respondents, in the open-ended section of the interview, stressed that their work environments had improved significantly over the course of their careers. One woman, for instance, said that she had been surprised to receive our initial letter because her work environment seemed fine; she said the fact that we were doing the study made her guess that harassment still was a problem in other newsrooms. Having established that harassment indeed is a problem for women newspaper journalists, we now need to turn our attention to understanding why this harassment occurs and, perhaps more important, how it can be stopped.

Further analysis of the open-ended responses from this study is helping us to understand how harassment victims typically respond to their harassers and which kinds of responses seem to be most effective. In addition, further research will be needed to determine how male journalists perceive the kinds of behaviours female journalists categorize as sexually harassing, the circumstances under which they may engage in such behaviours, and how action by newspaper management affects harassment of journalists both in the newsroom and by sources outside.

Regardless of the reason, it seems clear that newspapers must begin to do a better job of addressing the issue of sexual harassment if they want to keep their best and brightest female employees. Research in other fields has demonstrated that the negative work-related outcomes of sexual harassment include high employee turnover, lowered self-esteem and decreased selfconfidence among harassment victims, deteriorating coworker relationships, and decreased job satisfaction and commitment to the organization. From their recent meta-analysis of studies of job stress among journalists, Cook and Banks concluded that there is a strong relationship between job stress and burnout and between job burnout and intention to leave the profession.

Sexual harassment may be only one source of job stress for women journalists, but it's an additional stress. Female journalists already face the same stresses male journalists face, and that one additional burden may be enough, in some cases, to send highly competent, top-performing women looking for somewhere else to work. As noted earlier, even when they stay in newspapers, sexual harassment may distract women from the work on which they really want to be concentrating. In that sense, sexual harassment of women journalists does a disservice not only to them but to newspapers' readers as well. For these reasons, as well as concern for common human decency and fairness, newspaper owners, publishers, and managers would do well to heed the comments of one of our survey respondents, a reporter from a medium-sized Mid-Atlantic newspaper. She said of her supervisors: "Sometimes, these people don't seem to think all the publicity about sexual harassment and sex discrimination applies to them and their behaviour."

Chapter 8

Anecdotes in News Coverage

Studies of framing effects have found that episodic and human interest frames-in which anecdotes are often an element-affect audiences' thinking in important ways. In particular, Iyengar found that episodic framing, focusing news coverage on individuals and events, tends to prompt television news audiences to attribute responsibility for issues to individuals rather than social factors. Valkenburg, Semetko, and de Vreese found that crime stories framed in human interest terms prompted readers to emphasize emotions and implications for individuals more often, and to recall less information about an issue.

The literature on exemplification, because it focuses explicitly on the use and impact of examples, carries particular significance for an ethical analysis of anecdotes. Zillmann and Brosius address the problematic nature of anecdotes in noting that the concept of exemplification calls for the representation of groups of events "by single events that are typical and characteristic of the group. Exemplification by atypical and uncharacteristic events is deemed inappropriate because it fails to provide reliable information about the group." Given the inherent difficulties of accurate representation through anecdotes, the prevalence of anecdotes in journalism stands out as an ethical issue.

Psychological research shows that exemplification can overwhelm the influence of base-rate information-broader figures or statements about the frequency or typicality of an event. In one study, subjects shown an article about a welfare recipient and an interview with a prison guard changed their minds about the population as a whole, regardless of what kind of information they received about how typical the case was. Mass communication researchers have found that different distributions of exemplars have differing effects on audience perception of issues.

Zillmann, Perkins, and Sundar varied the ratio of exemplars to counterexemplars in a story about keeping weight off after dieting. The exemplars either all followed the focus of the story (selective exemplification), or were proportional to the situation in the broader population (representative), or disproportionately favored one side (blended).

Audiences' perception of the overall incidence of weight regaining proved most accurate for the representative condition and least accurate for the selective. Likewise, Brosius and Bathelt found that the perception of majority and minority opinions on public issues followed the distribution of exemplars. Zillmann et al. found that changes in the kinds of exemplars used in a news report on the plight of family farmers altered readers' perceptions of the prevalence of family farm failures.

Other research has examined the impact of using examples from extraordinary or highly emotional cases. Gibson and Zillmann found that estimates of the frequency of deaths in carjackings increased as exemplars were tilted more and more toward the unusual case of a fatal carjacking. A study of television news found that exemplification using emotional victims fostered perceptions that food poisoning problems and random violence were more severe than when unemotional or no victim exemplification was used.

Even the use of quotations in exemplars, a conventional journalistic practice, has been found to influence audiences. Gibson and Zillmann found that direct, one-sided personal testimony in print reports changed perceptions of amusement park safety. They also found that personal testimony about the plight of family farmers swayed readers' views. In addition, studies have found effects from the use of both threatening images and innocuous images, for example, changes in perception of risk of skin cancer. Findings about use of images are relevant to the evaluation of anecdotes in broadcast news because of its dependence on images. Viewed as a body, empirical studies on the power of exemplars indicate a need for careful consideration of the ethical implications of anecdote choice.

ANALYTICAL PERSPECTIVES

Three analytical perspectives are useful tools for assessing these ethical implications because they point both to the potential ethical good and the ethical dangers of anecdote use. A framework developed previously for studying coverage of news with an ethical dimension involves evaluating stories based on how thoroughly they portray the ethical issues relevant to a topic, the parties connected with those issues, the levels at which the ethical issues play out (individual, organizational/institutional, professional, and social), and the legal backdrop for those issues. Although each story about ethics-laden topics cannot be expected to address all four of these elements comprehensively, coverage that addresses these areas well is considered to be ethical.

The normative assumptions about journalism in this framework are in keeping with social responsibility and communitarian press theory, both of which emphasize the importance of not merely reporting events but also serving society.

The attention to levels of analysis reflects the importance of portraying individuals in news coverage. News coverage should include the ways that individuals and families are affected by decisions or events-such as a health maintenance organization's decision about whether to approve or deny coverage for a kind of cancer treatment.

Anecdotes shine light on the difficulties that individuals face, and as such they are tools of ethical journalism. The importance of the individual notwithstanding, journalists should go beyond that level to examine issues at the organizational/institutional, professional, and social levels. Attention to only one level of analysis, in an in-depth piece or a body of coverage, falls short of the moral obligation of journalists. In this light, anecdotes are morally a double-edged sword. While they can bring attention to the plight of individuals in riveting fashion, and even place that plight in institutional, professional, and social contexts, the attention remains on a representative, or perhaps unrepresentative, individual or family, as exemplification studies have shown.

Furthermore, previous work suggests that news coverage should include an array of sources, including neither exclusively professionals (such as doctors or businesspeople) or nonprofessionals (patients or customers). Good anecdotes, although they focus on an individual, may point out how that individual interacts with other people, as well as with organizations and institutions.

Attention to a range of relevant parties at a variety of levels, both in the anecdote and elsewhere in the story, can mitigate the potential ethical harm from anecdotes' narrow focus. But the exemplification literature suggests that the anecdote still would have power to shape readers' or viewers' perception of the broader issue.

Christians, Ferre, and Fackler's communitarian media ethic also provides ethical justification for using anecdotes to highlight the situations of individuals while it draws attention to the limitations of anecdotes. The idea of mutuality is central to this perspective, which has a variety of intellectual underpinnings including communitarian political theory and theology.

Mutuality views humans as having their identity in relation to others and living both for others and themselves. The relationship of persons and communities takes priority over either alone. This ethic is profoundly concerned with both society and the individual. The priority of justice creates a profound interest in the needs of the hurting or marginalized. "A press nurtured by communitarian ethics requires more of itself than fair treatment of events deemed worthy of coverage. Under the notion that justice itself-and not merely haphazard public enlightenment-is a telos of the press, the news-media system stands under obligation to tell the stories that justice requires." Part of telling "the stories that justice requires" involves telling the stories of individuals. This is because justice addresses fair treatment of individuals. One of the most powerful ways, in fact, to draw attention to such individuals is through the telling of their stories, in words and images, in print and broadcast media.

Even as it provides an ethical underpinning for use of anecdotes, communitarian media ethics, with its deeply grounded concern for the good of society, calls into question the structure and choice of anecdotes. Again, this ethic does support the use of compelling individual cases to highlight broader social injustices.

However, sloppy use of anecdotes can undermine an effort to portray the broader issue, not simply because of the natural tendency of anecdotes to highlight individuals, but also because the particular choice of individuals can skew understanding toward one side of a controversial issue, resulting potentially in neglect of social justice. The issue is not formulaic balance in news coverage; communitarian ethics calls for more than "fair treatment of events."

Consonant with Durham's notion of "strong objectivity," Christians, Ferre, and Fackler call for highlighting the perspectives of the marginalized and, where needed, giving those perspectives attention that is out of balance with the play given to the stories of the powerful. However, since communitarian ethics also implies a concern for faithful portrayal of the whole community, it implies a need to portray the breadth of the community's concern.

Gilligan's feminist ethic of care supports the use of anecdotes because it, too, is concerned with persons in relationships. This perspective, developed out of psychological studies of women's distinctive conceptions of morality, underlines the importance of relationships and responsibilities. Discussing one of her interviewees, Gilligan writes: "Her world is a world of relationships and psychological truths where an awareness of the connection between people gives rise to a recognition of responsibility for one another, a perception of the need for response." Commenting on how another interviewee viewed activities of care, she writes: "The ideal of care is thus an activity of relationship, of seeing and responding to need, taking care of the world by sustaining the web of connection so that no one is left alone." This ethic of care in relationships, however, is not relevant only to women, Gilligan argues. "To admit the truth of the women's perspective to the conception of moral development is to recognize for both sexes the importance throughout life of the connection between self and other, the universality of the need for compassion and care."

Anecdotes are ethically significant in the context of this perspective because they can help to portray the web of personal relationships and responsibilities involved in ethical situations. Anecdotes can dramatically represent the difficulties that individuals, including women facing illnesses such as breast cancer, face in relation to their families and others outside their families, such as physicians. In fact, use of anecdotes is in keeping with the attention to particulars that Gilligan found women bringing to their moral analysis. She discusses what happens when women go beyond hypothetical dilemmas:

However, the reconstruction of the dilemma in its contextual particularity allows the understanding of cause and consequence which engages the compassion and tolerance repeatedly noted to distinguish the moral judgments of women. Only when substance is given to the skeletal lives of hypothetical people is it possible to consider the social injustice that their moral problems may reflect and to imagine the individual suffering their occurrence may signify or their resolution engender.

This passage implies that anecdotes may awaken attention both to the suffering of individuals and the social context of their difficulties. It suggests that, despite the danger of distortion of the broader picture that the exemplification literature suggests, deep concern for the people behind issues that journalists report may arise only through telling the stories of individuals. Even as it underpins the ethical value of anecdotes, the ethic of care also implies a need for careful attention to what anecdotes are chosen and what they portray. It implies a need for accurate understanding of responsibilities of individuals in the broader context of society, so that the web of relationships and people's responsibilities within them is rightly understood.

All three perspectives suggest that anecdotes are best when they situate individuals they mention in the broader context of the issues being discussed. These three perspectives all draw attention to the value of the individual and therefore imply that it is ethically justifiable to use anecdotes to draw attention to the needs and concerns of individuals. The communitarian ethic and the ethic of care complement the ethics coverage framework by emphasizing the individual in relationships.

Communitarianism puts priority on the hurting and marginalized. The ethic of care draws attention to the importance of the circumstances of the lives of individuals in prompting a depth of concern for them. Even as they draw attention to the individual, however, all three perspectives emphasize the need to think beyond the individual to the broader contexts of a problem, thereby implying that anecdotes should be carefully chosen for how they may limit or draw attention to these contexts.

Method for Case Analysis

These three analytical perspectives will be applied to three anecdotes taken from larger bodies of stories about human embryo research, physician-assisted suicide, and HMOs, all topics that have received attention from the media and professionals during the past decade. These topics lend themselves to powerful use of anecdotes because of their life-and-death import.

Even though both the exemplification literature and the analytical perspectives used here suggest this power may be a mixed blessing, it is appropriate to study these kinds of topics because of the priority that journalists place on powerful, compelling anecdotes. Stories used here were published or aired during a key period of public discourse on each topic.

For human embryo research, this was 1994-1995, amid federal debate on the subject. For physician-assisted suicide, it was 1997-1999, which encompassed a Supreme Court ruling that there is no general constitutional right to assisted suicide, passage of law in Oregon legalizing the practice, and the trial of Dr. Jack Kevorkian for euthanasia. For health maintenance organizations, 1997-1998 was a time of increasing legal and political attention to HMO practices. For each topic, both print and broadcast stories that dealt significantly with the ethical dimension of the issue were examined.

The anecdotes analysed as cases were chosen for their vivid language and emotional power. In these respects, they represent the kinds of anecdotes that journalists strive to include in stories on many topics. Thus, while it is inescapable that they cannot fully represent the range of anecdote use, even in the topics studied, they represent an aspect of standard journalistic usage. They are, therefore, appropriate for ethical analysis of the strong and weak points in this usage. Although space limits consideration to one anecdote from each topic, both print and broadcast cases are included to make the ethical analysis more relevant to both.

Analysis of Cases

George Strait used an anecdote to help illustrate an ABC TV news story about human embryo research, aired just after a federal advisory panel recommended that federal funding be used to pay for research on human embryos. The story outlined arguments for and against human embryo research. This anecdote, shown in the middle of the piece, was the second of two that illustrated potential benefits of human embryo research. The story showed a girl born after genetic testing of her mother's embryos, and Strait talked with the girl's father. Strait described the treatment that enabled this girl to be born, against the backdrop of video that included shots of her:

This research on human embryos has vast potential, from improving fertility and contraceptives to better screening for genetic diseases. Take Brittany Abshire baby is shown wearing a bow on her head and a fancy dress. Her parents, Rene and David Abshire, were afraid they might never have a healthy baby. Their first child, Meaghan face is shown close-up in a still portrait, died of a rare genetic disease called Tay-Sachs. They got help here at the Jones Institute, where doctors recently developed a way to test an embryo for defective genes. Her deformed embryos were discarded; only healthy ones were implanted through in vitro fertilization. The result is Brittany the dressed-up baby is shown again.

By showing compelling video of real people affected by embryo research-especially children-Strait brought home the reality that this ethical topic touches individuals deeply. He thus drew attention to the individual level while remaining consistent with the ethic of care, by showing the web of family relationships in which the individuals are affected profoundly by decisions made about in vitro fertilization. In addition, he used professionals elsewhere in the story to show others involved in these kinds of cases, including a doctor at the institute the Abshires used. He thus represented a range of parties.

In this case, the communitarian ethic does not apply as strongly in the sense that the people involved were not poor or marginalized. But the decisions paralleled those faced by thousands of other families-all of whom, in communitarian terms, should be concerned about people who face similar situations. The story served to highlight the difficulties faced by couples seeking in vitro fertilization, and it pointed appropriately to ethical questions raised about embryo research as well as the benefits.

However, especially given television's ability to use emotional visuals, the use of anecdotes may overshadow broader issues. Strait's anecdote about the Abshire family used a still portrait of their now-deceased child, Meaghan, and shots of dressed-up baby Brittany, born after tests of other embryos for genetic defects and the use of in vitro fertilization. The story also used as sources two doctors, a Catholic leader critical of embryo research, and a member of a National Institutes of Health panel on human embryo research. This sourcing shows that Strait was seeking to place the issue in broader organizational, professional, and social context. But shots of a child who died and of a cute, living baby may overshadow the discussion of the broader context, especially since this and the only other anecdote in the story were used to illustrate potential benefits to individuals.

The second anecdote examined came from an NBC Nightly News story reported by Mike Boettcher. After anchor Brian Williams' introduction, Boettcher opened his reporting this way: Mike Boettcher reporting: No matter what Barbara Oskamp does, no matter how simple the act, the terminally ill woman writes it down video shows list of simple things she must write down to remember, otherwise she'll forget when she takes a bath, when she washes clothes.

A brain tumor slowly is taking her memory as it takes her life, and she wants the option to end her suffering before the pain becomes unbearable close-up of her. She supports Oregon's Death With Dignity Act, the only assisted suicide law in the nation. cMs. BARBARA OSKAMP: I don't know I'd be brave enough to actually do it. But the feeling that I had a choice, if the pain, maybe, was too awful, just as I said before, gave me a feeling of relief.

The use of this anecdote is commendable from the standpoint of the ethics coverage framework in that it drew attention to the difficulties of the terminally ill at the individual level. From the standpoint of communitarian ethics, with its priority of mutuality and its attention to the marginalized, it amounted to a call for better support-emotional and medical-for this woman and others like her. Similarly, through the lens of the ethic of care, this examination of the particulars of Oskamp's daily life might evoke empathy for her suffering and consideration of the justice of the system of care for her (as well as concern about what seems in this anecdote to be an absence of relationships).

However, again these perspectives point to ethical lapses. Oskamp's plight was heart-rending, and it likely would evoke empathy from the audience because she was suffering. However, the very power of this portrayal of suffering may obscure consideration of issues such as, at the professional level, the role of better pain management or counseling, and, at the social level, the implications of legal assisted suicide for people with disabilities and terminally ill individuals who cannot pay for insurance.

Social-level issues would be particularly important in the communitarian ethic-which, while supporting the attention to Oskamp and the concerns her situation raised, would also call for more direct attention to these other areas. A doctor was quoted as raising concern about impact on the poor-also important context under the ethic of care -but this professional voice was not as compelling as Oskamp's.

The third anecdote case concerns HMOs, which have become controversial in recent years because of the impact of HMO cost controls on patients. One repeated feature in the HMO stories, particularly the television pieces, was the use of anecdotes that were sympathetic to patients dealing with the fallout of HMO cost controls and related issues. A lengthy story in the Los Angeles Times, part of a series on "The HMO Backlash" in Ventura County, opened with that kind of account:

- Norma Barry had been treated by Simi Valley family doctor Elvin Gaines all her life. She trusted him so much he delivered both of her babies.
- She believed in his judgment to such a degree that she never argued when Gaines prescribed common painkillers after she complained of headaches and dizziness.
- Then, in late 1996, she died at age 26 of a massive brain hemorrhage, and evidence suggests she may have suffered from a series of small brain bleeds.
- "I blame myself so much for not making her go to another doctor," said her husband, Simi Valley truck mechanic Jerome Barry.

Just a few years ago, the Barry case would have represented nothing more than a routine, though tragic, claim of malpractice-a lawsuit not yet resolved in court: Gaines insists he did nothing wrong, and his attorney says medical records do not show a history of chronic headaches. But in this y ear of HMO reform, it stands as a purported example of how HMO financial incentives to cut costs can interfere with a doctor's treatment of his patients-and as a reason that lawmakers, doctors, and patients are trying to change managed-care medicine.

Jerome Barry claims not only negligence, but that his wife was mistreated by Gaines because an HMO contract required the doctor to pay out of his own pocket for the costly special test the young mother needed, but never got. This anecdote, too, riveted attention on the plight of an individual, consistent with the three analytical perspectives and especially the ethic of care's concern with the particulars of such a plight.

It also placed Norma Barry in the context of her relationship with her husband, who was obviously agonizing over her death, and a relationship of trust with her doctor-in keeping with both the communitarian ethic and the ethic of care. The account also drew readers toward the organizational/ institutional and professional levels because the example was placed in the context of the HMO reform debate that touched on business, medicine, and politics. This paragraph of context also implied concern with the justice of HMO interference in the treatment of patients.

Again, though, there are ethical problems, particularly in the fact that the anecdote, although couched in broader terms, may limit attention at the broader levels. Medical costs must be controlled. Because of the serious nature of medical problems, how costs are to be controlled becomes a profound issue of social ethics. Even though the story pointed to the broader issue of cost-cutting, exemplification research suggests that readers may better remember the individual, tragic case and thus miss the broader attention to economic reality.

Daniel Callahan, a medical ethicist, sees the use of anecdotes as hindering consideration of broader resource questions. His comment regarding use of anecdotes in the assisted-suicide debate is also cautionary regarding HMO coverage and portrayal of other topics that involve social ethics: "I'm endlessly on programmes with people who tell these sad stories, and it's very hard to talk about the larger social dangers of physician-assisted suicide when somebody's got a sad story." The analysis of anecdotes about assisted suicide and HMOs bolsters the argument that anecdotes are ethically problematic if they ignore broader consideration of social-level concerns, such as just treatment of the terminally ill and just allocation of health care resources.

Applying the three analytical vantage points to the three examples suggests the importance of careful consideration of how and when anecdotes are to be used in news stories, especially against the backdrop of the exemplification literature's findings on the influence of exemplars. This section will suggest an approach that adapts the advantages of anecdotes but avoids some of their liabilities. The suggestions for more critical thinking about choice of anecdotes arise out of an application of David Boeyink's discussion of use of casuistry in journalists' ethical decision making.

Casuistry is an appropriate method here because it is case-based, as is anecdote choice. Casuists consider comparison of cases to be highly important in determining whether an action is morally justifiable. The anchor for the comparison and judgment is a paradigm case (or cases), in which the decision made is morally unambiguous.

In classical Jesuit casuistry, such a case might involve a clear breach of the biblical command against killing. In terms of journalism ethics, it might mean taking an expensive gift from a news source - or, at the ethical end of the spectrum, accepting a free cup of coffee. In either realm of decision making, ambiguous cases are compared to clear-cut cases before choices are made. The choice of paradigm case thus becomes critical to the decision maker's understanding of the ethical issues at hand.

In situations in which reporters are striving to portray the ethical dimension of a news story, the notion of a paradigm case could be applied in two senses: anecdotes (cases) could be chosen to represent the possible extremes (the clearly ethical and the clearly unethical), or-in a twist on the notion of paradigm case-an anecdote could be chosen to represent the most morally ambiguous situation (as perceived in relationship to clear-cut cases). Without referring to casuistry, many reporters undoubtedly already seek to choose anecdotes that represent the ethical topics they are covering, and they focus on cases that highlight the difficult choices people face. However, the analysis in this chapter suggests that anecdotes could be used more appropriately if more conscious attention were given to how they represent the ethical issues in the situation being covered.

Two examples using stories about the topics discussed above will suggest more concretely how this adaptation of the use of casuistry could refine journalists' choices of anecdotes:

- Use of two anecdotes from "ethical extremes": a story on assisted suicide could use one anecdote that reflects a situation in which both opponents and proponents would come closest to seeing it as ethically unsupportable and one in which they would come closest to agreeing that it was supportable. The writer or TV reporter using this approach need not ignore the ethical concerns of opponents who would object even in this case, but by using this kind of template for choosing anecdotes, the reporter would reflect the breadth of viewpoints more fully. A review of the body of stories on assisted suicide from which the case anecdote was taken did not show any single story with both kinds of anecdotes. However, examples of anecdotes that come close to reflecting both ethical extremes appeared in separate television stories. One depicted Emerson Hoogstraat, whose body was "in excruciating pain from bone cancer" and whose wife said, "He would go to bed at night and say to me, 'I hope I don't wake up in the morning.'" If this pain were too excruciating to be relieved, both sides would be closer to agreement on the appropriateness of assisted suicide than in other cases. Another story had an anecdote that portrayed Karen Mortensen, for whom better pain treatment had made her able to sleep at night and able to think about things other than dying. In this case, both sides might agree that assisted suicide would be inappropriate. Using both these anecdotes in one story would present the viewpoint spectrum. This suggestion is not meant to imply that balance of ethical viewpoints should be the norm for all ethics coverage. In fact, writing which makes explicit a journalist's ethical views may do more for readers' understanding than ethical neutrality. But this suggestion retains the notion that audience understanding is enhanced by exposure to more than one viewpoint.

- Use of one anecdote with maximum moral ambiguity: a story about the practices of health maintenance organizations could use one anecdote that reflected the difficulty of moral choices involved by showing both ethical and unethical sides of HMOs. An ABC story about how to get the care one wants from an HMO focused on Cathy Patti, an Olympic skiing champion who had lost her right leg to cancer at age 9. She was initially denied the kind of prosthetic leg she needed, but eventually the company responded to her research and to her efforts to answer its questions by compromising on price with the prosthetic maker so she could get the leg, at no cost to her. The two sides in this case each individually represent clear-cut cases, but combined in one situation they reflect the ethical tension that arises in connection with HMOs. Although this application of casuistry applies most directly to stories with a clear ethical dimension-such as stories on bioethical topics, or controversial practices in business or government-it also has implications for stories where ethics may not be as prominent. Use of anecdotes reflecting extremes of the positive or negative impact from a public issue, such as a city council decision on subdivision zoning, would help to paint a broad picture for readers or viewers. Similarly, an anecdote that reflected the most mixed impact would, in a different way, represent more than one side of the issue.

Yet another way that journalists can personalize topics while keeping attention to their broadest dimensions is to accompany a broad issue piece with two or three sidebars, each centered on how the issue is playing out in the life of an individual or family.

This idea of expanding anecdotes-personal stories-to full sidebars is not unfamiliar to journalists, but the use of more than one person-centered sidebar would broaden reader or viewer understanding of the impact of the issue beyond what might be gained from a single sidebar. In addition, applying the discussion of casuistry above to the choice of these "superanecdotes"-by using the notions of ethical extremes and maximum moral ambiguity-could help make journalistic portrayals more ethically balanced.

These sidebars could be written in third person like conventional news stories, with the sources cited, or they could be first-person pieces by the individuals themselves. In either case, they are consistent in particular with Gilligan's emphasis on the importance of relationships and voice. This approach can address the relationship dimension better than conventional anecdotes by shedding more detailed light on individuals and how they are wrestling through an issue such as genetic testing for a disease that runs in the family.

A sidebar with an issue piece from the first day of the Los Angeles Times series on HMOs noted earlier provides an excellent example of use of "super-anecdotes." The sidebar, headlined "Faces and Voices," looked at the perspectives on HMOs of ten people including doctors, a nurse, and a hospital administrator.

Each person was introduced in the reporter's voice; then each was quoted directly for several paragraphs, which empirical studies suggest will be more engaging to readers than paraphrasing. In addition, the series that day included a sidebar focusing on one surgeon. The ten-person sidebar provides one example of "maximum moral ambiguity": a cardiologist cites improvement in the quality of health care and greater accountability for time and resources, but also a deterioration in relationships among doctors and between them and patients as medicine becomes more competitive.

Training readers and viewers to expect anecdotes is problematic if stories without anecdotes are ignored or devalued. But, it is unrealistic to expect journalists to avoid using anecdotes, given their potential power to get the attention of readers and viewers. Thus, both journalists and researchers should think critically about the choice and use of anecdotes.

This analysis suggests that a good anecdote:

- Provides the fullest possible insight not merely about an individual but also about individuals in relationship with one another.
- Provides the fullest possible insight about the broader organizational, professional, and social contexts of a topic.
- Illustrates the tug of different viewpoints within the same situation or works with one or more other anecdotes to reflect multiple viewpoints.
- Is not so highly emotional that it overshadows the broader point of a story.

These criteria suggest lines for further research. Additional studies growing out of this analysis could provide ethical evaluation of the use of anecdotes in larger sets of stories on a variety of topics, with an eye to how well the stories reflect these criteria. This kind of research would further the kind of critical analysis that can help bring readers and viewers stories that have both a powerful personal dimension and the context of social meaning. The debate rages over why journalists' ethical decision making goes wrong, whether they are capable of doing it well, and how to improve it.

Since the 1970s, journalism has been occupied with its own "ethics movement" -media ethics courses have tripled, and ethics is a staple at annual conferences and in academic and professional literature. Despite this scrutiny, no study has yet examined the ethical reasoning of a large-scale sample of journalists in the objective and quantitative way that other professions have been studied. Instruments that measure moral development have been administered to tens of thousands whose professions require them to make moral choices.

Doctors, nurses, dentists, accountants, military personnel, and myriad others have been measured and ranked along a continuum of moral development, but not journalists. This study helps fill that void by gathering baseline data on a national sample of 249 journalists in order to compare journalists to other professionals, to compare subgroups of journalists, and to discover what characteristics of journalists best predict high quality ethical reasoning.

This work is important for understanding how journalists reason about ethical issues and for placing those findings into a larger, professional context. The ethical choices journalists make are crucial to the profession's credibility. By knowing the level that journalists are starting from, we can design better educational and professional efforts to move journalists to higher stages.

By expanding on the foundation they have already established, these programmes can address the specific areas where journalists are weak, and build on the strengths they have mastered. With specific information about the influences that significantly predict higher levels of moral development in journalists, we can focus our efforts at those factors for maximum effectiveness.

Literature Review

Classical Ethical Theory and Moral Development. The concept of moral development has roots in classical philosophy. Aristotle believed ethical character was developed through daily living. This concept of virtuous people doing virtuous things was carried forward essentially unchanged until the twentieth century when scholars began to document how the human psyche grows and changes, what psychologists now label "development." Moral development is the change in how people think about ethical issues over time, partly in response to the development of other portions of the individual, for example, the intellect, and partly in response to the environment. Piaget provided the academic foundation for the field when he studied boys playing marbles and found the way stations of moral growth.

As the boys aged, their understanding of rules changed according to a pattern. Younger children were aware of a codified set of rules but played individually. The rules themselves were sacred, emanated from authority figures, lasted forever, and applied to all-absolutely. In later stages, the boys internalized the rules and the reasons for them. They assumed responsibility not only for following the rules but for making sure the spirit of the rule was followed, too. This paralleled Rawls' concept of distributive justice and its principles of maximizing liberty and protecting weaker parties.

Piaget inaugurated the idea that moral development proceeds in stages and others followed, including Kohlberg, who theorized that people moved through three main stages of moral development, each of which could be subdivided into two parts. The first stage was called the pre-conventional and was defined by simple obedience to the rules, and then the emergence of self interest, in other words, following the rules only when it is in one's own interest. In the latter half of this stage, reciprocity and fairness begin to emerge in a self-serving way. In Kohlberg's second stage, conventional reasoning, the first half was characterized by conformity, or doing what other people expected.

The second half included the notion of social systems, or doing what is expected to maintain social order. Thinking at this stage acknowledged the role of duty. In the final stage of post-conventional reasoning, there was an awareness of the process by which rules are arrived at as well as the content of the rules. In this stage's first half, people are aware of concepts such as a social contract that demands citizens uphold laws even if they are not in an individual's best interest. Thinking at this stage includes understanding that some rights were beyond debate, for example, life and liberty. The second half of the post-conventional stage was characterized by the adoption of universal ethical principles that guided choice even if laws were violated. Those at this stage had internalized such principles and applied them evenhandedly. Kohlberg and others found that most people function in the conventional stage most of the time. This study uses Kohlberg's theory as its foundation.

James Rest made Kohlberg's stages easier to study by developing a quantitative instrument called the Defining Issues Test (DIT), which results in a "P score" measuring the percentage of time that people use universal principles. A P score of 40 means the highest stage is used about 40% of the time, with lower stages being used 60%.

Rest and colleagues also reconceptualized Kohlberg's idea of hard-and-fast stages using schema theory. Schemas, which are expectations about the ways events usually unfold, are developed through previous interactions. People also hold schémas for ethical problems that they use when making decisions about new dilemmas.

Rest and colleagues theorized that schemas activate understandings from long-term memory to help people process new information. If a person has acquired a schema for the highest stage of ethical reasoning, statements at that stage on the DIT will activate those schemas; otherwise lower stage schemas are used. Rather than being "in" one discreet stage or another, Rest, Narvaez, Bebeau, and Thoma theorize that people are primarily in one stage, but can use ethical reasoning from lower or higher stages as well. Rather than a staircase with steps, moral development is seen as a shifting distribution.

Journalists' Moral Development. To date, only two small-scale studies have examined journalists' moral development using the theories of Rest et al. and Kohlberg with the DIT. In both, professional journalists showed higher levels of moral development than many other professionals. In one study, sixty-five journalists outscored all but three other groups. All of those-seminarians/philosophers, physicians, and medical students-had mean education levels higher than the journalists', which is important because education is consistently one of the strongest predictors of moral development. In the other study, seventy-two professional journalists again outscored the same four groups. This study attempts to replicate and broaden these works.

Quantitative studies of journalists' ethical reasoning have primarily sought to identify influences on journalists' ethical decisions. They include external influences such as laws and organizational policies, informal work groups, the newsroom environment, competition, professional values such as codes of ethics, news subjects and sources, advertisers, and the audience.

Another important influence was motivation. Singletary and colleagues developed an Ethical Motivation Scale consistent with Kohlberg's stages. External motivators were important, but intrinsic motivations proved more predictive of behaviour. One of the ways to enhance individuals' reliance on intrinsic motivations is to increase their feelings of autonomy, also a crucial variable in Kohlberg's theory; it is important for individuals to feel autonomous to attain the postconventional stage.

Other data suggest that choice, a construct related to autonomy, is important in moral growth. Other variables not studied specifically in journalists but shown to be significant predictors of moral development in other populations include expertise in a particular field. Higher levels of ethical reasoning result when the dilemmas are in the same domain.

Religion has been positively correlated with moral development to a point. More fundamental or conservative beliefs are correlated with lower levels of moral development. Some theorize that a higher ethical orientation requires critical reasoning that may be opposed to fundamental religious beliefs. Business research shows managers tend to score lower than nonmanagers and entrepreneurs.

Two other variables-investigative reporting and civic journalism-have been linked to moral development in journalists in qualitative work. This study attempts to test those ideas quantitatively. It has been shown that investigative reporters make moral decisions regarding wrongdoing then abandon objectivity to push for the public good, serve as moral judges, and deal with ethical issues more than other types of reporters. While no study has yet examined civic journalists' ethical orientation, that orientation has been linked to communi-tarianism and characterized as a higher stage of moral development than libertarianism. Before civic journalism, Culbertson studied activist journalists, to whom civic journalists have been likened, and found they bordered on Kohlberg's highest stage.

Age and education are the primary determinants of moral development. Longitudinal studies have found significant changes in DIT scores from high school into adulthood and moral development plateaus when formal education stops. Gender has been studied extensively but with arguable results. A review of DIT studies shows 90% of them find no gender differences, and when they do, the differences are better explained by education. Some studies find women consistently score significantly higher than men. Guided by the theories of Rest et al. and Kohlberg, and empirical evidence of journalists' ethical reasoning and moral development in other populations, this study asks:

- *RQ1*: How do professional journalists score on the DIT, and how do journalists' scores compare with the scores of other professionals?

Journalists have consistently ranked fourth highest among all professionals tested in two previous studies. However, these two studies used small samples, so we ask a research question designed to gather baseline data.

- *H1*: Journalists will have significantly higher moral development scores for journalism dilemmas than nonjournalism dilemmas.

Past studies that show expertise in a domain leads to better ethical reasoning.

- *RQ2*: Are there significant differences between subgroups of journalists, including women and men, managers and nonmanagers, print and broadcast journalists, and civic/ investigative journalists and traditional journalists?

This research question is derived from studies of subgroups. Since Gilligan contested the finding that women scored lower than men on Kohlberg's test, it has become traditional to ask about gender differences, even though no systematic bias has been found with Rest's DIT.

The focus on rank in an organization follows studies suggesting that serving in management roles may lead to compromised ethics. The broadcast and print comparison comes from a popular notion in the industry that broadcasters will "stretch the ethical envelope" farther than their print counterparts. The comparison of civic and investigative journalists to traditional journalists arises from qualitative work.

- *RQ3*: What best predicts high moral development in journalists? The predictor variables tested included religious beliefs, motivations, job autonomy, investigative and civic journalism experience, age, education, and gender.

This question derived from studies of journalists' ethics showing that motivations matter, and studies that identified religious beliefs, autonomy, age, education, and gender in other populations. The civic and investigative journalism variables are exploratory.

METHOD

Dependent Variable Instrument. Rest's Defining Issues Test, the instrument used to operationally define moral development, has been given to hundreds of populations in its thirty-year history. It poses six ethical dilemmas and asks respondents to rank twelve statements after each dilemma according to how important each was in making a decision (5-point scale, with 1 = "no importance" and 5 = "great importance").

These statements reflect schematic thinking at one of Kohlberg's six stages. For example, "What would most benefit society?" is a universal principle at stage 6. Next, participants rank their top four statements from the twelve. From the ratings and rankings, a P score is calculated that reflects the relative importance the person gave to principled considerations, that is, judgments at Kohlberg's highest stage. The DIT has been tested for validity in more than 400 studies and can be modified to include two new dilemmas since domain-specific stories can be more predictive of behaviour. This study included two new dilemmas for journalism, one about hidden cameras, the other about whether to run a controversial photo.

The four original DIT dilemmas were about whether a high school principal should censor a student newspaper; whether to turn in an escaped prisoner who has led a model life; whether a doctor should help a patient commit suicide; and whether a man should steal a drug to save his ill wife. Independent Variables. Autonomy and religion questions were from the General Social Survey. Autonomy (Cronbach's alpha =.76) included: "How independent does your job allow you to be?"

"How much say to do you have over the assignments you work on?" and "How much are you allowed to take part in making decisions that affect your work?" (1= "none" and 7 = "a lot"). Religiosity was measured with the following: "Would you describe yourself as extremely religious (7) to extremely nonreligious (1)?" and "Where would you place your religious beliefs from extremely fundamentalist (7) to extremely liberal (1)?" ($r = .57$, $p < .01$).

Investigative reporting and civic journalism used two questions each (7-point Likert scales) about the journalists' own involvement with and their news organization's commitment to investigative ($r = .53$, $p < .001$) and civic journalism ($r = .60$, $p < .001$). Participant job titles were dichotomized as management or not management (managers included broadcast news directors and higher, and newspaper managing editors and above).

Sixteen items from the Ethical Motivations Scale asked how important several criteria were when making ethical decisions (1 = "not at all important" and 7 = "very important"). For example, "Whether our competition has the story" and "How my colleagues would handle the same story" were offered as criteria. These were submitted to factor analysis and used to predict level of moral development. This study sampled 249 journalists chosen with a form of multistage cluster sampling.

To determine the proportions of the subsets of the population of U.S. journalists, we used the most recent national, random samples of working journalists as a guide. We initially stratified by geographic region, developing lists of news organizations from the 2001 and 2002 Editor & Publisher and Broadcasting & Cable yearbooks for the West, South, North, and Midwest. Next, we stratified the news outlets by size in the categories of large (> 100,000), medium (25,000100,000), and small (< 25,000) newspapers.

Letters were written to top managers of news organizations in each size category from each geographic region explaining the study; up to three follow-up phone calls were made asking for participation. Next, we identified categories shown to be important in moral development or for other variables-age, education, race, gender, and political party-in order to employ stratification techniques at these levels.

It proved extremely difficult or impossible to obtain lists of all journalists working in the newsrooms, so we were unable to randomly sample individuals at these levels. Instead, we selected individuals constituting the same proportion of the population on important stratification variables. Babbie says this is "likely to be more representative on a number of variables than would be the case for a simple random sample." We accomplished this by analyzing demographic data after each round of data collection; typically, one to three newsrooms per site were visited with 5 to 20 journalists from each newsroom participating.

This allowed us to modify the selection of news organizations for the next wave of data collection in order to conform to the proportions of individuals in the population. For example, if we found we had more journalists age 20 to 24, we would next visit larger news outlets where older journalists were typically found. We were interested in maintaining proportions at the individual level, not the organizational level, so this modification resulted in a sample that was potentially more in proportion to the population of individual U.S. journalists than a simple random sample of news organizations.

For example, Weaver, Beam, Brownlee, Voakes, and Wilhoit found 33% of journalists were women; this sample included 38% women; 90% of the Weaver et al. sample were Caucasian, 89% were Caucasian in this sample; 42% of the national sample of journalists were Democrats, 37% were in this study; 14% were at broadcast outlets in the national sample, 18% were broadcasters in our sample.

Because of the purposive sampling of journalists at the individual level, this was not a probability sample and findings should be considered suggestive rather than definitive; however, that should not discount the importance of the results for several reasons. First, it has been recognized that when probability sampling is not feasible, nonprobability sampling is acceptable.

In this study, random sampling was not feasible or even appropriate. The primary ways random samples are collected are by mail and phone; a mail survey would have generated too low a response rate since this survey took forty-five minutes to complete and was on a sensitive topic.

A phone survey would have introduced too much random error since the dilemmas require reflection and the ability to consider response choices; having choices read over the phone does not let respondents consider them the way they could if they saw them together and compared their importance. Instead, the surveys were administered in person on site-visits to newsrooms, an approach that almost all DIT studies have followed for more than thirty years.

Second, the purpose of this study is descriptive and explanatory, focusing on gathering baseline data on an unstudied population and understanding relationships between moral development and other variables. Never in the history of moral development research has there been an attempt to generalize to the population in the same way as electoral polls and surveys. Of more than 400 DIT studies, almost none was a random sample, and almost all were administered in person by researchers. Thus, these results are appropriate for comparison with studies of other professional populations.

Furthermore, this study satisfied the three conditions that justify the use of nonprobability sampling. The material being studied was difficult to obtain since ethics is possibly the hardest topic to get journalists, or anyone, to talk about in a revealing way. The ethical quandaries on the DIT do not compare in complexity to the simple demographics or even questions about ethical influences in Weaver and Wilhoit's survey.

The ethical questions in this survey reach the depths of a person's core values and beliefs rather than the more simple attitudes and opinions of most surveys. Furthermore, it would have been prohibitively expensive to generate a random sample of the population of journalists by administering surveys in person; it took two years to collect these data in person.

Also, this study explored an under-researched but important area; journalists are one of very few professional groups for which baseline ethical data have yet to be collected. Finally, it is not the intention of this study to generalize to the population in the sense that random sample surveys do; our purpose is to explain relationships and for general comparison, for which Babbie says a nonprobability multistage sample design is sufficient.

Science is a cumulative process and consistent results from a number of convenience samples can suggest important questions, to paraphrase one text. This is the third study of journalists, and the three results are consistent. As is traditional with DIT studies, generalizable statements become possible after many smaller studies of different participants from the same profession have been conducted over time.

All the populations we compare with our DIT results were collected in this manner, not with large random samples; therefore, the comparisons are fair. As the third such study of journalists, this represents one more step in a cumulative process of knowledge acquisition about journalists' ethical development.

RESULTS

Descriptive Statistics

In this sample, 62% of the journalists had a bachelor's degree, 13% had some graduate training, 17% had a graduate degree. Only 8% of those taking the DIT had "some college or a high school degree." Of these DIT respondents, 36% were Protestant, 29% Catholic, 4% Jewish, 10% listed other religious preferences, and 21% said they had no religious affiliation. The journalists in this study averaged 14 years in the profession, and were 38 years old oil average.

Twenty-eight per cent said they had done civic journalism, 7.2% said they had done investigative reporting, and 46% said they had done both. Thirty-one per cent had management-level job titles. Journalists' autonomy scores ranged from a low of 1 to a high of 7 on a 7-point scale with a mean of 5.3. The ethical development scores of the journalists in this study were normally distributed. Data fell within a normal curve and rose in a straight line on a normal probability plot. The data met three other tests for normality; the standard deviation was one-fourth or less the value of the mean, and skewness (1.25) and kurtosis (-.75) indicated normality. The sample was statistically normal and met the assumptions for regression analysis.

Journalists in this study scored quite well compared to other professions, mirroring the results of the two smaller studies. This larger sample of journalists again ranked fourth highest of all professionals who had taken this test. The mean moral development score, or P score, was 48.68. These journalists ranked below three professions-all with higher mean education levels than our journalists-and above 14 other groups, including four with higher education levels than journalists.

- *H*1: When the P score was broken down into journalism and general dilemmas, journalists in this study did significantly better on dilemmas in their field than other types of ethical problems. The mean P score for the three nonjournalism dilemmas was significantly lower than the mean P score for the three journalism dilemmas, supporting this hypothesis.

- *RQ*2. The only significant difference in moral reasoning between subgroups was related to the types of work they did. Journalists who had experience with investigative journalism, civic journalism, or both, scored significantly higher than those who did not do either.

There were no significant differences between men and women, between broadcast and print journalists, or between managers and nonmanagers in this study.

- *RQ*3. To discover the predictors of high levels of moral development, a regression model was developed based on factors formed from questions on the Ethical Motivations Scale, religion, type of journalistic work, and autonomy. A factor analysis with varimax rotation resulted in five factors accounting for 57% of the variance. Requirements for factor retention included an eigenvalue of 1.0 and a minimum of two items with a primary loading of at least.30 and no secondary loading as high as.20.

The factors were labeled external motivations, internal motivations, competition, religion, and law. The external motivations factor dealt with influences outside the journalists themselves such as how colleagues would handle the story. The internal motivations factor involved the journalists' ethical values, including their own sense of right and wrong. Religion reflected journalists' religious beliefs.

The law factor referred to specific legal constraints such as advice from legal counsel. The competition factor referred to media pressure, both outside the journalist and "within," such as whether the competition had the story. The five factors and other variables were submitted to a hierarchical regression to find which were predictive of high levels of ethical reasoning. The most parsimonious model was significant ai p <.001 and explained about 15% of the variance. The significant factors were religion, internal motivations, autonomy, law, and investigative reporting. Education approached significance at p =.062.

Just as in other studies, the religion factor was negatively correlated with these journalists' P scores. For every one-point increase in religiosity, there was nearly a two-point decline in moral development scores. The factor that measured how participants viewed the law and employer rules also was negatively correlated with higher P scores. For every one-point increase in importance of the law, there was nearly a two-point decrease in moral development scores.

The internal motivations factor was positively correlated with higher P scores; for every onepoint increase in the importance of internal motives, there was a threeand-a-half-point increase in moral development scores. Journalists in this study who had more autonomy on the job were significantly more likely to have higher P scores; for every one-point increase in autonomy levels, there was a half-point increase in moral development scores. Doing investigative reporting also predicted higher P scores; for every one-point increase in investigative reporting, there was nearly threefourths-of-a-point increase in P scores.

The journalists in this study appear to be strong ethical thinkers. This is the third and largest study to gather data on the moral development of journalists. In the first, journalists' mean P score was 48.1,76 in the second it was 48.17,77 and in this study it was 48.68. While this was not a random sample, the study reported here mirrored the population on important characteristics, and the numerical consistency in the three sets of findings gives us confidence that they are reasonable and may represent something of a larger whole.

These journalists appear to have reached a level of moral development that equips them to reason well about ethical problems. In this and three other studies, professional journalists consistently scored higher than adults in general and several professional groups including nurses and orthopedic surgeons, and dental and veterinary students. When ethical problems are professionally focused, journalists perform even better. This suggests that giving journalists the opportunity to work through more ethical dilemmas, whether they are real, occurring on the job, or hypothetical in seminars and workshops, bodes well for the profession. This also indicates there is a journalistic domain of knowledge and that journalists think even better about ethical problems in that domain than they do about general problems.

This evidence of domain expertise adds to the debate over whether journalism should be considered a profession or a craft. This suggests there is more to being a journalist than learning to write in inverted pyramid and mastering nonlinear editing. Thinking like a journalist involves moral reflection, done at a level that in most instances equals or exceeds members of other learned professions.

There is some irony is this result; public opinion would not support such an assessment of journalists as sophisticated moral thinkers. As is frequently the case, conventional wisdom is not always supported by empirical evidence. Professional opinion, the one that holds broadcasters are less ethical than print journalists, also finds no empirical support from this study. When analyzing these journalists' ranking against other professions, one should note that all the professionals who rank above journalists have more formal education than the bachelor's degree of most journalists. The same is true for dental students, who ranked slightly below journalists. Thus, formal education appears to be influential in how professional groups score on the DIT. Education clearly matters, and, as the demographics indicate, journalists are slowly becoming better educated.

This study also has added empirical evidence to the qualitative work that suggests investigative reporting builds ethical muscles. This correlational study cannot not tell us whether this form of reporting helps create better ethical reasoning or if the journalists practicing it already possess higher ethical development. Previous studies have indicated that investigative reporting entails making moral judgments and that the journalists who do this sort of work wrestle with ethical issues as a part of the reporting process. It makes some sense that journalists whose professional work foregrounds ethical thinking would outscore other professionals because they are regularly practicing and refining their ethical skills. Future research should sort out whether these forms of reporting help build ethical journalists or merely attract them. This study and others like it using self-reports do not address what participants would actually do in an ethical dilemma. The disconnect between attitudes and behaviour is well documented.

Hundreds of studies have looked at the link between moral judgment and behaviour; in general, moral judgment is statistically associated with many different measures of behaviour, but the correlations are not strong. For the DIT in particular, more than sixty studies have found evidence that the hypothetical dilemmas do tap something important to behaviour; there are many links to behaviour measures outside the test such as job performance ratings. Ethical behaviour is determined by several co-acting psychological processes; moral reasoning is only one.

Of course, all these conclusions should be supported with replication, and caution is urged in generalizing these findings. However, the findings of this study suggest that if you give journalists autonomy in the work they attempt, expose them to the rigors of investigative reporting, and moderate the influence of work-based rules and religion, then journalists are capable of high-level ethical thinking.

Just as others have found, the journalists in this study exhibited quality reasoning about their profession. Knowledge about journalism, as a set of practices and as an institution that performs an essential societal role, provided a significant and measurable level of domain expertise. Other studies, using different methods and asking different questions, have uncovered much the same kind of reasoning.

The journalists who participated in the interviews for a 2001 book, Good Work: When Excellence and Ethics Meet, maintained both high professional ideals and the practical knowledge that the economic nature of journalism-as-business represented a corrosive element within the profession. The authors of Good Work characterized these seemingly conflicting understandings as evidence of a profession that is "out of alignment" with some of its more basic understandings. Rather than focusing on the internal cross-signals, the authors suggested that the contradiction itself represented the opportunity for significant professional growth in both an individual and institutional sense. As Kohlberg noted, moving up the stages of moral development often occurs when the conflicts in one stage can be resolved only by a change in thinking. In an institutional sense, journalism as a profession appears to be at the same nexus, one that has potential for development.

Bibliography

Benjaminson Peter. Death in the Afternoon: America's Newspaper Giants Struggle for Survival. Kansas City, Kans.: Andrews, McMeel and Parker, 2004

Brand Stewart. The Media Lab: Inventing the Future at MIT. New York: Viking, 2002

Burkett Warren. News Reporting: Science, Medicine, and High Technology. Ames: Iowa State University Press, 2001

Charnley Mitchell. 2000. Reporting. New York: Holt, Rinehart and Winston.

Cohen Elliot D., ed. 2001. Philosophical Issues in Journalism. New York: Oxford University Press.

Goldstein Tom, ed. 2004. Killing the Messenger. 100 Years of Media Criticism. New York: Columbia University Press.

Graber Doris A. 2002. Mass Media and American Politics. Washington, D.C.: Congressional Quarterly.

Hallin Daniel C. 2000. We Keep America on Top of the World: Television Journalism and the Public Sphere. New York: Routledge.

Lavine John M., and Daniel B. Wackman. Managing Media Organizations. New York: Longman, 2001

Likert Rensis. The Human Organization. New York: McGraw-Hill, 2003

McCombs Maxwell, Donald Lewis Shaw, and David Grey. Handbook of Reporting Methods. Boston: Houghton Mifflin, 2002

Index